TYPE AT

AT

ORK

Type at Work

Type at Work

The Use of Type in Editorial Design

Andreu Balius

A book by Index Book, S.L.

English edition published and distributed by:
BIS Publishers
Herenbracht 370-372
1016 CH Amsterdam
The Netherlands

Tel: +31 20 524 75 60
Fax: +31 20 524 75 57
bis@bispublishers

ISBN 90-6369-041-x

Original Spanish version published and distributed by:
Index Book, S.L.
Consell de Cent 160, local 3
08015 Barcelona
Spain

Tel: +34 93 454 55 47
Fax: +34 93 454 84 38
ib@indexbook.com

English translation: Ted Krasny

Composition and design: Andreu Balius

Lithography and layout:
Nova Era Fotocomposición, S.A.
Josep Irla i Bosch 1-3 local
08034 Barcelona
Spain
Tel: +34 93 204 19 04
Fax: +34 93 204 19 07
English layout: Bite Graphic Design

Production and printing:
Printer, Industria gráfica, S.A.
Ctra N-II Km 600
08620 Sant Vicenç dels Horts
Spain
Tel: + 34 93 631 01 99
Fax: +34 93631 02 06

Printed in Spain

Prologue

Over the last two decades of the 20th century, graphic design (in the West, at least) underwent major transformations, perhaps comparable only with those produced by the invention of the printing press.

The sudden emergence in the design world in 1984 of a new tool, the Macintosh computer, brought radical change not only in work methods but – insofar as it made possible a series of practices that led to the exploration of new formal recourses – in aesthetic approaches as well. People began to speak of the 'MacStyle', a style based on the possibilities that the Mac and its programs offered: skewed typography, three-dimensional and/or shaded letters, layered, blurred or pixelated images, etc., which would define the second half of the eighties and a large part of the nineties.

But the Mac also appeared on the scene at a time of a debate – strongly marked by post-structuralism – that touched on all realms of design. This debate revisited a whole range of issues regarding design: its language and construction; its role as a bearer of ideas and messages; the place, use and abuse, invention and reinvention of history; the relations with advertising; the links, in a continually changing context, with popular culture and with technological development; and, finally, the ethical stance and social responsibility of the designer.

Over these last two decades design has likewise explored the possibility of applying theoretical models taken from other fields such as language theory, philosophy and cultural studies. Thus the importance of questions (belonging to post-modern thought) such as the shift from logocentrism to iconocentrism, communication and consumption.

Deconstructionist theory held a pre-eminent place within language studies in particular. Fathered by Jacques Derrida in the late sixties, the theory would have special resonance in graphic design following the experiences of the Cranbrook Academy of Art – beginning around 1983 – and fostered as well by the presence of the Mac.

Deconstructionist theory stressed the mutability of things, highlighting the limitations of objective analysis and underscoring the importance of historical and social context to explain the objects around us. It sees these objects as texts that continually fill with new meanings, depending on the time, place and culture. The need to locate everything in a specific historical and cultural context pointed up the futility of the Modern School's quest for universality.

Derrida's approach to writing made his ideas especially relevant to typography. In the French philosopher's view – placing writing and speaking at the same level, as opposed to the structuralist vision of the former as an instrument of representation of the latter – writing influences the construction of language and culture. The deconstructionist vision also encouraged readers to grasp the complex differences in meaning when something means one thing at one level and the contrary at another. Deconstructionism thus showed that design is not a one-way relationship between designer and receiver.

The practical application of Derridian theory to design produced the intrusion of the visual form in the verbal content and, thus, the invasion of ideas by the graphic signs, making typography a means of interpretation. Font was conceived as discourse, rejecting the traditional distinction between seeing and reading, arguing that designers can actively combine both experiences, such that an image can be read and a written word seen.

Aware or not of the contents of post-structuralism, but certainly heavily influenced by them, the last two decades of the 20th century accordingly saw rise to predominance of the image. In an increasingly visual world, texts, words and letters have become images, woven among and filling with them new associations and meanings. Designers became aware again – and I say again because such awareness, as we can see in baroque if not earlier typography, had long existed in the past – that letters are more than just abstract signs.

This concept of the letter, favoured by a technology that facilitated formal experimentation, brought about (at a time when some were proclaiming the demise of a printing press rendered obsolete by the new technologies) our current situation of veritable typographic euphoria. Thus, it could be said that a 'conscious typographic culture' is emerging, which, on the other hand, has permitted

Introduction

The Font is the Message

In this book editorial design is understood as a specialised area of graphic design concerned with the visual organisation of essentially textual contents.

We can safely say that, in publishing, the most common supports for text are books, newspapers and magazines. In these media, where text predominates, typography plays a fundamental role. In the hands of the designer, typography a realm traditionally reserved for bibliophiles and specialists to intrude on the terrain of popular manifestations thanks to the computer's capacity for producing texts, combining them with images and generating new fonts. What we now call desktop publishing has placed typographic knowledge within the reach of practically anyone.

This change, of course, did not come about without certain conflict. The nineties saw struggles in favour of the democratisation of typography, and for a time the sacred principles of font, legibility among them, were turned inside out.

With these conflicts resolved and the new ideas admitted, typography is now an open territory in which we find an enormous variety of uses and manifestations: from those for whom it is an abstract vehicle that, by not interfering in the structure and meaning of the text, remains invisible – and in which the typographer acts simply as a text editor more concerned with structural clarity than formal expression – to others who seek visual impact and where the style becomes part of the content.

And thus on a daily basis we find everything from fonts that are so familiar – with hundreds of years of historical baggage, located within the most traditional austere classicism in search of invisibility – that we hardly notice them, to others that seem to appear out of nowhere and, created for a single project, vanish just as quickly: fonts that seek to captivate the reader, demanding her or his visual involvement in what she or he is reading and that suggest a new vocabulary of the masses.

In any event, graphic designers are again aware of what fonts have always meant for them: crucial elements in facilitating communication and the basic grammar of design – a tool used to structure the contents, whose expressive power helps manifest the designer's own sensitivity while transmitting an identity or the interests of a given society.

This reacquired awareness has had, of course, its most immediate reflection in the territory most closely associated with typography since its origins: editorial design, a world in which since the invention of the printing press a whole tradition has been built up. Over the course of that development a series of typographic conventions have evolved, which, hardly affected by the avant-garde trends that have emerged over the centuries, remained practically unchanged until the appearance of the new technologies in the late 20th century.

These new technologies have fostered fundamental changes in the publishing world, with an impact at all levels of production: from design and printing to distribution, coinciding with the diversity and fragmentation associated with our time that has given rise to a proliferation of formats and contents heretofore inconceivable.

Perhaps post-modern thought itself has favoured this proliferation. If we advocate the presence of fragments, mixtures and references to high and low culture, what better means to materialise our discourse than periodicals, where different discourses and references are so often combined?

While some have been predicting the imminent death of the printed page – for the time being apparently still not in the offing – we have witnessed the emergence of innumerable small publishers capable of covering the needs of minority readerships, in addition to the large firms whose goal is market dominance through mass production.

Meanwhile, the boundaries between the traditional roles of the author, publisher and designer have begun to blur, giving rise to professionals who, in their ability to deal with all aspects of text, recall the monks of the medieval scriptorium.

And, as occurred with font design, desktop publishing has made it possible for anyone, even those with no training in design and scarce professional experience, to tackle an editorial design project, and do so successfully, even contributing a bit of freshness. This is the case of David Carson, who turned the magazine **Raygun** into a cult publication while setting the standard for a generation of young designers of the nineties especially interested in font.

Moreover, as Mark Porter[1], head of design at **The Guardian**, points out, the new technologies have permitted the creation of more sophisticated publications at lower costs, something that before the appearance of the Mac was only possible for the big publishing houses.

Yet, perhaps as a reaction to the relentless technological advances of our times, designers are is a necessary tool for shaping the personality and character of a given publication. It is an essential element in written communication, since both its formal design and its use and handling are factors that influence – and even determine – how the transmission of the messages, the very essence of communication, is established.

In recent years, in part thanks to the application of digital technology to the design processes, typography has undergone a revolution unprecedented in its history, assuming new roles and pushing back its formal and conceptual limits. Its function is no longer restricted to the verbal: its formal, aesthetic and cultural features now contribute to the meaning of the text as well. This is seen in the broad range of work taken on by graphic designers – a profession in the midst of transformation, in this period straddling two centuries.

At present, different practices and attitudes coexist in editorial design. There are two different supports – monitor and paper – entailing different approaches to the use of typography. The mutual influences are palpable in a present shared by two great generations of designers: those brought up on the old technologies and those who from the outset have naturally taken to the computer. The transition from a traditional support to another more modern one as the result of technological advances will change the way textual content is viewed and organised in the future.

now attempting to humanise publishing, treating books and periodicals as artefacts, as physical elements or, what comes to the same, as objects of intimate and personal use which appeal to all our senses, thus acquiring their permanence not only through their contents but through their form as well. Perhaps, given the current scenario, this is the only way to compete.

That is why there are those who once again conceive books as complete works of art, as happened in the latter 19th century with the reaction to the Industrial Revolution and its undermining of the art of publishing. And in the complete work of art care is required both within and without: one must be meticulous with all details, from the cover to the subtlest typographic recourse. The book thus becomes an experience that goes beyond the purely intellectual.

Even the academic publishing world, once seemingly immune to new graphic ideas, is undergoing genuine renewal. Thus, for example, recent years have seen the emergence of magnificent books on architecture, philosophy and even the sciences – in addition to splendid exhibition catalogues – which, thanks to an intelligent use of typography succeed in offering something more than an elegant collection of images. And the same may be said of company reports and bulletins, which in the many cases are no longer the staid publications we are used to seeing.

The impact of the new technologies and a more versatile use of typography are giving rise to richly evocative publications in which design takes a leading role, at the same time as it serves to highlight the personality of each product.

It is precisely this desire to create a personality that often leads to the design of exclusive, unique fonts specially conceived for a specific publication, or to a layout that breaks many of the traditional typographic rules with the aim of underscoring the meaning of the text. Despite the growing power of images in the contemporary world – or perhaps because of it – words have not lost their strength.

Thus, at the same time as images seemingly prevail over type, the latter is becoming more and more physical, more bodily, more patent. And while photography is growing more and more sophisticated and capable of captivating the gaze of the least interested reader, designers are increasingly fascinated with fonts, having some time ago breached its traditional boundaries and learnt to handle typefaces with great skill. Type at Work includes excellent examples of this fascination.

Raquel Pelta

[1] Cited by John O'Reilly in Visual Journalism. Magazines and technology, Eye no. 36, Vol. 9, summer 2000.

Type at Work, The Use of Type in Editorial Design aims to reflect this broad scene, as eclectic as it is fascinating, one which we cannot fail to see as the product of our contemporary reality. Through a small number of publishing projects by designers, studios and agencies, we explore different approaches to the use of typography, attempting to shed light on the processes and experiences in order to understand better the results.

The works selected – out of many other possible choices – encompass different areas of editorial design, from book design in its most classical sense to fanzines, electronic publications, catalogues and magazines. We have categorised these publications by area, according to the usefulness of typography: its functionality, expressiveness and conceptuality.

In editorial design many courses are open to the designer. Technology pushes the limits but it is the designer who must remove the barriers. The computer is now the means. The letter will continue to be the message.

Andreu Balius

Index

"Typography can be
with which the read
vated, while the grap
on which the voices
ters – the letters –
each other".

he shout or whisper
r is seduced or capti-
cs comprise the stage
of the leading charac-
onfront and speak to

xplicit typography

Why Not Associates

Why Not Associates
London, United Kingdom

"The Image of the Text"

Why Not Associates is a long-established, multi-disciplinary design firm which emerged in the nineties as a point of reference on the European graphics scene.

Why Not was founded in 1987 by three friends who had recently graduated from the Royal College of Art, Andy Altmann, David Ellis and Howard Greenhalgh, later joined by Patrick Morrissey after he graduated from the London College of Printing in 1994.

Why Not's creative and innovative work can be seen in a wide variety of graphic products, from postage stamps to large-scale installations and exhibitions. Their work succeeds in reconciling their particular vision of design and experimental attitude with the wishes and expectations of their clients. Why Not believe that the result depends on the client getting involved in a project and sharing a similar sense of adventure.

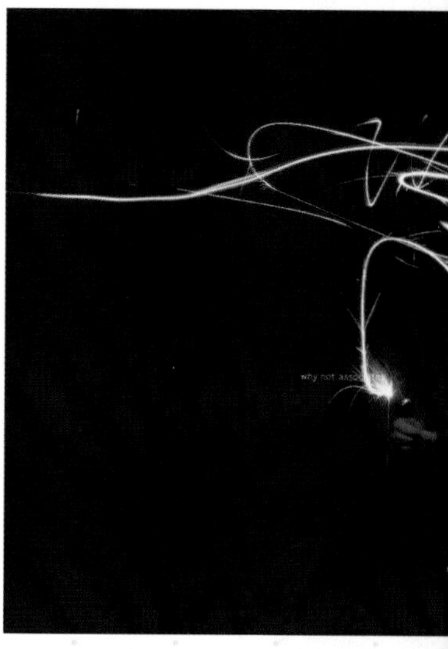

With an interrogative for a name **Why Not Associates** questions the need to justify absolutely everything that forms part of a graphic solution.

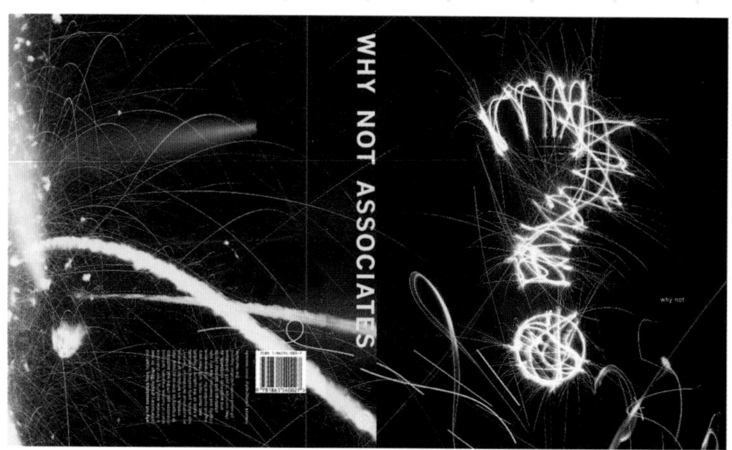

Why Not Associates Book
1998

Jacket of the commemorative book including the most representative works by the Why Not Associates studio in their first ten years.

Why Not Associates Book
1998

Double inside pages

Using a book to present a studio's work always represents a tricky design problem. One of the most important tasks is choosing the works and deciding how they are to be presented.

Why Not do an excellent job of producing a book with a value of its own, and go beyond merely compiling a series of images.

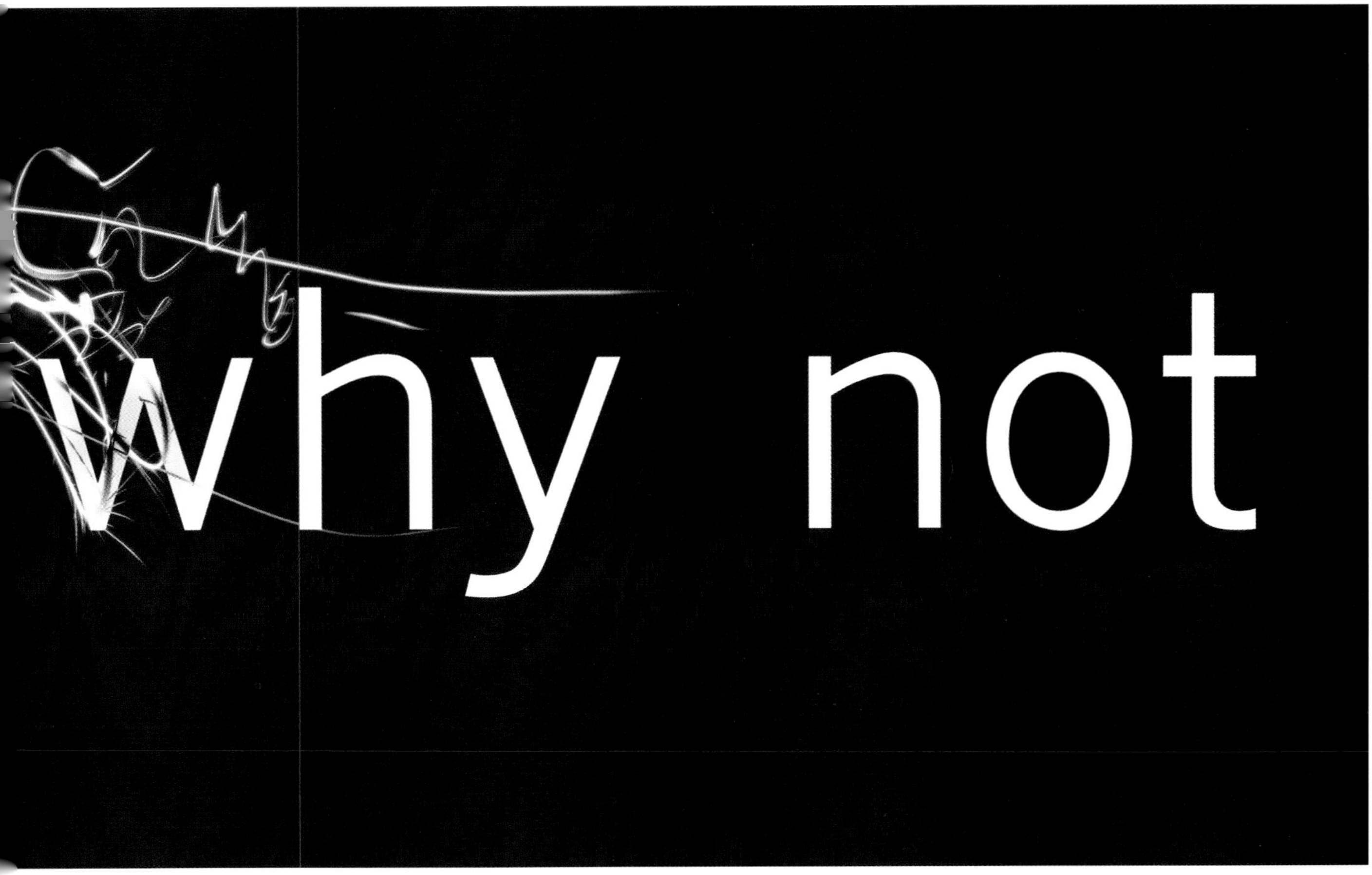

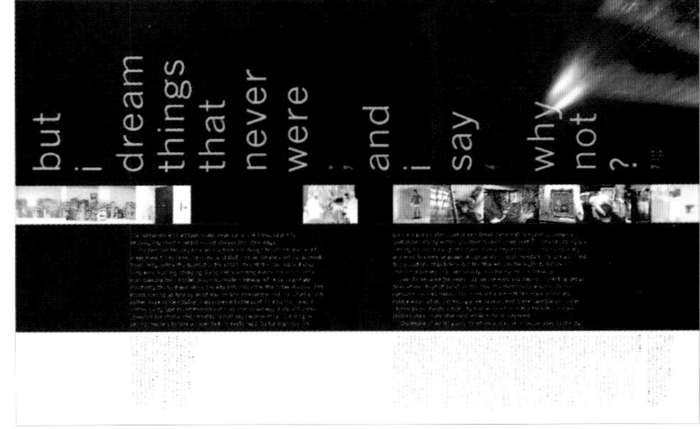

Why Not Associates

BITE:99 – The Beckett Festival (1999)
Design of the publicity leaflet for the theatre season at the Barbican Centre.

Front cover and inside pages

GATE THEATRE DUBLIN
THE BECKETT FESTIVAL
CONTEN
2 Introductions
3 Samuel Beckett: a chronology
4 From Nowhere? Beckett's Ireland by Eoin O'Brien
7 'The Brink of Shrieks' by Carol Ann Duffy
8 But not in the eye: Beckett's comedy by Fintan O'Toole
10 Waiting for Godot
12 Happy Days
14 Endgame
16 Come And Go | Act Without Words II | Play
18 Krapp's Last Tape
20 Not I | What Where | Act Wit
22 Footfalls | Rough for Theatre
24 Ohio Impromptu | Rough for
26 Breath | That Time | A Piece
28 Biographies
32 Visual Arts
34 Beckett on Screen
35 Exploring Beckett; Beckett E

CAST
BREATH
THAT TIME
Listener Niall Buggy
A PIECE OF MONOLOGUE
Speaker Stephen Brennan
Director Robin Lefèvre
Designer Giles Cadle
Lighting Designer Alan Burrett
BREATH
THAT TIME
A PIECE OF MONOLOGUE
26
BREATH
Written in response to a request from Kenneth Tynan for an anonymous sketch to be included in the revue Oh! Calcutta! First produced in New York in June 1969 with unauthorised additions and withdrawn, at Beckett's insistence, from the London production of the revue.
This is the most compressed of Beckett's dramatic works, taking about a half a minute of stage time from start to finish. Life is reduced to a brief interval of dim light between two cries and two darknesses. The brief light illuminates a small heap of miscellaneous rubbish ('no verticals'). It is an elegant and gruesome footnote to Pozzo's complaint in Waiting for Godot: 'They give birth astride of a grave, the light gleams an instant, then it's night once more'.
THAT TIME
Written in English during 1974 and 1975
In this piece Beckett returns to the formal experimentation of the earlier Play (1963). That Time, however, intercuts three monologues not from three separate characters but from three strata in the past experience of one character. The pattern for the intercutting is precise: each voice speaks four times during the course of each of three 'scenes'. The scenes are marked off from each other by silences. The first and second scenes offer precise parallel patterns whereas the third offers a pattern repeated three times: this may imply that (a) the pattern is endlessly repeatable or (b) that it is closed and final. Beckett frequently has recourse to such ambiguities. Each voice is burdened by time, memories and visions of nullity, and at the end the isolated head on stage smiles ('toothless for preference') at the prospect of happiness, sans everything.
JENNY DISKI, NOVELIST
A PIECE OF MONOLOGUE
Written in English in 1979 and first performed in New York the following year
The nature of this piece is aptly summed up in the title: it is a piece of staged monologue. The Speaker tells a fragment of story about birth and death in which the narrative details almost match those visible to us as the theatre set. The gap between the narrative and the set dramatises a process of atrophy or winding down which is implicit or immanent in the opening words: 'Birth was the death of him'. The piece is contemporaneous with Heard in the dark I and Heard in the dark II, both of which were fragments towards Company (1980). These connections are invoked because A Piece of Monologue dramatises a successive loss of company: firstly, in the account of the destruction of the photographs and secondly, in the memories of a funeral in the rain. At another level the story opens a window on the past, a window begrimed by the accumulation of years, and the Speaker's eyes turn to the viewing of the inner dark where are 'seen': 'The dead and gone. The dying and the going. From the word go. The word begone'.
27

One More Kiss
1999

Front cover and inside pages

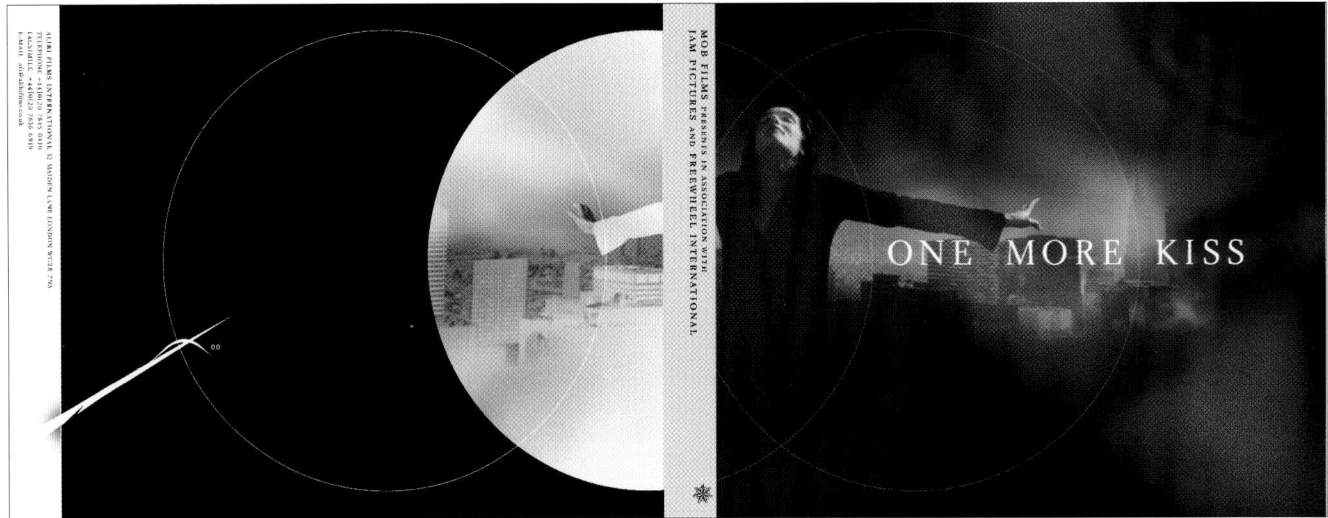

One More Kiss
Promotional leaflet

Year: 1999
Client: Mob films / Alibi films
Photography: Vadim Jean, Photodisc

Font used: Charlotte

25 x 19 cm. 14 pages. Full colour printing (cover) and two inks (inside pages)

The Poetry of Text and Image

Before the computer opened up the possibilities for visual manipulation, the team at **Why Not Associates**, trained in the principles of modern typography, opted to break the ground rules and establish their own guidelines for how typography should be used in design. They see type as a medium for creating and transmitting messages subliminally: **"Good typography communicates beyond the written word. It can provoke people, anger them or relax them; it can inform and entertain."**

Why Not's graphic work is characterised by transgressive layouts without losing sight of readability. Text flows between fragmented images or crosses them on overlaid planes, creating discontinuous blocks which, with the aid of other graphic elements (fillets, geometric shapes, backgrounds, textures) create sensations which go beyond the strictly literary. The typography is laid out on the page in complete harmony with the images, achieving pleasant overall reading. Blank space is the main unifying recourse for the variety of resources used in these graphic compositions. Beneath the formal complexity, however, lies a love of decoration which recalls the late-19th-century English tradition.

The promotional design work for the film One More Kiss is a good example of this particular way of laying out text and fostering dialogue with the images to achieve visually attractive pages.

The double page is conceived as a single entity. Although there may be no graphic structure, the arrangement of the elements seems to obey a preconceived order.

"We didn't want to use a grid. We wanted to create something fluid and poetic," says Patrick.

Taking as its starting point the film's plot, in which the main character leaves New York for her native Scotland, Why Not combines iconographic elements from both places. So the colours are determined by the blues and greens of the Statue of Liberty and the typical hues of the Scottish countryside.

› Following pages:
Poster (front and back) for **Plazm** magazine, based on the theme of human identity and creation. Insert for issue no. 22 of **Plazm** magazine (1999).

Font used: Interstate

NOR COULD I CONSIDER THE MAGNITUDE AND COMPLEXITY OF MY PLAN AS ANY ARGUMENT OF ITS IMPRACTICABILITY.
IT WAS WITH THESE FEELINGS THAT I BEGAN THE
CREATION OF A HUMAN BEING.

AFTER DAYS AND NIGHTS OF
INCREDIBLE LABOUR AND FATIGUE,
I SUCCEEDED IN DISCOVERING THE
CAUSE OF GENERATION AND LIFE;
NAY, MORE, I BECAME MYSELF
CAPABLE OF BESTOWING
ANIMATION UPON LIFELESS
MATTER.
WHENCE,
I OFTEN
ASKED
MYSELF,
DID
THE
PRINCIPLE
OF
LIFE
PROCEED?

ReDesign

Petr Krejzek, Klara Kvizova
Prague, Czech Republic

"Experimenting with Type"

Petr Krejzek (1965) and Klara Kvizova (1970) founded the **ReDesign** studio in Prague in early 1999. They work in a number of graphic areas, including corporate identity design, website design, editorial design – books and magazines – as well as catalogues, annuals and electronic publications in CD format.

They do all their work on computers and combine their commissions with personal projects in which they experiment with fonts.

They see the design of the magazine **Zivel** as the perfect opportunity for experimenting with fonts.

Zivel

Magazine covers
Double page Zivel n. 4

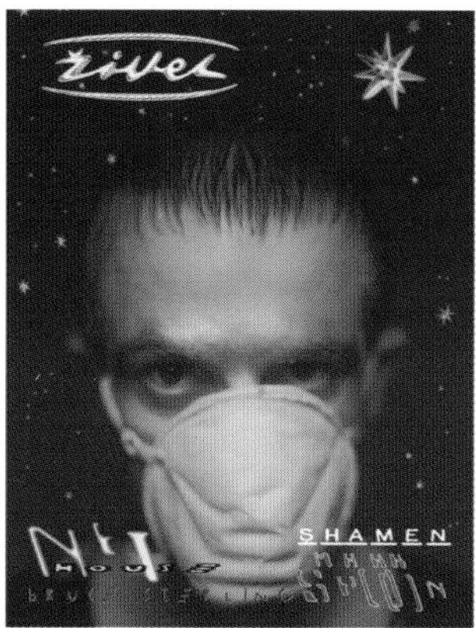

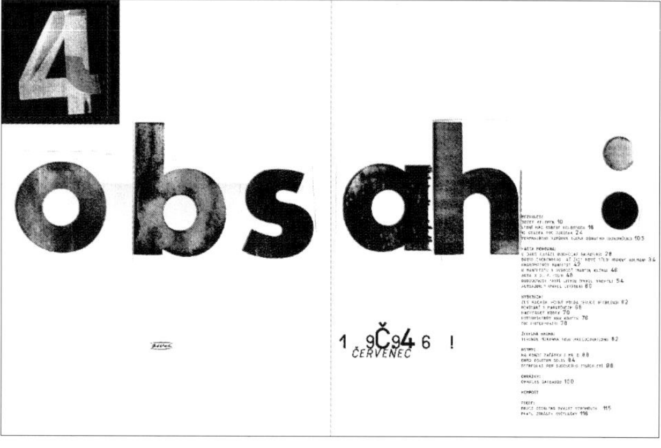

Zivel

Double page Zivel n. 4

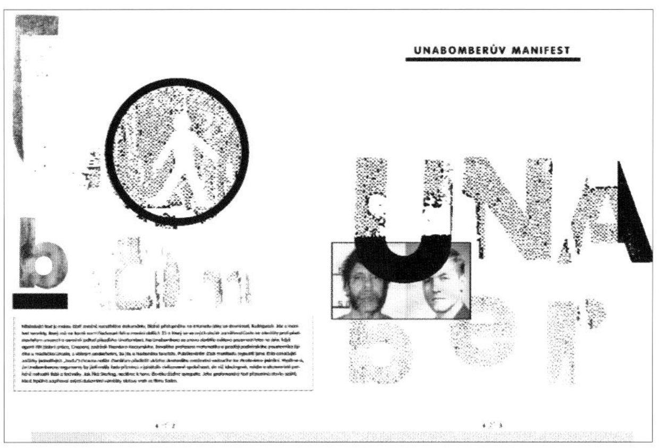

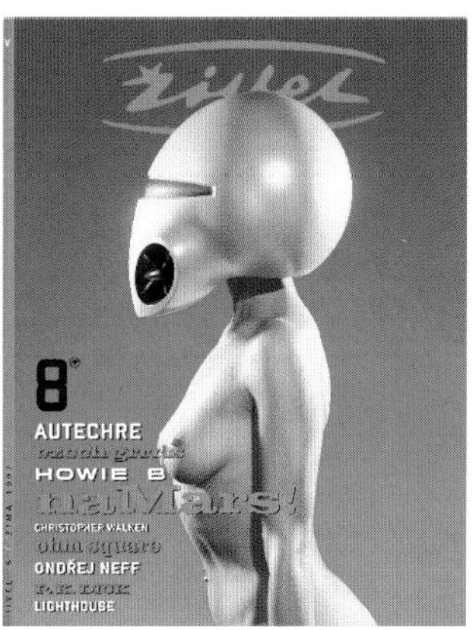

Zivel

Magazine covers
Double page Zivel n. 4

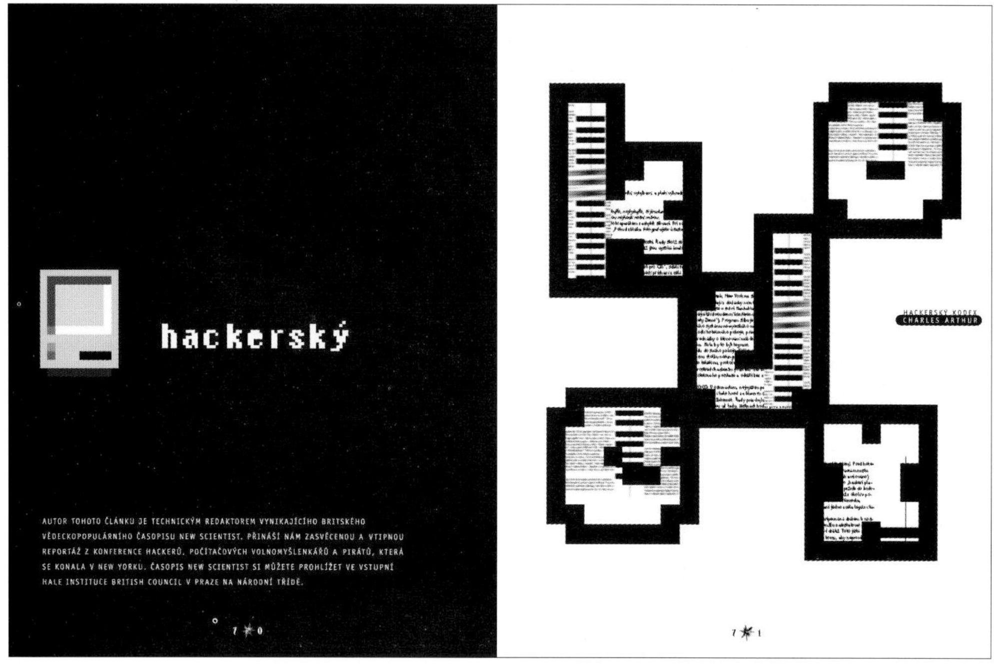

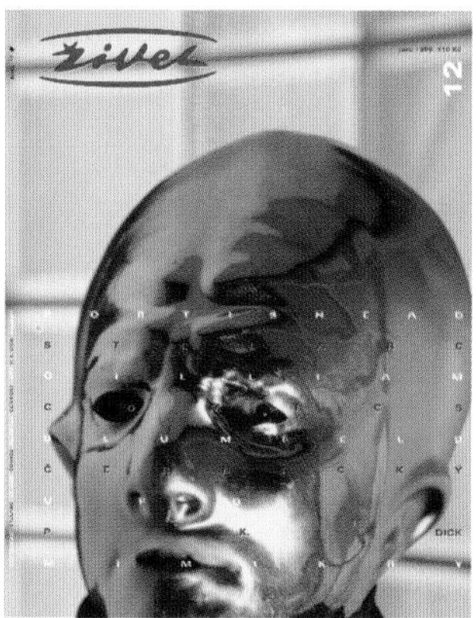

Zivel
Magazine

Year: 1995
Client: Zivel House

21 x 25 cm. 2 inks

Fonts Made to Measure

Zivel magazine was created in 1995 as a diploma project for the University of Fine Arts of Prague. With a solid experimental base in the use of fonts, from the outset Zivel was conceived as a magazine for the diffusion of the alternative lifestyle of a new generation of Czechs. The contents range from social issues to cyberculture, techno music and any other theme that Czech youths might be concerned with.

"Considering that it targets a young readership, we can take more risks with the legibility," Petr says.

One feature of the magazine is that it uses its own typefaces, designed by Klara Kvizova and her colleagues Petr Krejzek, Marek Pistora and Radim Pesko.

They often design their fonts specially for the contents of a single issue; fonts that demonstrate the expressive and emotional force of designs based on intuition and the spontaneity.

Indeed part of the magazine's appeal is the change it undergoes from one issue to the next.

"Because of our tight budget we began designing it in black and white. And eventually we realised that that gave the magazine

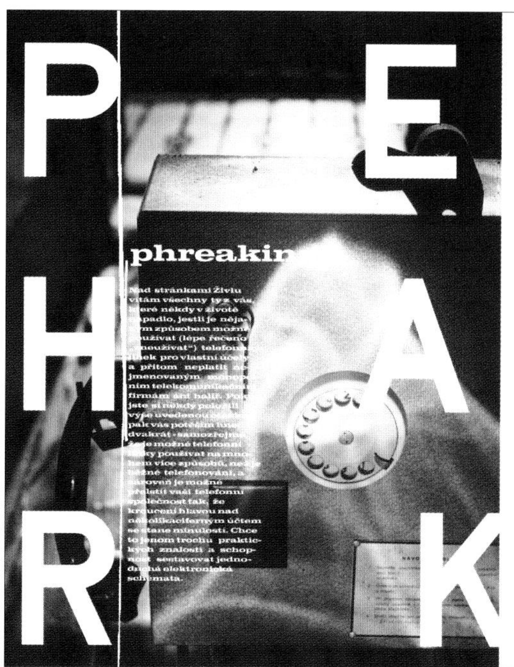

Zivel

Double page Zivel n. 8
Double page Zivel n. 14

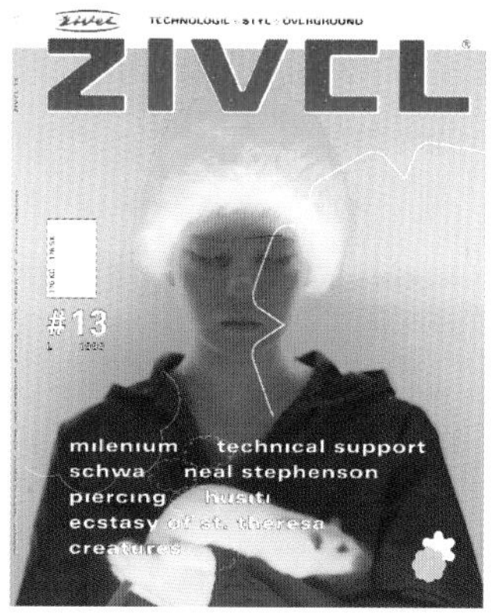

an interesting character, midway between pop and underground."

Zivel provides the ReDesign studio with a proving ground for its own fonts and experimentation with the graphic structures. A magazine by young designers for young readers, one of the few examples found in the Czech print media today.

Zivel

Magazine covers

Double page Zivel n. 12
Double page Zivel n. 17

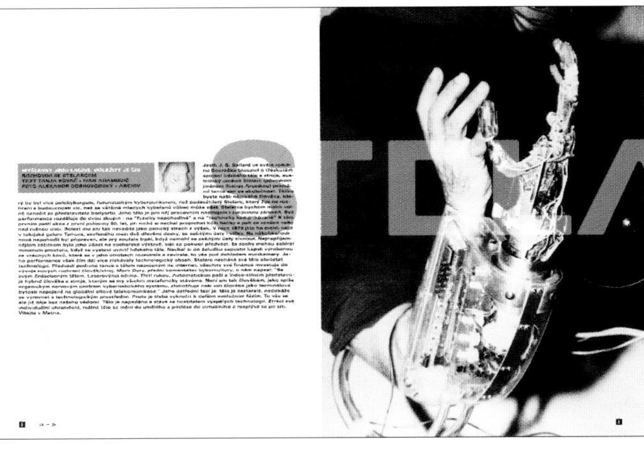

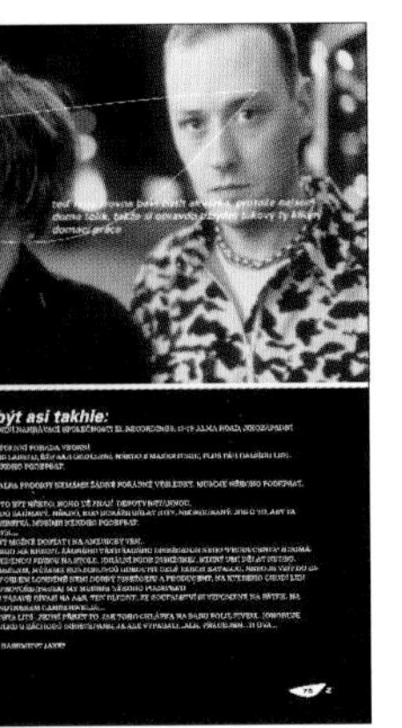

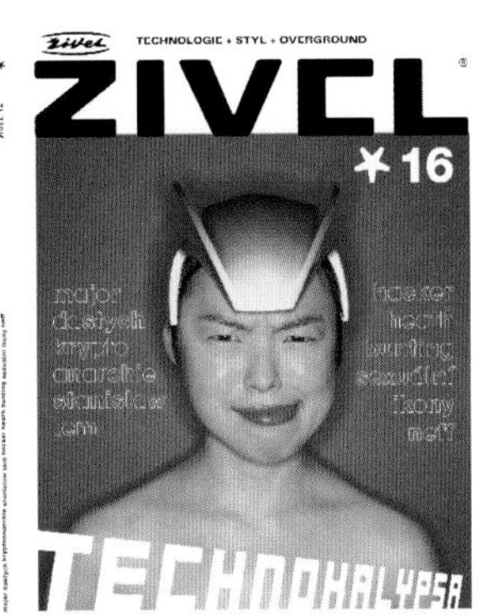

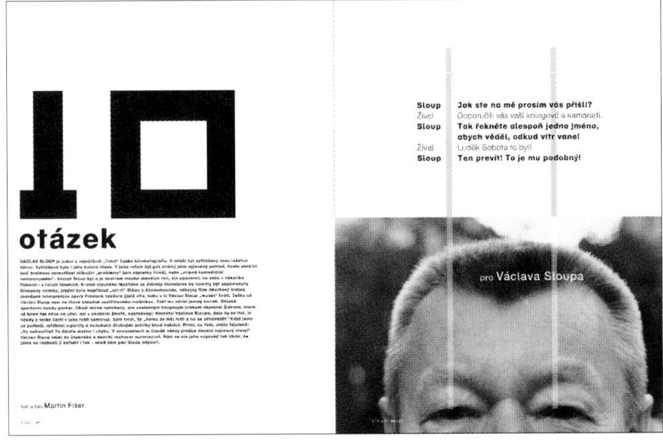

Zivel
2001

Cover Zivel n. 19

technognose industriální speleologie laser slash vernor vinge felix da housecat josef nesvadba benjamin diamond etymologie kyberpunku futuristický rock

Typerware

Typerware
Santa Maria de Martorelles, Spain

Faust v 3.0 / La Fura dels Baus
1998

Page from the libretto

"Two Fellows and Some Fonts"

Joan Carles Pérez (Barcelona, 1969) studied graphic design at the Elisava and Bau design schools in Barcelona.

Andreu Balius (Barcelona, 1962) studied Sociology at the Autonomous University of Barcelona and graphic design at the IDEP school. He combined his studies with work, contributing to **Ajoblanco** magazine and working for various design firms before setting up his own studio in 1990.

Andreu Balius and Joan Carles met in 1993 at the Bau design school where Andreu was teaching. They began working together under the name **Typerware**, designing fonts eventually included in the **Garcia fonts & co.** catalogue.

At first their collaboration was closely linked to the playful typography project **Garcia fonts & co.**, which Andreu had launched a short time before. But their work as designers was soon to expand into other graphic territories.

Their interest in type means that it takes a leading role in most of their graphic work.

Some of their fonts are included in the **ITC** (International Typeface Corporation) and **FontFont** (FontShop International) catalogues.

Andreu and Joan Carles worked together up until the end of 2001, when they both struck out on their own.

Manes / La Fura dels Baus
Book-object based on the basic ideas for a production by La Fura dels Baus.
A font generated by the use of a fax – FaxFont – served as an expressive vehicle for laying out the texts accompanying the images of La Fura del Baus.

El Fausto de Goethe es una obra monumental

Monumental por la amplitud y profundidad del pensamiento literario que genera, por la condición de obra de toda una vida -una obra que Goethe retoma una y otra vez desde su juventud y sólo deja definitivamente acabada meses antes de su muerte, pero también por la calidad de las versiones que ha dejado como secuela. La leyenda de Fausto, la posibilidad de un pacto entre el hombre y las potencias infernales, puede rastrearse, sin embargo, desde la Antigüedad y es, por lo tanto, anterior al personaje histórico en que se basa. Georg Sabelicus Faustus Junior, nacido en 1480 y muerto en 1540, fue históricamente un personaje oscuro, doctor en teología, astrólogo, nigromante y servidor del diablo. La obra anónima Historia del Dr. Johann Faustus (1587) fue escrita en tiempos de luchas de religión y de caza de brujas e identifica el afán de saber propio del Renacimiento con las artes diabólicas. Significativamente, sin embargo, es el afán de saber el elemento que, más allá de la literatura popular (donde cabe incluir la versión para títeres que impresionó al Goethe niño), se encuentra en el origen de las reelaboraciones cultas de la leyenda y, especialmente, de las dos partes (1808 y 1832) del Fausto de Goethe. El Fausto de Goethe es un clásico, es decir, una obra que es preciso leer y releer y que, en cada relectura, ensancha su vastísimo universo de sentido. Pero hay más. El Fausto de Goethe es una obra en verso y resulta prácticamente intraducible porque la sonoridad y el ritmo de los versos forman parte del contenido. Ambas circunstancias hacen que cualquier aproximación al Fausto de Goethe sea siempre e inevitablemente una versión.

¶

El F@usto, versión 3.0 toma como referencia inmediata el Fausto I y II de Goethe. Es una versión libre porque, además, había que traducirlo al lenguaje escénico que caracteriza a LA FURA DELS BAUS. En cualquier caso, la libertad del F@usto versión 3.0 no es pura arbitrariedad, ni pura modernidad estética: intenta interpretar el pensamiento de Goethe desde unas coordenadas de actualidad dentro de las cuales Dios (¿qué dios?). Mefisto (¿metáfora de qué?) o el afán de saber de Fausto (¿qué Naturaleza nos queda por leer?) no pueden tener el mismo sentido. Nuestro presente nos aboca sin escapatoria a una nueva forma de conocimiento marcado por herramientas ya tan habituales, y sin embargo de posibilidades aún inexploradas, como el ordenador e internet. El desbordamiento de la información en la red informática, leído a menudo desde un optimismo heredero del optimismo del progreso, no mejora ni transforma la condición del hombre, creado sin finalidad por las leyes del azar de la evolución y ligado a las perentorias exigencias de unos instintos primarios contra los que se elevan los muros de contención de las normas sociales. F@usto, versión 3.0 utiliza para explicar la historia una diversidad de lenguajes que son los de la sensibilidad del hombre actual. Teatro, música, vídeo, objetos, luces, acción se entrelazan para explicar la historia original sintetizada, fragmentada, desdoblada. Sin perder su resonancia trágica, todos los personajes son personajes con biografías posibles en nuestras ciudades. Fausto es, en la versión 3.0, habitante de la desolada imagen del universo surgida del Big Bang, el hombre inmerso en la insatisfacción de la incapacidad de vivir. Mefisto no es el diablo de la tradición cristiana, sino el desdoblamiento de Fausto, es el ser oscuro, diablo interior de los instintos, capaz de arrastrar la razón hacia los delirios de la pasión y la muerte. Su viaje atraviesa la cara oculta de la realidad social. Margarita es, en definitiva, la víctima universal, paradigma de cualquier violencia cometida contra el débil. A su alrededor, los personajes conforman el mundo contemporáneo que habitamos. F@usto, versión 3.0 es el desenfreno del deseo, de la pasión del amor y la muerte, el desenfreno de ese ser dual, monstruo sin finalidad ni paz que son Fausto y Mefisto. Hemos realizado un proceso de digitalización de Fausto hasta llegar a su dualidad binaria: 0-1.

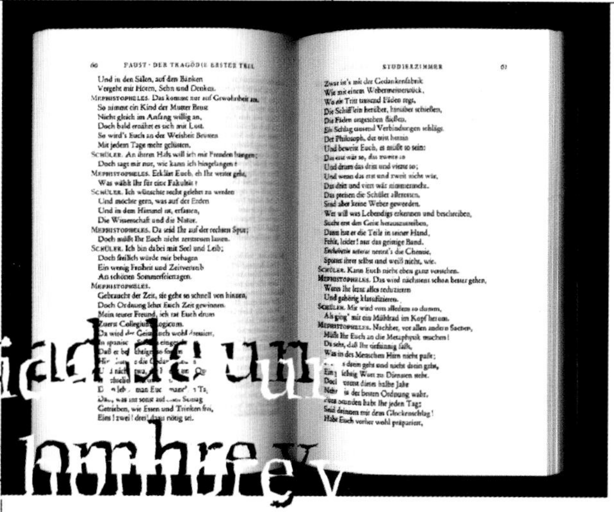

la posibilidad de un pacto entre el hombre y las potencias infernales,

la llibertat del F@ust versió 3.0 no és pura arbitrarietat, ni pura modernitat estètica: intenta interpretar el pensament de Goethe des d'unes coordenades d'actualitat dintre de les quals Déu (quin déu?), Mefist (metàfora de què?) o l'afany de saber de Faust (quina Natura ens queda per llegir?) no poden tenir el mateix sentit.

El Fausto de Goethe es un clásico, es decir, una obra que es preciso leer y releer y que, en cada relectura, ensancha su vastísimo universo de sentido.

Faust v 3.0

Cover of the libretto and inside pages

Faust v 3.0
Theatre libretto

Year: 1998
Client: La Fura dels Baus

Fonts used: Beowolf, Gutenberg (digitalised blackletter typeface)

21.5 x 29 cm. 44 pages. Full colour printing

The Libretto as Theatrical Support
La Fura dels Baus, one of Spain's most innovative theatre companies, commissioned Typerware to design a libretto for its production 'Faust v 3.0'.

La Fura's production draws on the well-known Goethe play to create a new work set in the present, where the new technologies and mass media play a key role in our everyday environment. In this work, La Fura combine theatre with music, video and special effects to reveal Faust's dual personality, whose existence is marked by love and death.

Typerware's design should be viewed in the context of this approach to theatre.

The booklet is divided into three parts. In the first, the company explains its particular interpretation of this classic piece of European theatre; the second is a brief chronological rundown of the different scenes that make up the production; and the third contains information about the company, including curriculum and credits.

Typerware use the ideas that inform the production and at the same time give shape to the tortured being Faust. The spread was con-

Fausto firma con sangre su entrega.

he very waters stirred by Faust, someone was waiting for him in the bath. Faust signs his commitment with

Faust signs his commitment with blood.

Faust firma el seu lliurament amb sang el seu lliurament.

Margaret fills the corridors of the mind of her creator.

"el gran mundo está hecho de mundc

Margarita ahueca pasillos en la mente de su creador.

"el gran mundo está he

"el gran món està fe

...the great world is made of small worlds"

stà fet de mons petits".

Amb paraules del mateix Mefisto s'accelera la fi de la noia. Penjada d'un ganxo, com un animal escorxat, es balanceja la primera personificació de la dona interna de Faust. Margarida eixampla passadissos en la ment del seu creador.

o está hecho de mundos pequeños".

Con palabras del propio Mefisto se acelera el fin de la joven. Colgada de un gancho, como una res, pende la primera personificación de la mujer interna de Fausto. Margarita ahueca pasillos en la mente de su creador.

d is made of small worlds".

With Mephistopheles' own words the death of the young woman is accelerated. Slung on a hook like an animal carcass, the first personification of the woman inside Faust hangs. Margaret fills the corridors of the mind of her creator.

Faust v 3.0

Double inside pages

Page devoted to the company's curriculum, with text arrayed according to the different languages: Spanish, Catalan and English.

ceived with complete freedom. The space was only divided horizontally in two, along a central axis, with the aim of expressing the character's dual personality. This horizon marks the fine line separating wisdom from insanity, the real world from the world of shadows, the conscious from the innermost self. The axis is the thread which links the visuals throughout the pages of the booklet.

The full colour images – printed in fluorescent ink so that the chromatic range is similar to that seen on the RGB screens – acquire enormous importance. In many cases the type is laid over them and competes on an equal footing on the printed page.

Typerware chose the Beowolf font, created by LettError, a type with a classic feel but which randomly changes shape when generated on a PostScript rasterizer – printed or on film. With the use of Beowolf, a font associated with computer language, they achieve a coherent resolution to the contradiction between Goethe's classical text and La Fura dels Baus' contemporary take on it. They also digitalised blackletter hand-drawn fonts, created before the invention of the printing press, for use as capitals at the beginning of paragraphs. This is another reference to the medieval tale of Dr. Johann Faustus which would later inspire Goethe in his Faust I and II.

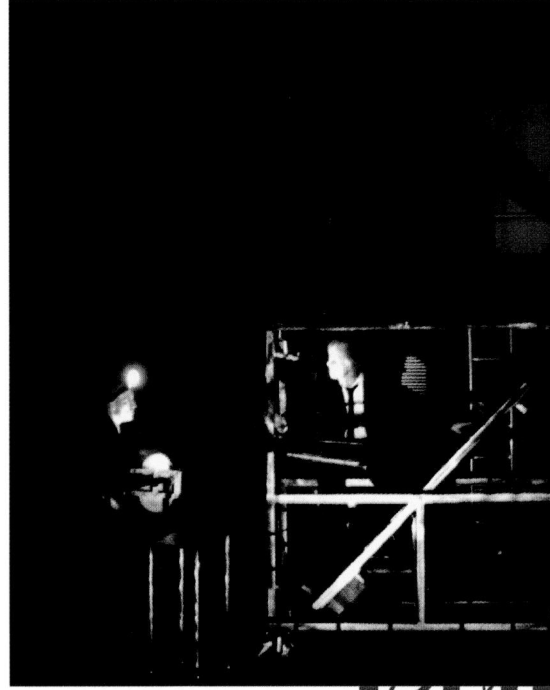

ACTOS I y II

Siguiendo el hilo c
encontramos al Doc
intimidad de su habitació
su cabeza. Deseos e invocac
sus exclamaciones al mun
incluso a través de internet
reciben repuestas vacías. S
cebando en los pasillos de l
iluminación puntual. su

ACTES I i II

ACTS I. II

Seguint el fil de l'"acció" trobem el Doctor Faust en la intimitat de la seva habitació sotmès al balandreig del seu cap. Desitjos i invocacions emergeixen entre les seves exclamacions al món, als esperits, fins i tot per internet. **Totes aquestes crides** reben respostes buides. reben respostes buides. El neguit va burxant els passadissos de la seva ment, subjecta a una il·luminació puntual, el seu remugueig intern.

Faust v 3.0

Double inside pages

The importance of the typography lies in the arrangement of the bodies of text and the rhythm which this generates.

Bored with himself he tries suicide. We will never know if he failed in the attempt or if all of Faust is an exhalation. What is certain is that Mephistopheles, manifest evil or even the shadow of Faust himself, depending on the vers on, presents himself to him willing to give him what he desires.

Avorrit de si mateix, prova el suïcidi. Mai no sabrem si erra l'intent o si tot el Faust és una expiració. Però el que és cert és que Mefisto, manifestació maligna o mera ombra del mateix Faust, segons les versions, se li presenta davant disposat a donar-li allò que desitja.

Aburrido de sí mismo, intenta el suicidio. Nunca sabremos si falla en el intento o si todo el Fausto es una expiración. Lo cierto es que Mefisto, manifestación maligna o simple sombra del propio Fausto, según versiones, se le presenta dispuesto a darle aquello que desea.

Todas esas llamadas reciben repuestas

Todas esas llamadas reciben repuestas vacías.

Todas esas llamadas reciben repuestas vacías.

Todas esas llamadas reciben repuestas vacías.

Todas esas llamadas reciben repuestas vacías.

s

n de

ntre

s.

adas reciben repuestas vacías. Su ansiedad se va cebando en los pasillos de la mente, sujeta a una iluminación puntual, su ron eo interno.

una

o.

Following the thread of the 'action' we find Dr. Faust in the intimacy of his room, subject to the oscillations in his head. Desires and invocations emerge from among his exclamations to the world, to the spirits, even through Internet. **All those** calls receive empty answers. His anxiety feeds itself in the corridors of his mind, subject to a specific illumination his internal purring. calls receive empty answers. His anxiety feeds itself in the corridors of his mind, subject to a specific illumination his internal purring.

Orange Juice

Garth Walker
Durban, South Africa

I-Jusi no. 13
2000

Poster designed by Scott Robertson

"Pure Juice"

Garth Walker (1957) studied graphic design at Technikon Natal (South Africa).

After a long stay at a small design firm in Durban, in 1995 he founded his own studio, **Orange Juice Design**. In the same year, he published the first edition of **I-Jusi** magazine with the aim of promoting and stimulating a design language rooted in South African culture.

"I started I-Jusi just after I'd set up my own studio, in 1995. I had no clients so the magazine was a way of keeping busy," says Garth. With his laid-back approach to his daily work he looks on graphic design as one of his hobbies, among which he also includes **"books, magazines, photography, wine tasting, travelling and cycling."**

In 1997, Orange Juice Design was acquired by Ogilvy & Mather as their design brand, and now has offices in Durban, Cape Town and Johannesburg.

I-Jusi
Magazine covers

I-Jusi no. 15. 2001
I-Jusi no. 13. 2000

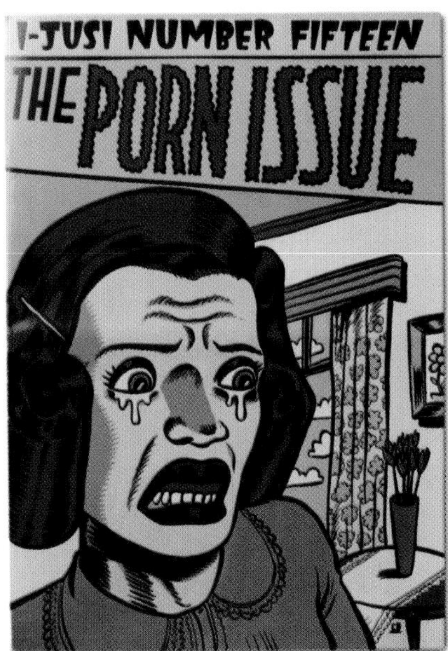

STADSAAL 19h00 • MOOI MEISIES • DRANK • VLOEK • WORS ROLLS • ROFSTOEI

VANAAND **WRESTLING** TONIGHT

A NEW CONSTITUTION GRUDGE MATCH FOR THE ALL AFRICAN INTER-CONTINENTAL TITLE

Die Boer

DIE BOER VS EL NEGRO

"DIE SWARTE"

WHITE GUILT vs BLACK POWER

Die Swarte

R15.00 ADULTS

KINDERS R10.00

FREE

DAAR IS NIKS GRATIS IN DIE LEWE NIE.

BROUGHT TO YOU BY

FEATURING LIVE AND LOUD

WOUTER BASSON EN DIE TRC TROMPOPPIES

HARDCORE

MOENIE DIE SKOUSPEL MISLOOP NIE!

Scott Robertson

Issue
Twelve
death

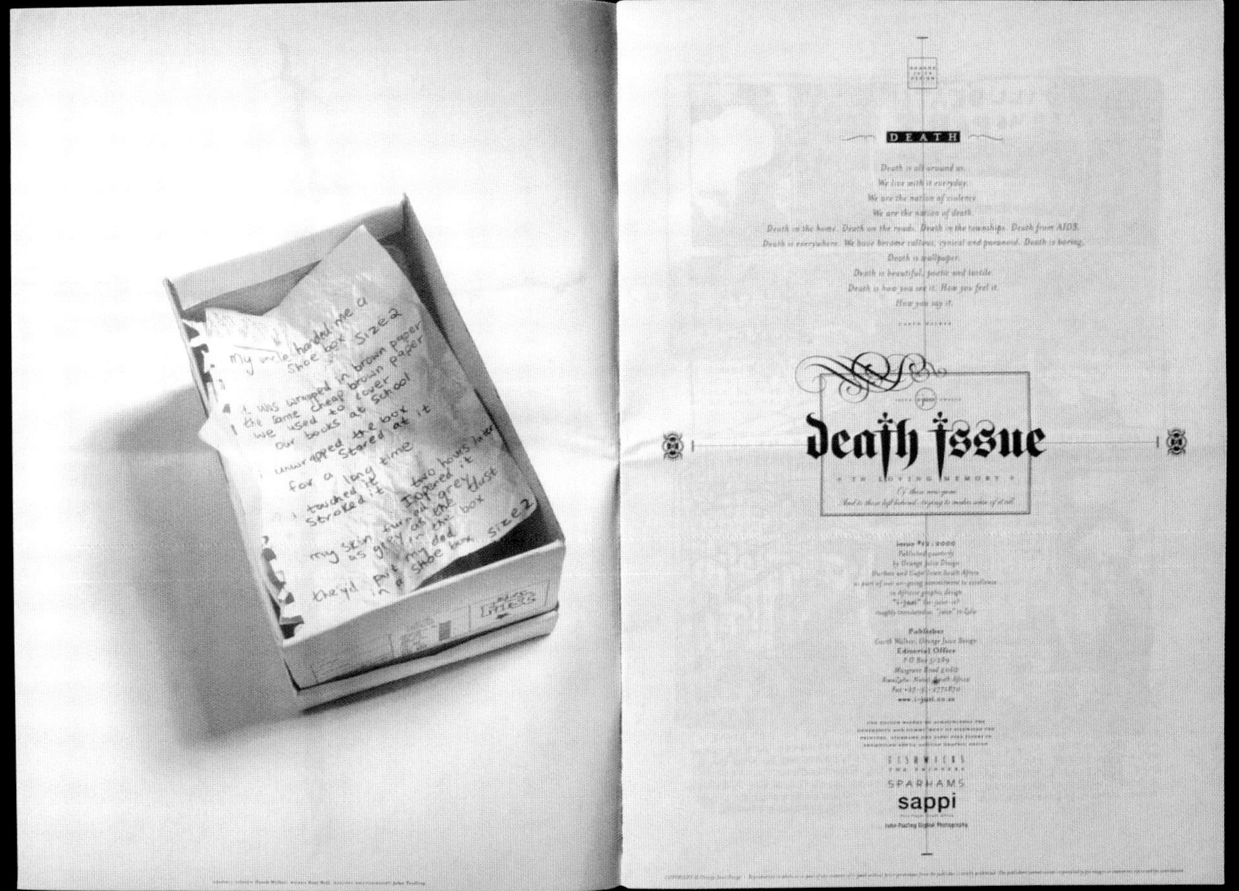

I-Jusi
Magazine

Year: 1995
Client: Orange Juice Design

29.7 x 42 cm. 16 pages. Full colour printing. Quarterly

Street Culture

I-Jusi – 'juice' in Zulu – appeared in 1995 with the aim of developing a graphic design language rooted in South African culture. The magazine, which is non-profit and published quarterly, acts as a platform for the expression and promotion of South African professional designers, design students, illustrators, photographers and writers.

As a personal project that he manages from his own studio, Garth has a completely free hand in the design of the magazine. Indeed it is just one of his hobbies.

Each issue of I-Jusi is devoted to one subject and designers and writers are invited to contribute. The page design follows very simple guidelines, so the designers are totally free to do what they want, how they want it. The editors do not interfere directly in the result or how individual designers interpret the theme. Instead they simply select the best work submitted for publication, although most of submissions are from members of the **Orange Juice Design** staff.

Garth defines I-Jusi as **"an experimental magazine".** He says his work is influenced to a certain extent by Russian Constructiv-

What will happen when I die?
Will I go to Heaven and see
God as was promised by the
Dutch Reformed Church?

Standing on the mountain at night
and looking at the glittering city lights:
How many lives are ending and beginning?

Imagine the immense relief in dying, no more worrying
about getting fucked over by the rest of the human race.

Design is Death
Death is Design

Sleep Eat Fuck Die

Will someone remember
the good/bad things I did?

CONFUSED

THINKING

Name: WHITE PUSSY FACE Age: 25

Subject: DEATH

I want to be cremated....

In my final hour
will I have regrets?

What makes me think of death is usually the stuff
that other people find happiness in, for example
going to the cinema to watch a "feel good" movie.

I am young ambitious, positive about life,
career driven, but I will die one day.

CARBON MONOXIDE
WASHINGTON
The way to go. I drive past a funeral parlour on my way home from work.
It is a gloomy grey building nestled between a run-down liquor store
and a shoe factory in the seedy semi-industrial part of town.
On certain days, brownish grey smoke trails from a tall thin chimney at
the back of the building and blends in with the pollution of the city.
GRAPHIC DESIGN Nadine Bindemann

I-Jusi no. 11
2000

Cover and inside pages.
National Typografika is a special issue devoted to typography. It showcases fonts designed by South African designers.

ism and by indigenous African craftwork. But his main source of inspiration is in the street: African vernacular graphics and popular culture, reflected above all in the use of illustration and the 'casual' arrangement of elements on the page. Sometimes this vernacular and spontaneous spirit is manifested typographically with handwritten texts.

Typography in I-Jusi acts as a catalyst between Western culture and indigenous graphics. For Garth, the basic rule is that the typography must be **"sympathetic to the message"**. This is the criterion he uses when choosing a particular typeface.

"When working with typography", he says, **"it's important to ignore boundaries of any kind. But there are certain rules that you do have to take into account."**

Garth sometimes creates typefaces specially for a particular issue of I-Jusi. He uses vectoral design programmes – such as FreeHand – to draw the letters which he then places one by one, composing the texts manually just like a traditional typesetter would. The task is laborious, but it permits him to avoid software-imposed standardisation and obtain results closer to the language of the street.

The combination of typographical forms and images – usually illustrations – helps to bring plenty of originality, authenticity and freshness to the finished pages of the magazine.

type issue
One Man's Search For A Boerewors Roll.
iZulu
i-jusi
Undertaker
CURTAIN LINEN BAZAAR
RAJ CHETTY
COCKROACH SPRAY

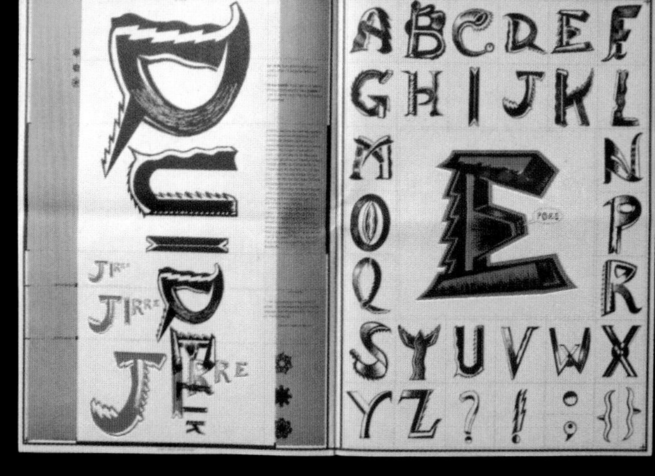
ABCDEF
GHIJKL
YZ?!:

CABO

FFIRKORN
OLONIAL

A B C D E F G H
KAFFIRKORN
KOLONIAL

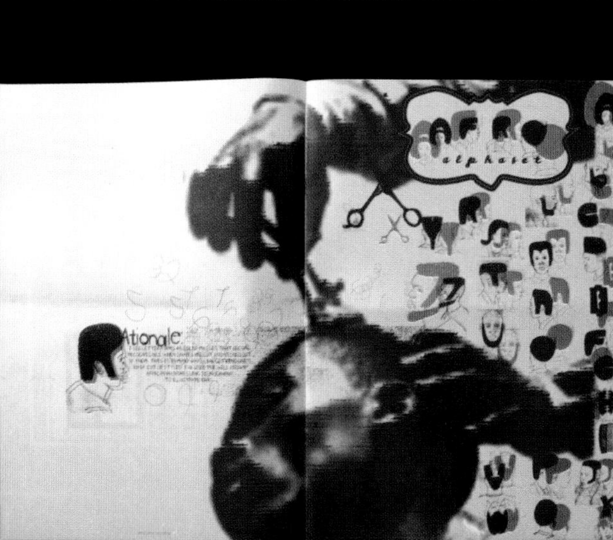
AFRO
alphabet
Ationale

Bis]

Pere Àlvaro, Àlex Gifreu
Figueres, Spain

"Typography as Graphic Expression"

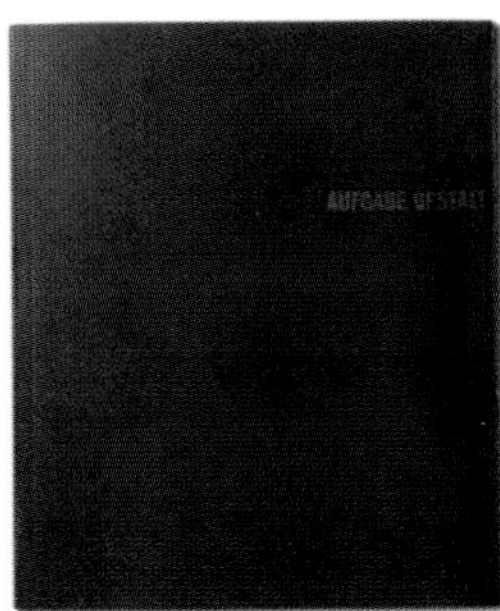

Pere Àlvaro (Palafrugell, 1967) and Àlex Gifreu (Maó, 1971) met in 1992 at the School for Applied Arts and Artistic Trades of Olot (Girona), where Pere taught design for several years. After working separately for some time while collaborating on the occasional project, they decided to join forces and set up Bis] in 1997.

Before founding their own studio, both Pere and Àlex had alternated between freelance work and collaborations with other studios in the US, England and Holland. This gave them the opportunity to know different ways of working, which they apply to their own design processes.

Their broad experience has enabled them to win the confidence of their clients and thus gives them certain liberty when it comes to designing.

In addition to commissions, they do personal work in the form of small, carefully crafted publications for artists and friends.

Their work pushes the boundaries, but has certain restraint – a quality hard to find in today's graphic design.

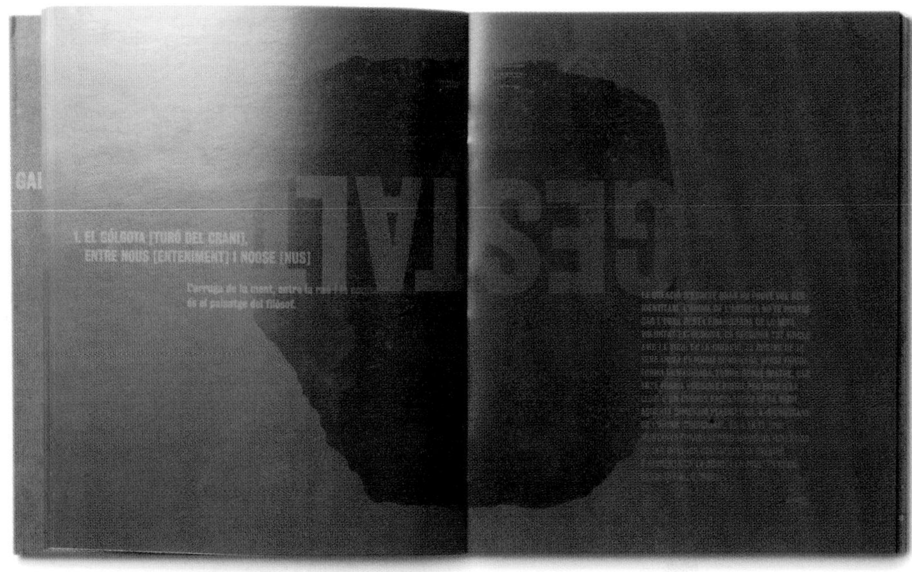

Listening Walls catalogue
2000

Publication designed for a sound art exhibition based on four posters, the reverse sides of which make up the catalogue itself. The austere composition on the fronts, consisting of the initials of the three artists in the exhibition, contrasts with the back structured in modules. The four catalogue-posters are folded up inside a cardboard box which also contains an audio CD.
The font used is Kebab, designed by Àlex Gifreu, based on the destination signs on Istanbul buses.

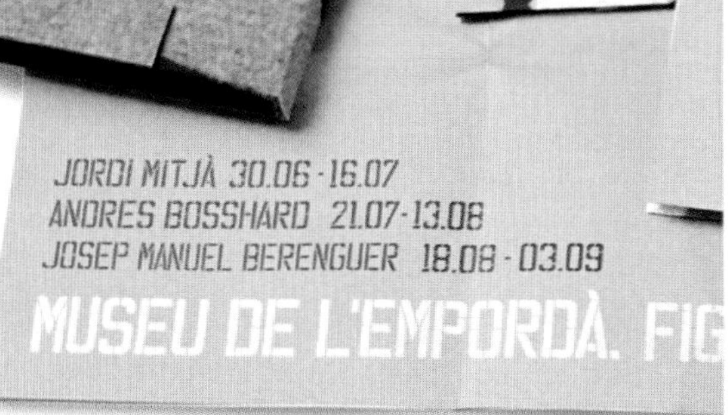

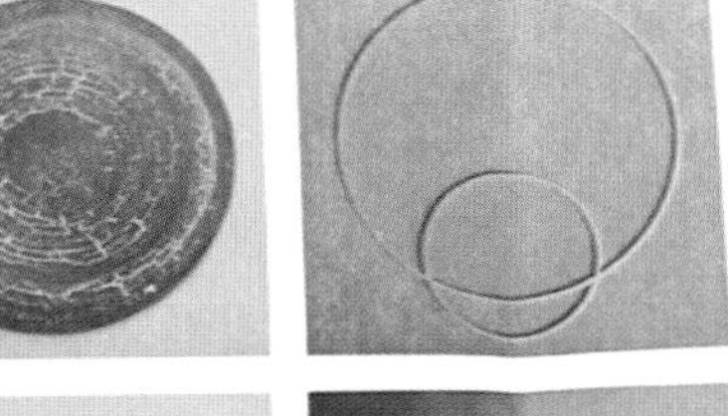

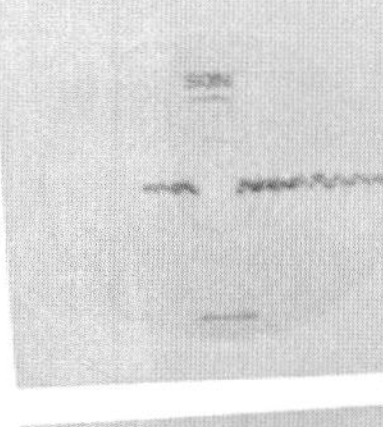

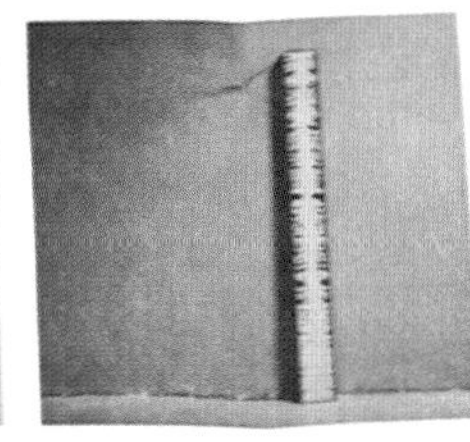

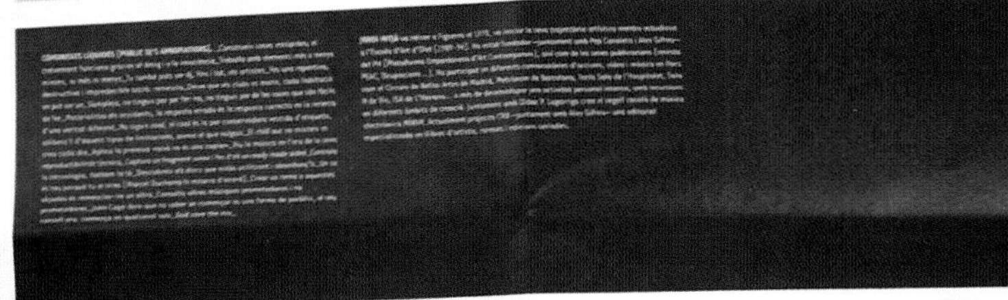

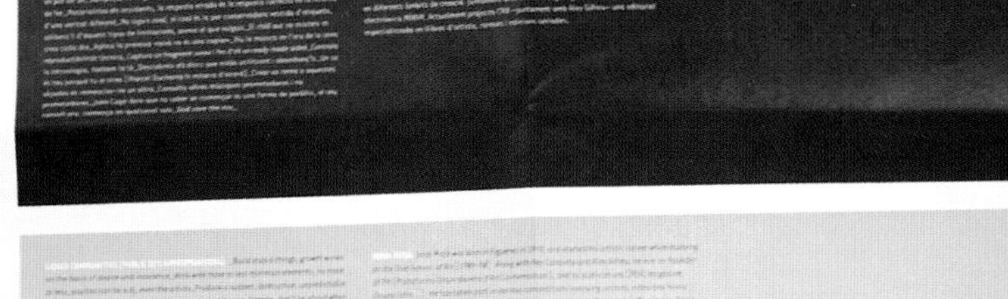

‹ **Aufgabe Gestalt** catalogue
1999

Catalogue designed for the sculptor Gabriel. Printed in three shades of black, using metallic inks and varnishes, it is only readable when the light strikes the paper at different angles. The reproduction technique is aimed at reflecting the work of the artist in the catalogue: sculptures and drawings, most of which are finished in different shades of black.

JORDI MITJÀ

PARÀSITS

art. the end
Xec imprès. Intervenció en una bústia bancària.
Rambla

ART
the end.

convertir el castell de Figueres en un altre mur de Berlin i fer de la vergony
un camp
d'atraccions
Cartell de 420 x 297 m
Intervenció a les
marquesines de la ciuta

convertir el castell
de Figueres en un
altre mur de Berlin,
i fer de la vergonya
un camp d'atraccions.

convertir el castell
de Figueres en un
altre mur de Berlin,
i fer de la vergonya
un camp d'atraccions

convertir el castell
de Figueres en un
altre mur de Berlin,
i fer de la vergonya
un camp d'atraccions.

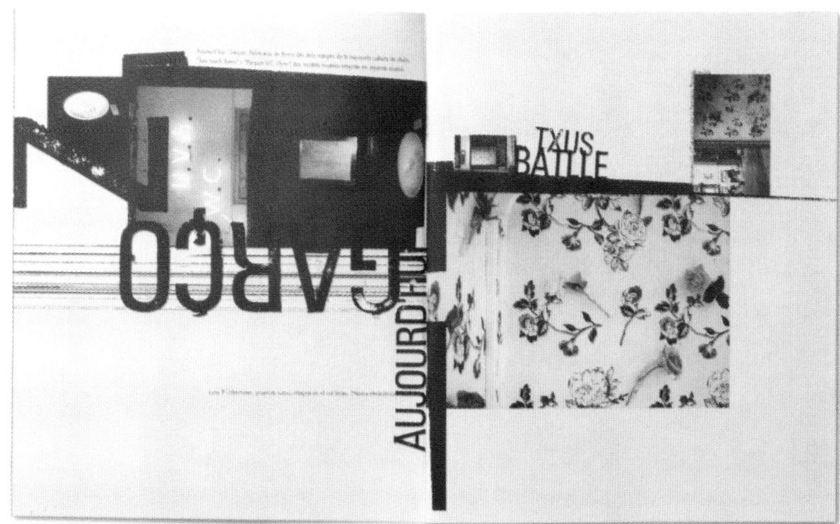

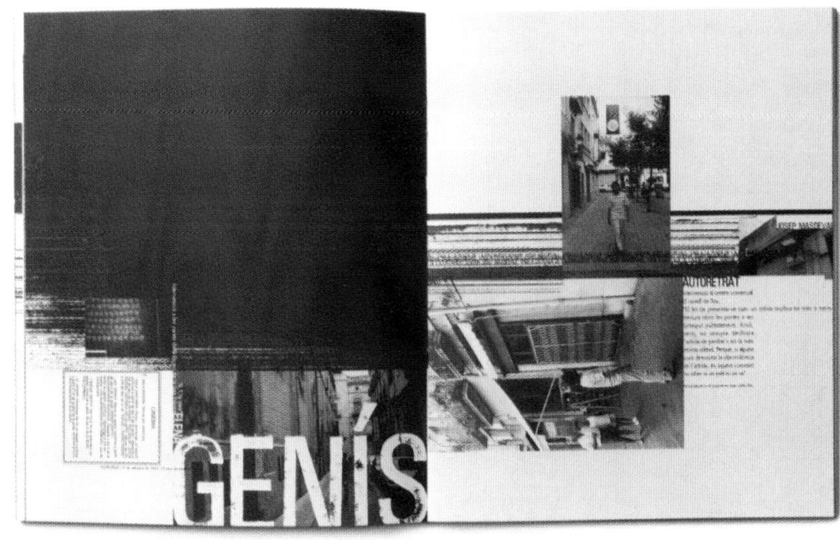

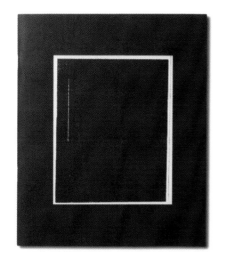

Catalogue [PH]
Cover and inside pages

As it is not based on a definite compositional structure or grid, the cohesion of the different components on the page – photography and typography – depends on the arrangement of the blank and inked spaces.
The absence of a grid and the formal play between the blocks of text and images is characteristic of much of Bis]'s work.

"We believe that an implicit order exists in the forms of the elements, which, if you can find it, permits you to create layouts that are much more effective than those determined by a simple grid."

[PH] Ocupacions
Catalogue

Year: 1997
Client: Plataforma Empordanesa d'Art Contemporani

Fonts used: Hector, Kennedy

21 x 25 cm. 36 pages. 1 black ink

Occupying Space

The Plataforma Empordanesa d'Art Contemporani [PH] (a platform for contemporary art in the Catalan region of Empordà) organised various street happenings, under the name Ocupacions, in the town of Figueres to protest the lack of spaces devoted to art. The campaign was open to anyone who wanted to transform public spaces – or anyone involved in the life of the town – with an artistic project. The [PH] catalogue, designed by Àlex Gifreu, records the different projects done by the artists who took part.

The contextualisation of their work in the cultural environment requires that Bis] be highly aware of the artistic phenomena they are dealing with. Àlex and Pere devote a lot of time to research and getting to know the subject-object of their projects: **"When we design a catalogue for an artist, we try to get an in-depth understanding of their discourse, their work, their attitude."** They both see the art catalogue as an extension of the artist's work and not as a mere 'publication-container' that exists for purely commercial reasons.

In the case of [PH], the catalogue is presented as just another piece within the body of work brought together by the event. Bis]

The fonts used in this work – Hector and Kennedy – were designed by Àlex Gifreu. Hector, digitalized from prints made with different wood types, is enormously expressive when used in large sizes. Its power lies in its imperfection, as it becomes integrated with the photographs and blends in with the darker areas.

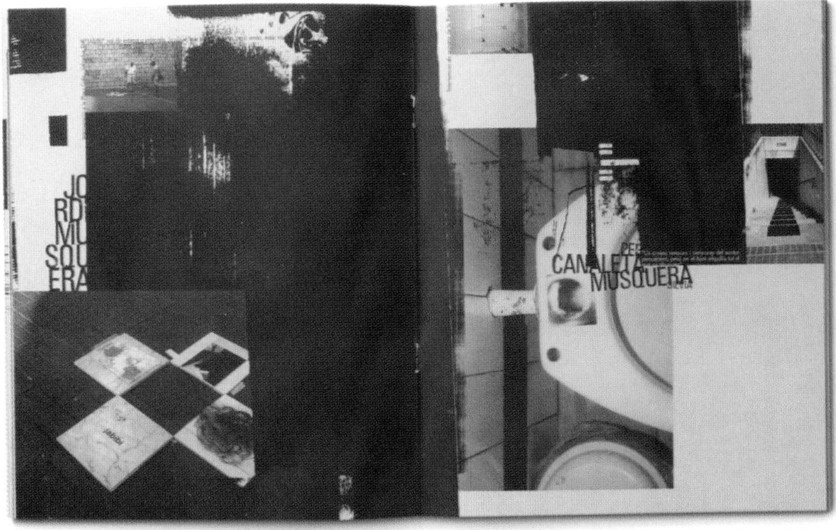

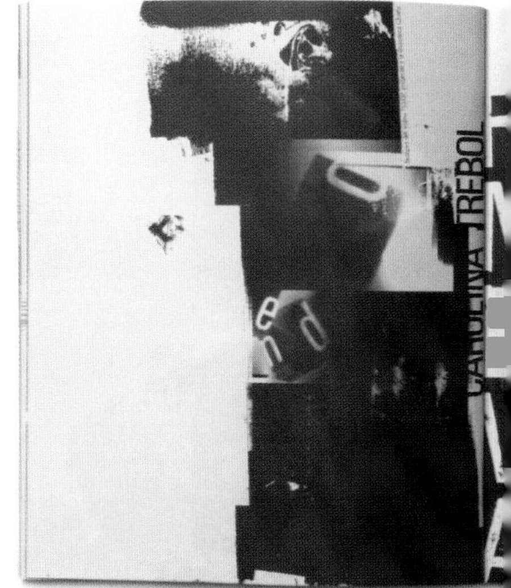

act as authors and use design to make their own artistic protest, in this case, through the occupation of a graphic space – a publication – and include photographs showing the different street happenings. Bis] lay graphics on top of the images – which show the work of various artists – in the shape of texts and ink stains, using a font, Hector, which imitates the texture of certain wood typefaces.

Bis]'s publishing work is characterised by the major role it allocates to typography as a vehicle for communication, at once verbal and expressive. In many cases, the shape of the letters becomes the image and competes on equal footing with the photography, as happens in this example.

"Typography is our favourite star. It's never given the supporting role," says Àlex. **"Although the relationship between the image and the text is important, rhythm and the expressiveness are fundamental when working with typography,"** adds Pere.

Posters de la programació del Talp Club. Temporada 96/97.

Intervenció a l'escorxador de Figueres.

Moniteurs

Heike Nehl, Heidi Specker, Sibylle Schlaich
Berlin, Germany

"Letters lend us their Character"

Founded in 1994 by three partners – Heike Nehl, Sibylle Schlaich and Heidi Specker – the Berlin design studio **Moniteurs** specialises in corporate identity development, broadening the terrain to apply graphic design to all the supports necessary for an identity's establishment.

The group work both in analogue and digital media, and this encourages them to examine the relationships between the two languages, achieving graphically interesting results.

As a design studio, Moniteurs has developed its own creative space in which to develop its projects. **"We see design as an active and emotional element within cultural processes, in which typography plays an important role."**

Workspace is a promotional publication by the Moniteurs studio.

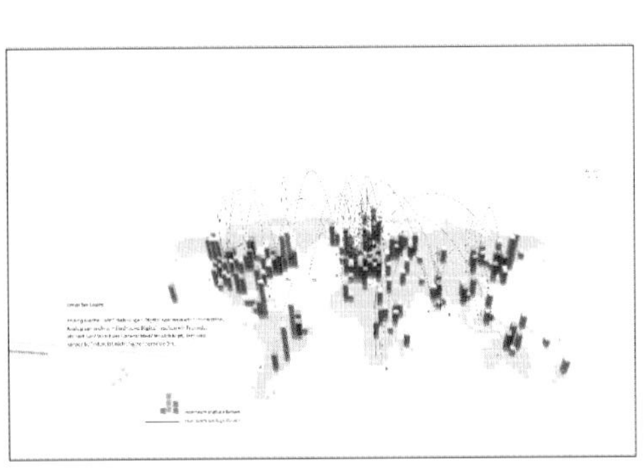

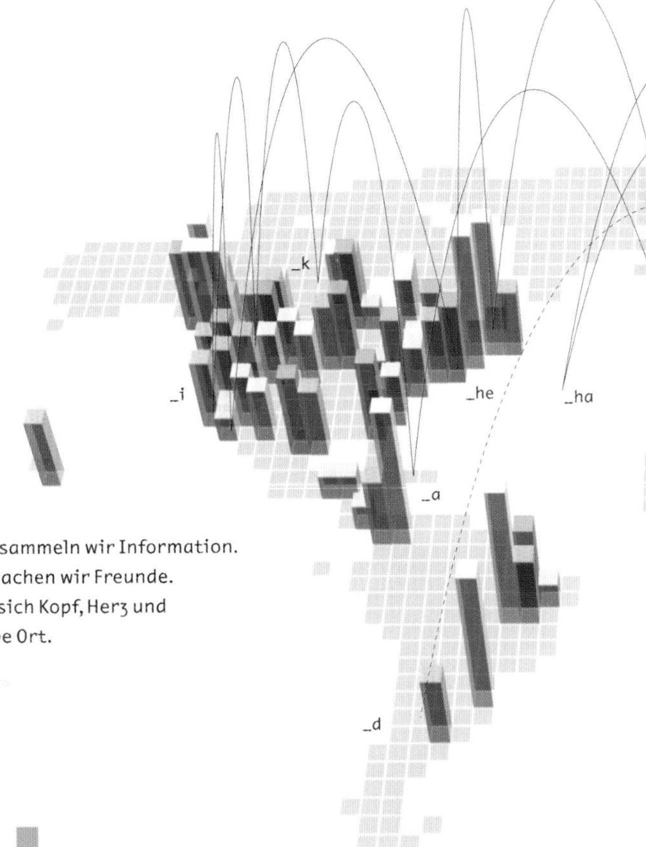

creative tours

Analog machen wir Erfahrungen. Digital sammeln wir Information. Analog sammeln wir Eindrücke. Digital machen wir Freunde. Stimmt das? Wo ist der Unterschied? Wo sich Kopf, Herȝ und Körper befinden, ist nicht immer derselbe Ort.

moniteurs digitale Reisen
moniteurs analoge Reisen

Emotional_digital
1999

Moniteurs was directly involved in producing this book, in both the design and the development of its contents.

Displaying a broad spectrum of design – fonts and their creators -demonstrates how expressive and personal contemporary typography can be.
As well as including articles on typography written by experts, the book reproduces examples of typography, posters, catalogues, leaflets and other promotional material published by these font houses, some with established reputations and others which are more recent and experimental.

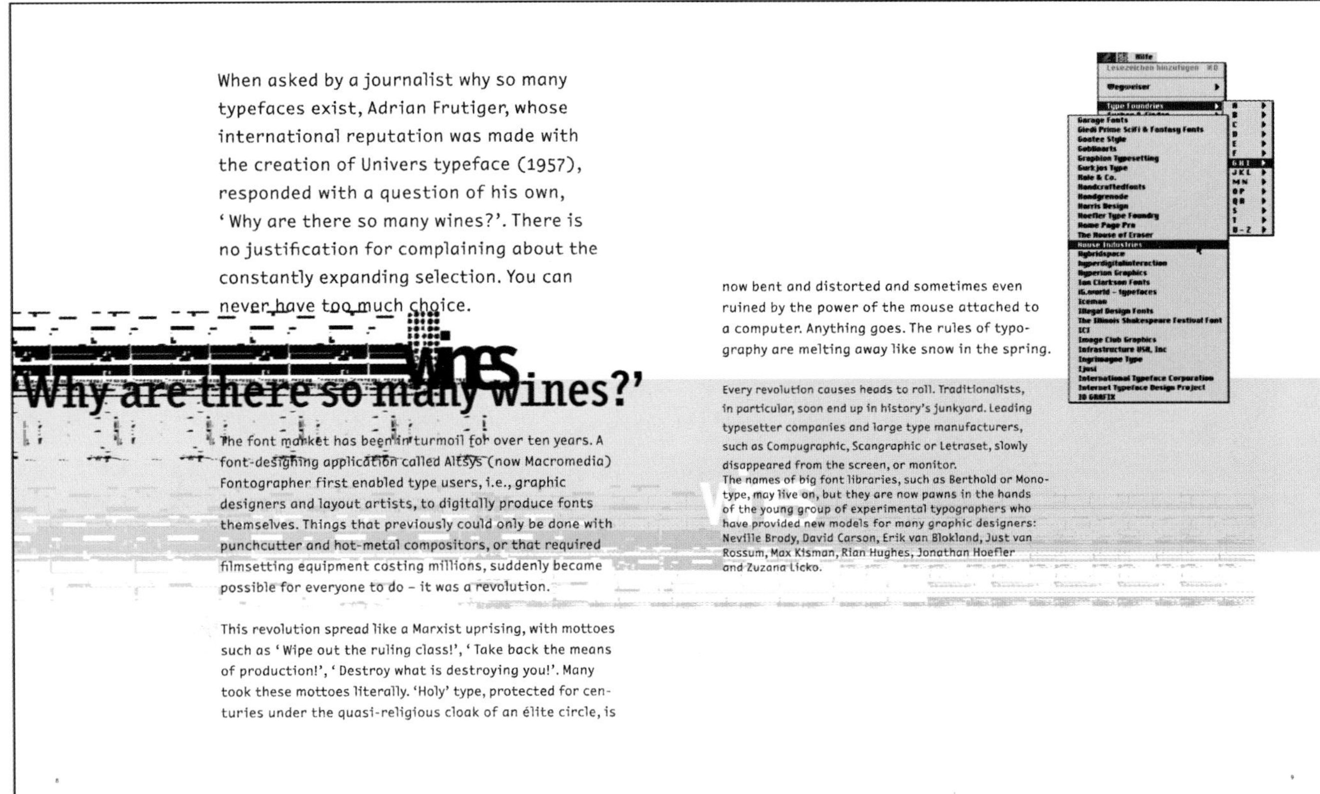

When asked by a journalist why so many typefaces exist, Adrian Frutiger, whose international reputation was made with the creation of Univers typeface (1957), responded with a question of his own, 'Why are there so many wines?'. There is no justification for complaining about the constantly expanding selection. You can never have too much choice.

'Why are there so many wines?'

The font market has been in turmoil for over ten years. A font-designing application called Altsys (now Macromedia) Fontographer first enabled type users, i.e., graphic designers and layout artists, to digitally produce fonts themselves. Things that previously could only be done with punchcutter and hot-metal compositors, or that required filmsetting equipment costing millions, suddenly became possible for everyone to do – it was a revolution.

This revolution spread like a Marxist uprising, with mottoes such as 'Wipe out the ruling class!', 'Take back the means of production!', 'Destroy what is destroying you!'. Many took these mottoes literally. 'Holy' type, protected for centuries under the quasi-religious cloak of an élite circle, is now bent and distorted and sometimes even ruined by the power of the mouse attached to a computer. Anything goes. The rules of typography are melting away like snow in the spring.

Every revolution causes heads to roll. Traditionalists, in particular, soon end up in history's junkyard. Leading typesetter companies and large type manufacturers, such as Compugraphic, Scangraphic or Letraset, slowly disappeared from the screen, or monitor. The names of big font libraries, such as Berthold or Monotype, may live on, but they are now pawns in the hands of the young group of experimental typographers who have provided new models for many graphic designers: Neville Brody, David Carson, Erik van Blokland, Just van Rossum, Max Kisman, Rian Hughes, Jonathan Hoefler and Zuzana Licko.

Emotional_digital
Book

Year: 1999
Client: Moniteurs

Fonts used:
Moniko, Bellczyk, Synaesthesis, mmm-teurs

23 x 28 cm. 312 pages. Full colour printing

Digital Emotion

Emotional_digital is a book about the 50 most influential font houses in the world, arranged in alphabetical order.

With the huge variety of material produced by these companies, it was a major challenge to unify formats and design a structure which would maintain unity throughout the publication.

Moniteurs opt for an open mockup, without formal restrictions, using a grid only for the introductory text for each of the font houses and the articles by specialists, interspersed throughout the book.

It is interesting to note how, by playing with proportions, blank spaces, overlaid images, fonts, alphabets, etc. in the layout of the material from the different font houses, a rhythm is achieved.

"Normally, the content of a book is expressed through letters, but in this case the letters are the content," says Sibylle.

Emotional_digital
Alphabetical dividers

Moniteurs, working jointly with the Xplicit studio, designed the Synaesthesis and mmm-teurs typefaces as additional fonts for the cover and inside dividers. These are experimental typefaces which 'whisper' – like background noise.

Emotional_digital

Inside pages presenting the different font houses included in the publication.

Moniko and Bellczyk were specially designed by Alexander Branczyk for the book's texts based on the Monaco — associated with Macintosh — and Bell fonnts.

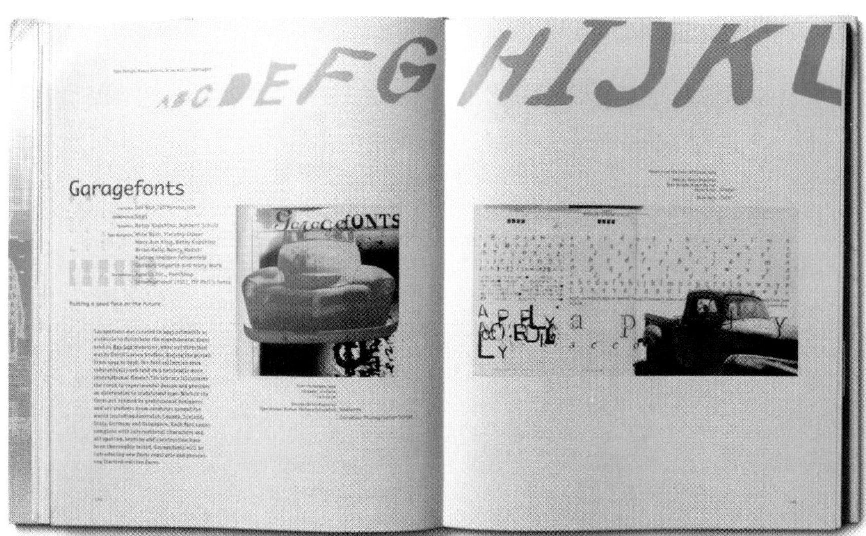

Gerrit Rietveld catalogue

Cover

Some of Moniteurs's publishing design work is directly linked to corporate image.
That is the case with this catalogue, designed for the Galerie Ulrich Fiedler as part of the graphic image applied to a publishing product.

Gerrit Rietveld
Exhibition catalogue

Year: 2001
Design: Heidi Specker
Client: Galerie Ulrich Fiedler

Font used: Super Grotesk

18 x 22.5 cm. 48 pages. Full colour printing

Graphic Identity

The Ulrich Fiedler art gallery (Cologne), specialising in early-20th-Century avant-garde design, commissioned **Moniteurs** to redesign its corporate image.

For the corporate typography, they looked for a font that would communicate both classical Bauhaus modernity and contemporary reality. Super Grotesk, based on the font by Arno Drescher (1930) and redesigned in the nineties by Svend Smital, was the perfect solution.

"For the Rietveld exhibition catalogue, we used the entire Super Grotesk family to present their Rietveld furnishings as masterpieces of industrial design," explains Heidi.

For Moniteurs, typography is the basis of corporate design. **"We like fonts which, for their individuality, suit our clients' identities,"** says Sibylle. If a suitable font is not available, Moniteurs design their own.

By designing exclusive fonts or by modifying existing ones, they find tailor-made communication solutions. In other words, they design their clients' 'writing'.

Gerrit Rietveld catalogue

Double inside pages

The design of this catalogue plays with proportions, with details and general views of the furnishings. There is an introductory text for each piece.
The numbering for each of the pieces establishes a relationship with the page number and with the year in which the piece was designed.

6

1

1919

Gerrit Rietveld

Kinderhochstuhl High Chair

Kurz nachdem sich Rietveld 1918 der De Stijl Gruppe anschloss, entstanden die bedeutendsten Möbel Rietvelds. Stücke aus dieser Zeit sah er als Experimente und Studien an, die er fast ausschliesslich selbst fertigte. Der skeletthafte, architektonische Aufbau dieses Kinderhochstuhls erinnert in seiner gesamten Anmutung noch mehr an konstruktivistische Skulpturen als die ersten noch nicht farbig gefassten Rot-Blauen Stühle. Die abgerundeten Kanten der Holzelemente, die ihn von anderen Stücken dieser Periode unterscheiden, sollten wohl seine Benutzung für Kinder sicherer machen.

Rietveld's most important furniture, which made a definite break with the tradition of his fathers craft, were created after he joined the De Stijl group in 1918. He viewed the pieces from this time as experiments and studies; they were built almost entirely by himself. The skill with which he crafted these pieces lends them a grace and charm that recalls sculpture rather than furniture. The rounded edges of its wooden pieces were meant to make the chair safer for children to use.

Peter Vöge, The complete Rietveld furniture, Rotterdam 1993, Seite 54-55, Nr. 36
M. Küper, I. v. Zijl, Gerrit Th. Rietveld 1888-1964, The complete works, Utrecht 1992, Seite 82, Nr. 48

7

1923

4

5

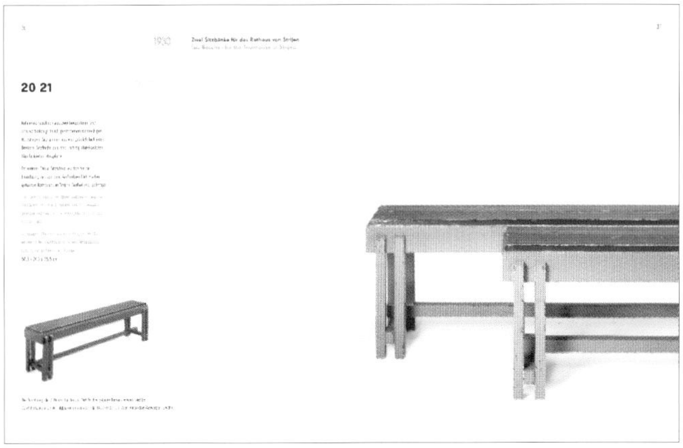

1930

20 21

Planet Base

Sebastián Saavedra
Barcelona, Spain

"A Magazine for our Friends"

In 1990, Sebastián Saavedra (Barcelona, 1971) and Antonio Kobau (Barcelona, 1971) shared a great passion for snowboarding, a sport barely known in Spain at that time. This passion was sufficient motivation for them to embark on a magazine publishing adventure: shutting themselves away in a small, damp basement, with the aid of a computer they came up with **Snow Planet**.

They never believed they would earn their living from what they thought of as a hobby. But snowboarding caught on in Spain, their dream became reality and their project blossomed from a photocopied sheet to a two-ink and, later, full colour magazine.

They studied graphic design at the Barcelona design schools IDEP and Eina and started working together on small pieces, combining their studies with freelance work.

Antonio and Sebastián, fellow snowboarders, childhood friends and now business partners, decided to set up their own studio, **Planet Base**, in 1999, as a platform for developing their publishing projects and those graphic design commissions they wished to take on.

Snow Planet no. 0
Dec-Jan, 1994

First cover of the magazine

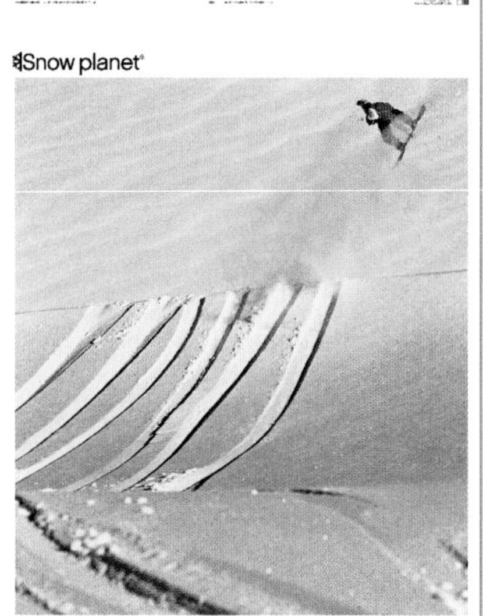

Snow Planet no. 32
Nov-Dec, 2001

Design of two different covers for the same issue

Snow Planet no. 32
Nov-Dec, 2001

Opening spread of feature article

SE TRATA DE UNA DE LAS PRIMERAS MONTAÑAS DE ARGENTINA DONDE SE PRACTICA EL SKI, PUES DEBEMOS REMONTARNOS HASTA 1938 PARA VER SUS LADERAS NEVADAS POBLADAS POR GENTE EN BUSCA DE SENSACIONES. SU NOMBRE RESPONDE A LA SIMILITUD DE SUS CUMBRES CON CATEDRALES GOTICAS.

MEETING POINT CERRO CATEDRAL

Snow Planet
Magazine

Year: 1994 - 2002
Client: Planet Base

Fonts used: Chalet, Swiss, Arcade

24 x 31 cm. 84 pages. Full colour printing
Five issues are printed each year in the winter season

Mad about Snowboarding

The Snow planet publishing project began in 1994 as Sebastián Saavedra's and Antonio Kobau's personal adventure. They started with the aim of informing and entertaining a small set who were "mad about mountains and snowboarding". "We had more high hopes and enthusiasm than experience," says Sebastián. "At first we did all the work, from going on trips, taking photos and writing the articles to the marketing, doing the design work, production and distributing the magazine on our scooter."

Lacking quality photographic material, typography was their only graphic resource for improving the appearance of their articles.

Now that the magazine permits them to work with more experienced professionals, the photos have the same communicative value as the text. They see the typeface is a 'patch', as they do the text layout and photos. All these elements are jumbled together. Blank spaces help to lend the page cohesion and create pauses within the apparent disorder. They are not overly concerned with legibility, or with keeping the photos free of text. When contributing photographers are shocked to see their

MEETING POINT

CERRO CATEDRAL

001 _ _ Juan Beveraggi

0025 _ _ 0029

SPOT
CERRO CATEDRAL (BARILOCHE)

Se trata de una de las primeras montañas de Argentina donde se practica el ski, pues debemos remontarnos hasta 1938 para ver sus laderas nevadas pobladas por gente en busca sensaciones. Su nombre responde a la similitud de sus cumbres con catedrales góticas.

Hoy es uno de los centros invernales más famosos del continente sudamericano, desde la cima el paisaje que se divisa es impresionante: múltiples lagos, la cordillera de los Andes y los entornos más alucinantes que te puedas encontrar en una bajada.

A tan sólo 11 km. de carretera asfaltada se encuentra la ciudad de Bariloche, que es la puerta de entrada a la Patagonia, a unas veinte horas en autobús al suroeste de Buenos Aires. Situada a orillas del lago Nahuel Huapi, rodeada de montañas y con sus casi 100.000 habitantes es la ciudad-snowboard más grande de Argentina y, en consecuencia, cuna de muchos y muy buenos riders.

A finales de los 80, cuando los locales volvían de hacer la doble temporada de Europa o USA, todos traían una tabla bajo el brazo. En 1992 se realizó el primer curso de instructor de snowboard, lo que juntamente con la fuerte tendencia de la moda favoreció a que el "surfero" formase parte del paisaje natural de la zona.

Actualmente en el Cerro Catedral existen tres snowparks permanentes

Snow Planet no. 28
Oct-Nov, 2000

Inside pages

Blank spaces, empty and pristine, speak to the reader of the spectacular beauty of the mountains. They suggest the virgin territory that true snowboarders yearn to slide over smoothly.

photos invaded by letters and signs, Sebastián explains: **"I'm very clear about the difference between a photography book and a magazine which uses photos."**

Sebastián and Antonio are still totally involved in the magazine's content. They intend to keep on entertaining themselves and their readers at the same time.

"A magazine allows you to adjust the different elements issue by issue, article by article. And the readers evolve with you too," says Sebastián.

Snow planet has been through many different formats and styles since it started.

In its current period, the magazine's graphics have recently become more settled. According to Sebastián, **"it's more coherent, a reflection of what's happening in snowboarding now, which is professionalism and respect for the environment."**

When Antonio and Sebastián started the magazine, as a fanzine, it was aimed at their closest friends and collaborators; despite the changes it has gone through, Snow planet has not lost its editorial direction. It still has the same spirit, which is not to give in to editorial pressures, either in content or advertising. **"We're not interested in snowboarding as a fashion,"** they say. **"We're still doing a magazine for people like us."**

People like them, snowboarders who are passionate about mountains and sport.

UNO issue 2
July, 2000

Magazine cover

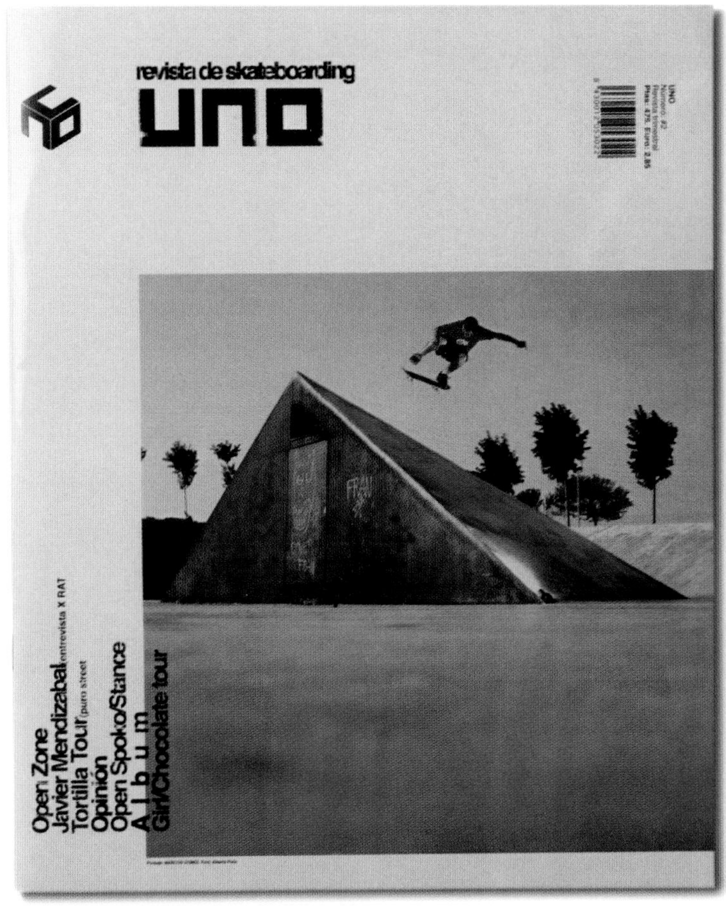

UNO
Magazine

Year: 2000
Client: Planet Base

Fonts used:
Century Schoolbook, Neue Helvetica, Swiss

24 x 29 cm. 84 pages. Full colour printing. Quarterly

Passion for the Street

UNO is a specialised skateboard magazine aimed at skateboarders. The typical skater attitude – tough and obsessive – and basically urban aesthetic are perfectly reflected in the pages of the magazine.

Like Snow planet, the setting in which the sport is practised influences the way in which UNO is done. The skateboard phenomenon happens in cities, a heterogeneous space where different colours and textures coexist side by side. This is the graphic concept of UNO. Its pages, without any stable structure or grid, become an urban environment. Low resolution printing, faxing, photocopying, paintbrushing – all of these resources are used to shape a baroque style abounding in textures and colours capable of exciting a young readership that reads about their favourite pastime without worrying whether the texts are properly laid out, or even legible.

The skating and snowboarding worlds are growing further and further apart, and the only thing they have in common, according to Sebastián, is that **"they share a love of 'riding sideways' on a board."** The aesthetics of the two magazines therefore reflect two readerships as different as their graphic treatments.

UNO issue 6
October, 2001

Idea for article-interview
(› current and following pages)

UNO issue 6
October, 2001

Magazine cover

Jimmy Fontecilla

INTERVIEW: Manuel Alca[illegible]

[illegible] que tengo para escribir alg[illegible]erca de Jimmy.
La primer[illegible] en relación a un simple check-out, pero en esta ocasión me refiero a él en palabras mayores; y mayor lo es también Jimmy, pues aunque no lo parezca los años han pasado también para él. Cierto es que estos años no pasan en valde, sin embargo, para algunos son años que castigan, y para otros favorecen. A Jimmy, sin duda alguna, le han favorecido. La experiencia ha incrementado y el espíritu del primer día sigue vigente, desde ese día que se subió a su viejo patín del equipo Pepsi, que alguien le regaló, muy oportunamente. Por supuesto, también ha pasado por malos momentos..., ya que las cosas tampoco han sido nada fáciles para él, pero decidió elegir el camino que muchos hemos elegido, que no es otra cosa que el del patín. Siempre he pensado que, con una mentalidad positiva y ganadora, las cosas siempre van hacia delante, y esta es la mentalidad que también comparte **JIMMY**.
Buenos sponsors (**Quicksilver, DC, Alien Workshop**), buenos amigos y grandes trucos, son algunos de sus más importantes logros, aunque lo más importante se lo guarda para él, y es quizás ese sentimiento de diversión y la satisfacción de cumplir consigo mismo y con lo que más le gusta.

P A G :40MES: OCT.

UNO: 6

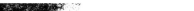

NOLLIE NOSESLIDE, en el puente de Juan Bravo, Madrid

¿Cuándo empezó el skate a ser una de las principales prioridades de tu vida?
Desde que empecé, patinar ha sido lo que me ha apetecido en todo momento, pero como era un niño de 10 años mi madre me presionaba para que estudiase. Si no hubiera sido por ella lo habría dejado todo por el patinete, pero hay que saber que no es lo único en esta vida, y de hecho, para mi se convirtió en lo "principal" desde que entré en Quiksilver.

¿En qué lugar y con que personas te darías una sesión de ensueño?
Eso sería en Colón con toda la peña: Esteban, Brasi, Jesús, Alfon, David, Chunque, Dani, Lebroni, Sete, Pichu, Victor, Pichi, Varo, Jebi, Musta, Michi, Manu, Sarmi, Casta, Tolo, etc... No sé, con estos patinaría en cualquier parte.

¿Con qué material es con el que te sientes más cómodo a la hora de patinar?
Con tablas Alien Workshop de 6 láminas, ruedas AWS de 52 mm, rodamientos Reflex, ejes Venture 5.0 Low, Zapas DC y ropa Quiksilver.

¿Qué te sugiere "patín nuevo y zapas nuevas"?
Engorile, *Nollie flips*, sesiones guapas hasta que se gaste, y volver a empezar otra vez.

Planet Base

The main source of inspiration for the magazine's designers is the setting in which these sports are practised and the personalities or typical characteristics of their devotees.

These typically overloaded graphic compositions are not far removed from urban **graffiti** aesthetics.

› Following page:
UNO issue 6
October, 2001

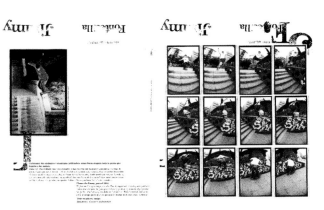

SWITCH FRONTSIDE flip a 5/0 en Colón, Madrid

SWITCH BACKSIDE HEELFLIP en Heroncity, Madrid

¿Qué crees que tiene más importancia, quedar bien en campeonatos o tener buenas partes en videos?
Los campeonatos son importantes, pero suelo patinar a disgusto. Hay mucha presión y poco tiempo, aunque esas cosas se van olvidando con el paso del tiempo. En cambio, el video es un formato, es algo más duradero, y tienes más tiempo para grabar, con gente que te agrada y con la que disfrutas. Es un día de patín con más "engorile". Prefiero el video a los campeonatos, pero sé que ambos son importantes.

¿Cómo te ha influido a la hora de patinar, el hecho de que tus sponsors te den todo el material que necesitas, que te paguen aviones para ir a campeonatos, o que te den cierta cantidad de dinero al año?
Eso empezó hace 3 años, cuando se formó el primer equipo Unity, hasta entonces me compraba todo el material con mi dinero. A partir de entonces, desde el primer día que comencé a patinar para ellos, no me ha faltado de nada, eso hace que sólo te preocupes de patinar, da igual que no tengas dinero, porqué sabes que de patines y zapas no te van a faltar. Luego vino lo de Quiksilver, y esta peña es pata negra: te llevan de viaje, te lo pagan todo, etc. No sé, cosas que parecían imposibles en España se hacen realidad. Todo esto te hace crecer y progresar como patinador y como persona.

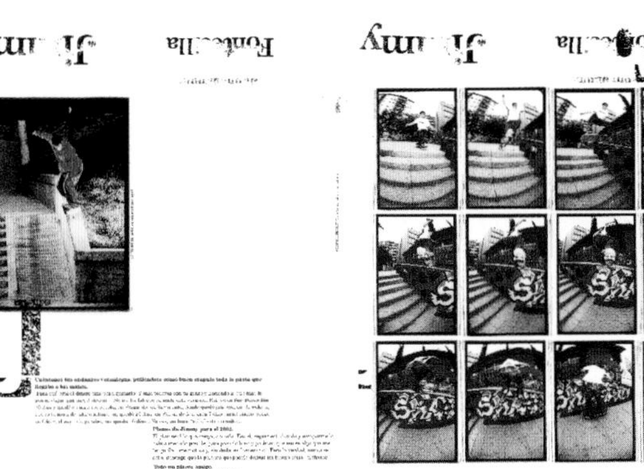

circuito nacional globe

TXT: Eduardo Saenz "Rat"

UNO: 6 MES: OCT.

Concluida la primera prueba de Lérida, donde Javi Mendizábal se llevó el primer puesto y Andreu Renau sorprendió por su soltu... hacer, el circuito GLOBE navegaba rumbo al ecuador del circuito. El puerto de destino, en Arroyo de la Miel (Málaga), está cerca de la casa del barco de Chanquete. La prueba estaba prevista que se celebrase el 9 y 10 de Junio, pero el achicharrante sol hizo cambiar los horarios y reducir el campeonato a un solo dia. Hubiera sido un crimen hacerles patinar en el hogar de Belcebú.

Así que el sábado, cuando las moscas dejaron de caerse, comenzó la segunda prueba en el parque de Arroyo de la Miel, con patinadores de toda España y en especial de Al Andalus, como debe ser. El parque, con tan sólo un año de vida de cemento, consta de dos quarters en dos de las esquinas colocados en diagonal, un fun box, una pirámide, dos planos inclinados bastante grandes, un bordillo doble y un grind box. La primera ronda de clasificación trajo algunas sorpresas, ya que skaters tan buenos como el Negro de Chiclana, Javier Mendizábal o David Ramos se quedaban a "two candels". El gran Alexis se hizo dueño del show con gracia, la lengua calva y un micrófono. Gracias a él, las rondas comenzaron a su debido tiempo y el público disfrutó de su arte lingüistico. En el panel de la gran final sólo aparecieron los skaters de lujo: Alain Goikoetxea, Roberto Alemán, Iván Rivado, Pitu, Adrián Morales, Héctor Garcia, Orlando Acosta, Christian Pujola, Gonzalo Aguilar, Fali, Bibi , Ricki Majoni y un crio Finlandés de nueve años (que, por cierto, no era el primo de Arto). Decidir quién de estos merecía la zapatilla de oro no tuvo que ser fácil. Roberto estaba patinando con autoridad y estilo; Alain, pues bien, ¿Qué se puede decir de esta maquina con más de una docena de años encima de un patin?, pues eso, que es una maquina; Pitu, aunque sin patrocinador, estuvo en estado de gracia todo el campeonato; Iván Rivado, Adrián y Christian demostraron perfección, estilo y técnica; y, Orlando Acosta lo dio todo, como siempre. Así que, cuando la calculadora escupió sus resultados, Orlando salió victorioso del duelo a doce bandas, tras él se situó Pitu, -sin sponsor, insisto-, y Gonzalo Aguilar, "pedaso de pan", completó el podium.

Labomatic

**Pascal Béjean, Frédéric Bortolotti,
P. Nicolas Ledoux**
Paris, France

› Next page:
Génération/s 2001

Poster

"Design as a Laboratory"

The Paris studio **Labomatic (U)** was founded in October 1997 by a group of artists and graphic designers with the aim of promoting team projects, with or without external collaboration, and establishing a new form of artistic and financial independence.

We might see Labomatic (U) as having a double personality, operating along the frontiers of graphic communication and art. This is expressed in the execution of commissions – from the conception of the idea to the final result – and the development of in-house initiatives under the Labomatic label (exhibitions, art projects, publications, websites).

They combine these twin facets – design and art – in order to attain certain 'mutability' in the work processes.

Bulldozer
Revue graphique à Paris

Magazine in foldout format created by Pascal Béjean and Frédéric Bortolotti in Paris.

Bulldozer n. 10.
1999

Génération/s 2001
2000

Cover n. 0

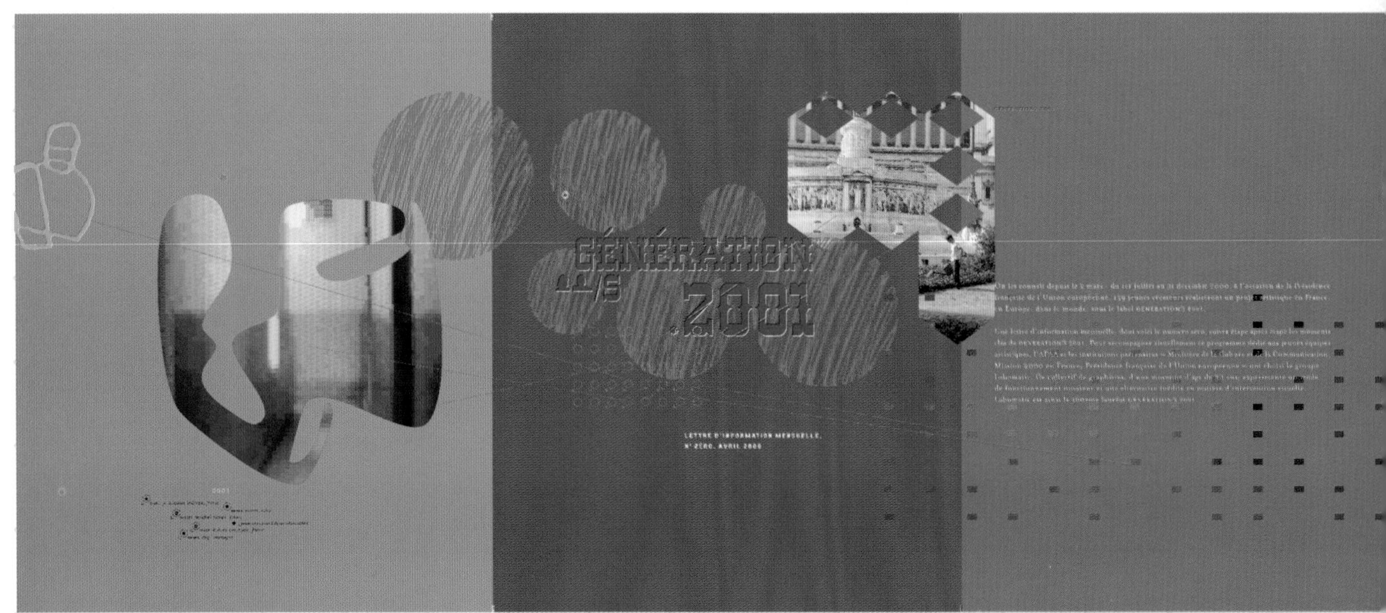

ÉRATION
2001

Labomatic

Génération/s 2001
2000

Informative bulletins published in the second half of 2000

POUR EN SAVOIR PLUS.

CARNET D'ADRESSES

ÉDITO.

Génération/s 2001

Cultural bulletin

Year: 2000
Client: Présidence Française de l'Union Européenne, Ministère de la Culture et de la Communication, Ministère des Affaires Étrangères

Fonts used: Eunuverse, Mrs Eaves

21 x 25 cm. 2 inks

Images for a Generation

Génération/s 2001 is a cultural programme targeting young artists and cultural mediators promoted by the French Presidency of the European Union. Under this name, 160 young creators were invited to present artistic projects.

Labomatic was one of those invited, in their case to design the visual identity for the programme.

The studio approached the commission from an artistic perspective, making it compatible with the client's requirement: to create an image that would reflect the multicultural and multidisciplinary character of Génération/s 2001.

On the one hand, Labomatic designed a small informative bulletin, of which various issues were published during the first half of 2000, the period in which France held the presidency of the European Union. On the other hand, based on the idea of mixture and mutability, the studio created a whole system for the visual identity of Génération/s 2001.

For this job Labomatic developed the Flux 2001 software, a graphic program that combines images and fonts. The result is a 'trademark', different each time, capable of materialising visually the different manifestations represented in Génération/s 2001. The program handles

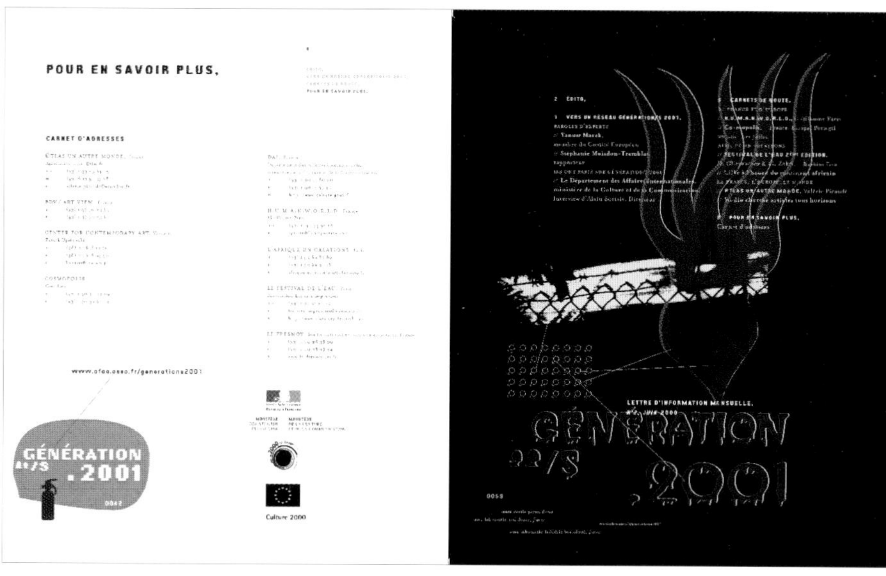

a vast database of the contributions from the artists and designers. **"Flux 2001 poses questions about the concepts of process, artistic identity and the intellectual property,"** Pascal says.

Labomatic employs this software to make a 'mutating' banner for their bulletin. This graphic image, inspired in the concept of sampling, uses a different font each time, which they combine with the images sent to Labomatic for storage in their graphic archive.

The unconventional use of font in this graphic image project helps express the playful and informal aspect of the Génération/s 2001 programme.

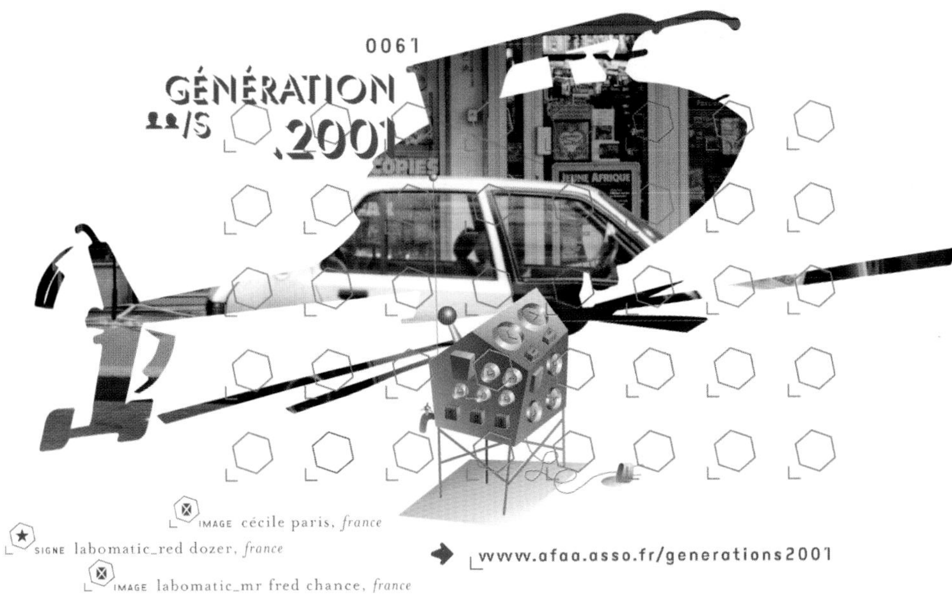

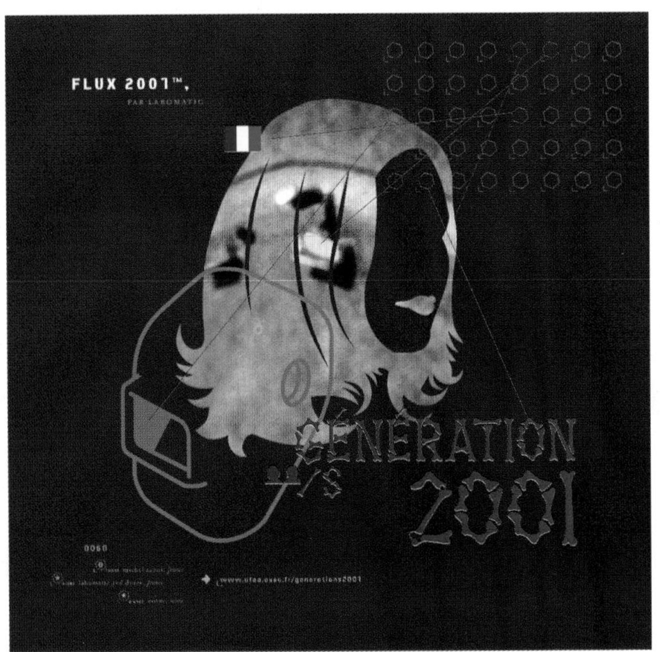

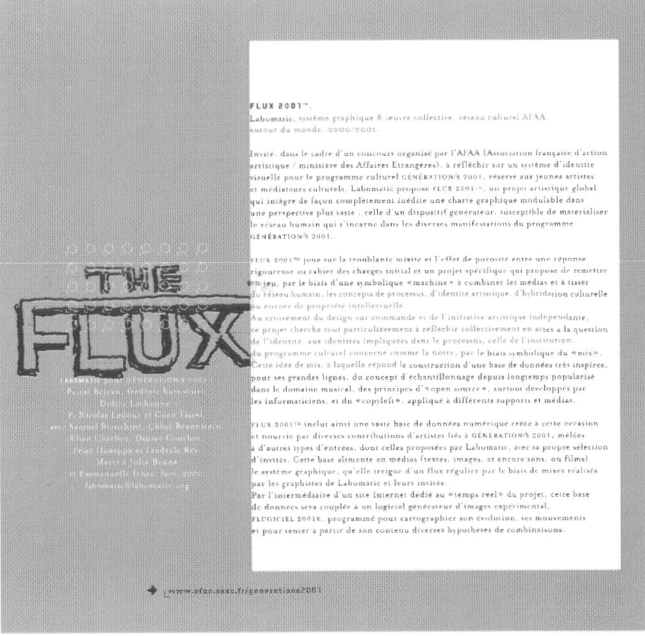

FLUX 2001™,
Labomatic, système graphique & œuvre collective, réseau culturel AFAA, autour du monde, 2000/2001.

Invité, dans le cadre d'un concours organisé par l'AFAA (Association française d'action artistique / ministère des Affaires Etrangères), à réfléchir sur un système d'identité visuelle pour le programme culturel GÉNÉRATION/S 2001, réservé aux jeunes artistes et médiateurs culturels, Labomatic propose FLUX 2001™, un projet artistique global qui intègre de façon complètement inédite une charte graphique modulable dans une perspective plus vaste : celle d'un dispositif générateur, susceptible de matérialiser le réseau humain qui s'incarne dans les diverses manifestations du programme GÉNÉRATION/S 2001.

FLUX 2001™ joue sur la troublante mixité et l'effet de porosité entre une réponse rigoureuse au cahier des charges initial et un projet spécifique qui propose de remettre en jeu, par le biais d'une symbolique «machine» à combiner les médias et à tisser du réseau humain, les concepts de processus, d'identité artistique, d'hybridation culturelle ou encore de propriété intellectuelle.
Au croisement du design sur commande et de l'initiative artistique indépendante, ce projet cherche tout particulièrement à réfléchir collectivement en actes à la question de l'identité, aux identités impliquées dans le processus, celle de l'institution, du programme culturel concerné comme la nôtre, par le biais symbolique du «mix». Cette idée de mix, à laquelle répond la construction d'une base de données très inspirée, pour ses grandes lignes, du concept d'échantillonnage depuis longtemps popularisé dans le domaine musical, des principes d'«open source», surtout développés par les informaticiens, et du «copyleft», appliqué à différents supports et médias.

FLUX 2001™ inclut ainsi une vaste base de données numérique créée à cette occasion et nourrie par diverses contributions d'artistes liés à GÉNÉRATION/S 2001, mêlées à d'autres types d'entrées, dont celles proposées par Labomatic, avec sa propre sélection d'invités. Cette base alimente en médias (textes, images, et encore sons, ou films) le système graphique, qu'elle irrigue d'un flux régulier par le biais de mixes réalisés par les graphistes de Labomatic et leurs invités.
Par l'intermédiaire d'un site Internet dédié au «temps reel» du projet, cette base de données sera couplée à un logiciel générateur d'images expérimental, FLUGICIEL 2001X, programmé pour cartographier son évolution, ses mouvements et pour tenter à partir de son contenu diverses hypothèses de combinaisons.

0056

SIGNE labomatic _ red dozer, *france*

SIGNES julie b. lorenz, *états-unis*

IMAGE labomatic _ frédéric bortolotti, *france*

www.afaa.asso.fr/generations2001

GÉNÉRATION/S 2001

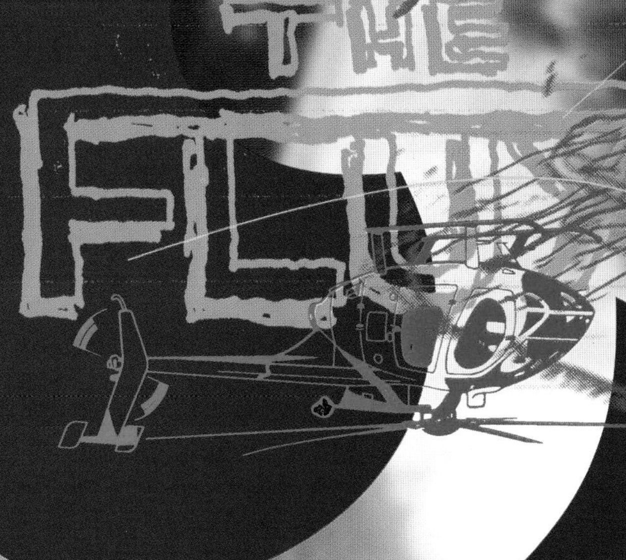

A CAR CRASH 2

பிரவேசிக்க
கூடாது

00665728 6

Social

Paul Driver
Leeds, United Kingdom

"Expressive Space"

Paul Driver founded **Social** in 2000 after working for the design firm Attik, first as a designer and then as art director at their New York office.

Paul started Social with the aim of specialising in graphic projects, both print and multimedia. With this new professional direction, Paul seeks to explore new, more personally gratifying territories. One of his priorities is find a balance between meeting the needs of the client and his own personal satisfaction.

Contrary to appearances, Paul avoids getting too tied to one trend or style. **"Relying on a single style is dangerous,"** he says. **"I believe a good designer should be able to adapt a little and cope with any design problem."**

He cites many influences and says they change all the time. He admires designers whose work endures and remains relevant over long periods, regardless of trends.

OLD STYLE . MD . REGULAR . ITALIC . MD ITALIC . BOLD . BOLD ITALIC . SUPER
abcdefghijklmnopqrstuvwxyz
ABCDEFGHIJKLMNOPQRST
DON'T BELIEVE THE TYPE
K-alpha
K-beta
4.30000E-02
ABCDEFGHIJKLMNOPQRSTUVWXYZ

TypeDirectorsClub

The Judges' Choices and Designers' Statements

TDC 46+ P.018

Type Director's Club 21

Dividers designed for different sections of the annual. The typography is totally subordinate to the image.

Type Director's Club 21
Annual

Year: 2000
Client: Type Director's Club

Font used: Bell Centennial, Akzidenz Grotesk, Helvetica

21.5 x 28.5 cm. 320 pages. Full colour printing

Typography Annual

Although Paul Driver's work emphasises the formal and expressive value of text, he considers typography to be an essential element in getting messages across. Thus he believes good page layout is crucial in any publishing design and says there must be a hierarchy of information so that the reader does not get lost or the message does not become clouded.

Paul is not in favour of using lots of typefaces, and points out the importance of avoiding information overload, striking the right balance between text and image.

The work that Paul Driver did in his former job at the Attik studio for the Type Directors Club annual was based on a very open brief: "At first we worked on the graphic image for the 'call for entries' campaign for the prize which is given out each year by the Type Director's Club. This included a poster that asked type designers to take part by donating their work. They gave work in exchange for recognition. That was the idea we wanted to get across."

"Our starting point was the medical theme of giving and receiving, which relates to the giving and receiving of blood. I worked with a small team of designers on many spreads.

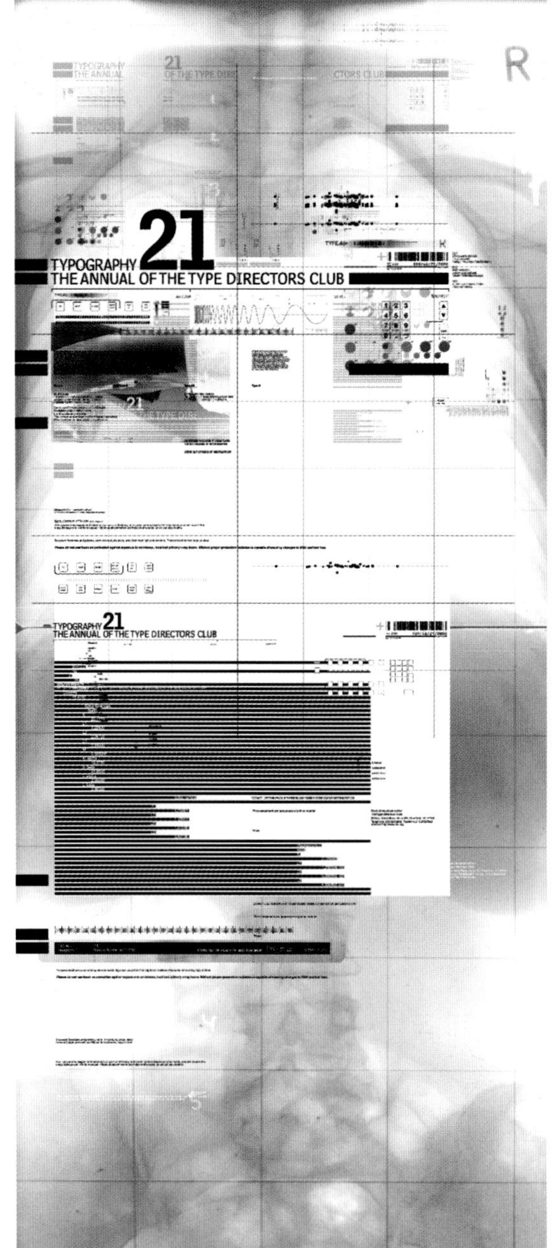

Type Directors Club 21

Original proposal for the design of the book's outer cover. The design is based on medical iconography. The text forms part of the image, integrated like a patch.

We didn't want the book to feel too rigid. We had the freedom to create images in any style we wanted. The main challenge was trying to keep everything consistently fresh."

The book shows a variety of different work selected by the Type Director's Club reproduced in different sizes. Paul constructed a grid that enabled him to achieve clean, ordered pages with minimal typography as neutrally as possible so as to avoid detracting from the submitted work.

Typography in the annual is used in two different ways. One, more rational, font is used for the texts accompanying the images of the works submitted, and is designed to look like technical specifications. The other, more experimental – or artistic – font is used to generate images. This is the case with the dividers inside the book, which help underscore the unity of the publication by means of a more experimental treatment of the typography.

For the texts, Paul used the Bell Centennial, Akzidenz Grotesk and Helvetica families, which he considered most appropriate due to project's influences – hospital graphics and medical packaging.

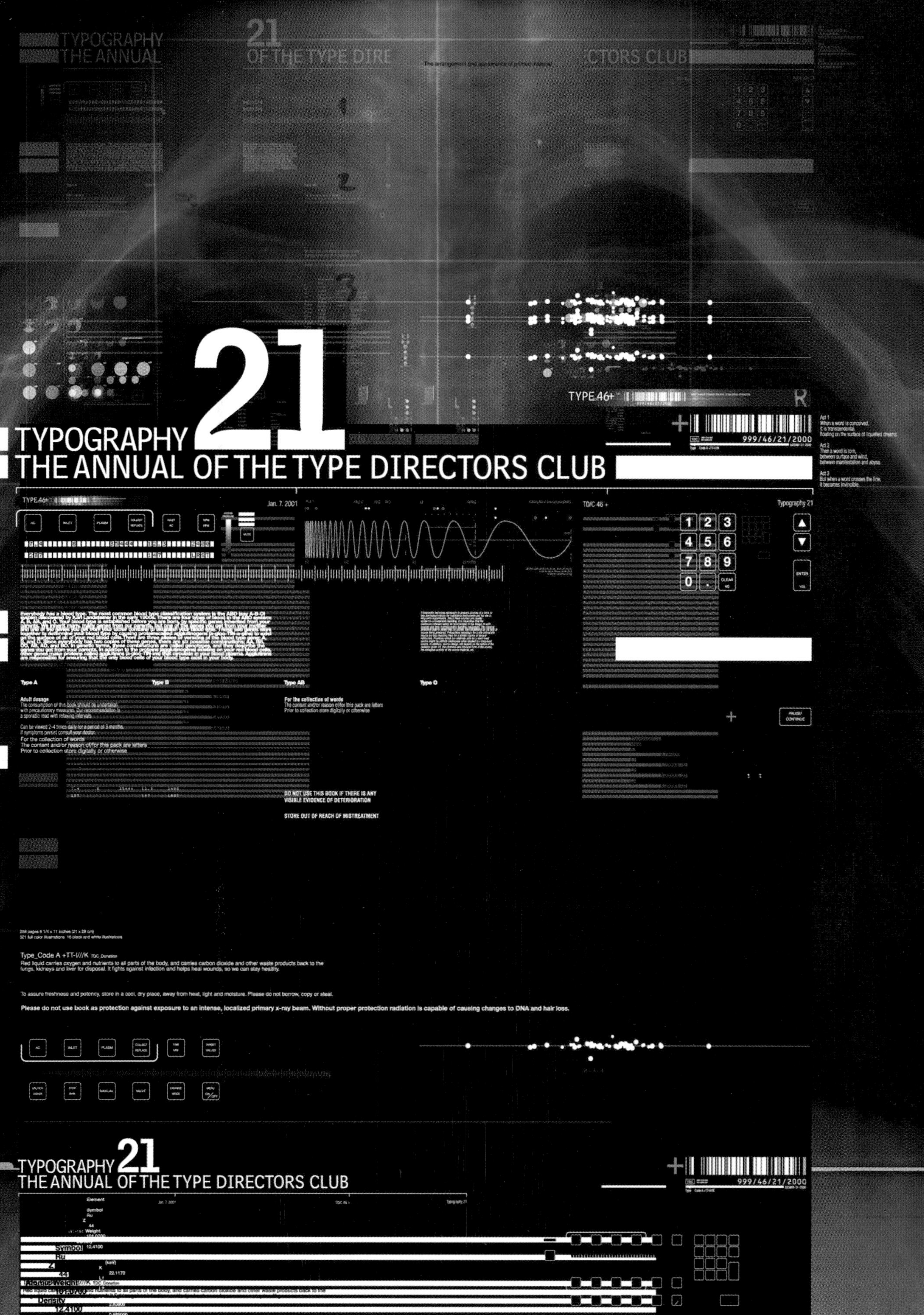

TYPOGRAPHY 21
THE ANNUAL OF THE TYPE DIRECTORS CLUB
TYPE.46+
999/46/21/2000
Act 1
When a word is conceived,
it is transcendental,
floating on the surface of liquefied dreams.
Act 2
Then a word is torn,
between surface and wind,
between manifestation and abyss.
Act 3
But when a word crosses the line,
it becomes invincible.
Jan. 7. 2001
TD/C 46 +
Typography 21
1 2 3
4 5 6
7 8 9
0 . CLEAR
Type A
Type B
Type AB
Type O
Adult dosage
The consumption of this book should be undertaken
with precautionary measures. Our recommendation is
a sporadic read with relaxing intervals.
Can be viewed 2-4 times daily for a period of 3 months.
If symptoms persist consult your doctor.
For the collection of words
The content and/or reason of/for this pack are letters
Prior to collection store digitally or otherwise
For the collection of words
The content and/or reason of/for this pack are letters
Prior to collection store digitally or otherwise
DO NOT USE THIS BOOK IF THERE IS ANY
VISIBLE EVIDENCE OF DETERIORATION
STORE OUT OF REACH OF MISTREATMENT
258 pages 8 1/4 x 11 inches (21 x 28 cm)
321 full color illustrations 16 black and white illustrations
Type_Code A +TT-I///K TDC_Donation
Red liquid carries oxygen and nutrients to all parts of the body, and carries carbon dioxide and other waste products back to the lungs, kidneys and liver for disposal. It fights against infection and helps heal wounds, so we can stay healthy.
To assure freshness and potency, store in a cool, dry place, away from heat, light and moisture. Please do not borrow, copy or steal.
Please do not use book as protection against exposure to an intense, localized primary x-ray beam. Without proper protection radiation is capable of causing changes to DNA and hair loss.
TYPOGRAPHY 21
THE ANNUAL OF THE TYPE DIRECTORS CLUB
999/46/21/2000

Appetite engineers

Martin Venezky
San Francisco, United States

"The Beauty of Typographic Ornamentation"

Martin Venezky heads **Appetite Engineers**, a small San Francisco-based design firm where he develops graphic projects for clients such as the San Francisco Museum of Modern Art, Chronicle Books, Blue Note Records and the Sundance Film Festival. He has also offered his services to non-profit organisations such as the San Francisco Aids Foundation and Q-Action/Stop Aids.

He was formerly the art director of **Speak**, a magazine devoted to popular culture, literature, art and music.

A graduate of the Cranbrook Academy of Art (1993), Martin sees design as useful but also decorative, adding beauty and mystery to things.

"For me, the job has meaning when I'm able to do something really new and which will last, even if only for a short time."

Martin values complexity in his graphic solutions, the use of ornamentation and the manual side of his work.

Speak magazine
Covers no. 13 and no. 18

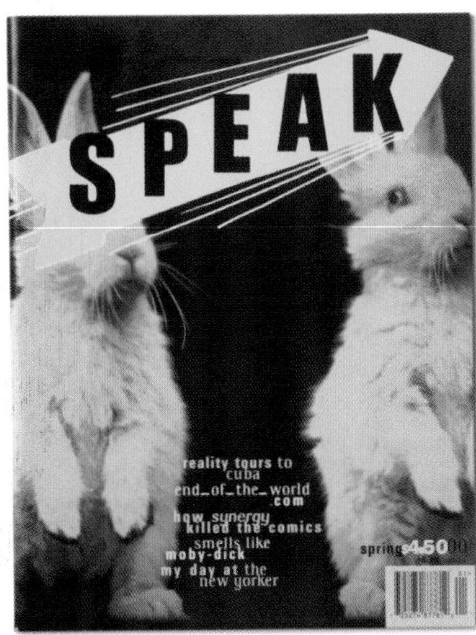

Speak magazine, no. 19
2000

Double-page introduction to an article

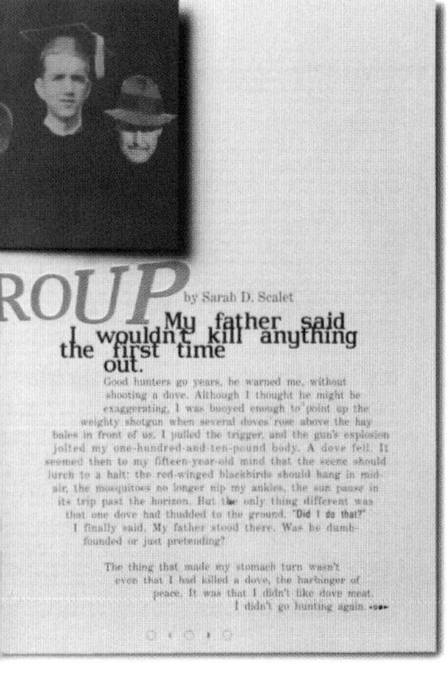
ROUP

by Sarah D. Scalet

My father said I wouldn't kill anything the first time out.

Good hunters go years, he warned me, without shooting a dove. Although I thought he might be exaggerating, I was buoyed enough to point up the weighty shotgun when several doves rose above the hay bales in front of us. I pulled the trigger, and the gun's explosion jolted my one-hundred-and-ten-pound body. A dove fell. It seemed then to my fifteen-year-old mind that the scene should lurch to a halt: the red-winged blackbirds should hang in mid-air, the mosquitoes no longer nip my ankles, the sun pause in its trip past the horizon. But the only thing different was that one dove had thudded to the ground. "Did I do that?" I finally said. My father stood there. Was he dumbfounded or just pretending?

The thing that made my stomach turn wasn't even that I had killed a dove, the harbinger of peace. It was that I didn't like dove meat. I didn't go hunting again.

Speak magazine, no. 19
2000

Typographic ornamentation
done for an article on American literature

SPEAK
Magazine

Year: 1995-2001
Client: Speak Magazine

21.5 x 27.5 cm. 108 pages. Full colour printing. Bi-monthly

Typographic Lab

Speak is a cultural and literary magazine whose contents conform to very broad criteria. Its aim is to showcase writers, artists and thinkers who do not get published in higher distribution magazines.

At first the magazine concentrated on music and fashion, until the editor, Dan Rolleri, found his interests shifting towards fiction, essays and feature articles.

The design has also changed from one issue to the next. The early ones are full of a typographical playfulness, much of it gratuitous. But as the magazine has matured editorially, the articles have come to be seen as an opportunity for graphic interpretation and poetic response.

Martin uses the magazine as a support for experimentation: **"I use the magazine as a lab, a space in which I can explore new ways of telling stories on paper,"** he says.

Sometimes his typographic experiments are closely linked to the content of the text; at other times, they spring from his own curiosity.

He usually uses the Univers and Century families for the texts, although they often mutate into different forms under Martin's intervention.

On the subject of legibility, Martin says

Speak magazine, no. 19
2000

Double page article

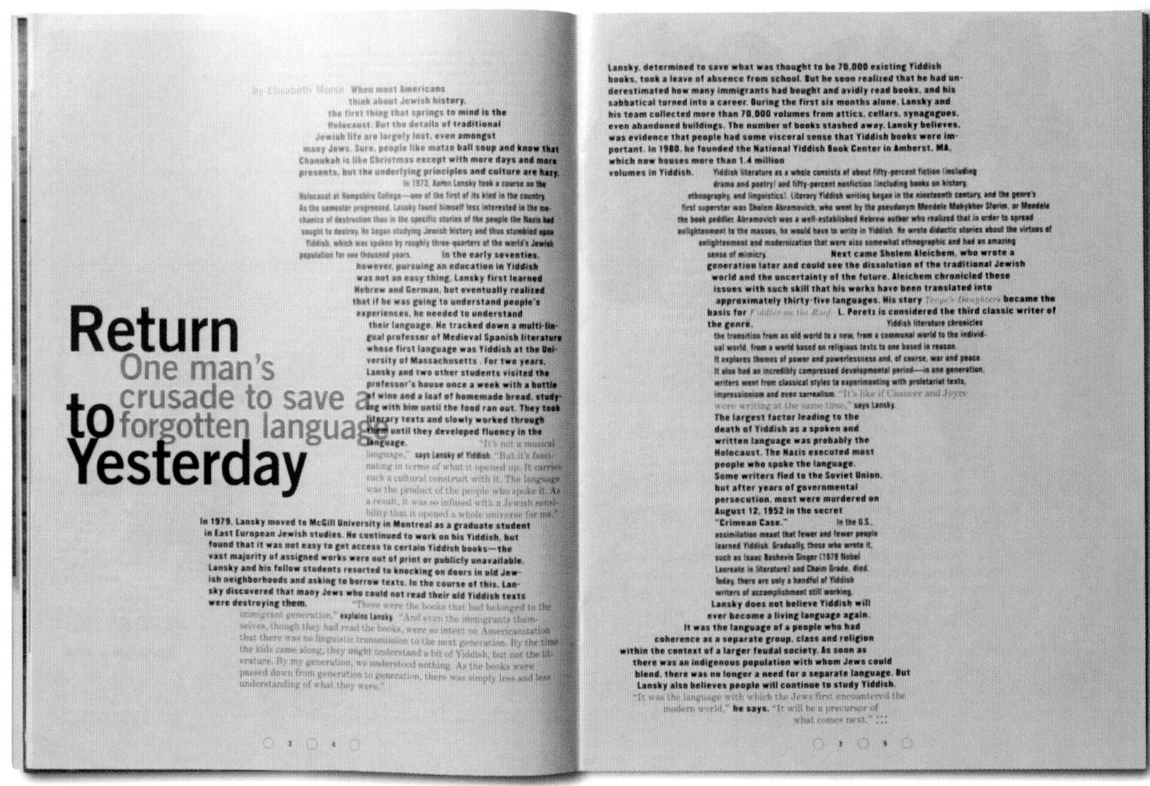

Return to Yesterday

One man's crusade to save a forgotten language

by Elisabeth Morse

When most Americans think about Jewish history, the first thing that springs to mind is the Holocaust. But the details of traditional Jewish life are largely lost, even amongst many Jews. Sure, people like matzo ball soup and know that Chanukah is like Christmas except with more days and more presents, but the underlying principles and culture are hazy.

In 1973, Aaron Lansky took a course on the Holocaust at Hampshire College—one of the first of its kind in the country. As the semester progressed, Lansky found himself less interested in the mechanics of destruction than in the specific stories of the people the Nazis had sought to destroy. He began studying Jewish history and thus stumbled upon Yiddish, which was spoken by roughly three-quarters of the world's Jewish population for one thousand years.

In the early seventies, however, pursuing an education in Yiddish was not an easy thing. Lansky first learned Hebrew and German, but eventually realized that if he was going to understand people's experiences, he needed to understand their language. He tracked down a multi-lingual professor of Medieval Spanish literature whose first language was Yiddish at the University of Massachusetts. For two years, Lansky and two other students visited the professor's house once a week with a bottle of wine and a loaf of homemade bread, studying with him until the food ran out. They took literary texts and slowly worked through them until they developed fluency in the language.

"It's not a musical language," says Lansky of Yiddish. "But it's fascinating in terms of what it opened up. It carries such a cultural construct with it. The language was the product of the people who spoke it. As a result, it was so infused with a Jewish sensibility that it opened a whole universe for me."

In 1979, Lansky moved to McGill University in Montreal as a graduate student in East European Jewish studies. He continued to work on his Yiddish, but found that it was not easy to get access to certain Yiddish books—the vast majority of assigned works were out of print or publicly unavailable. Lansky and his fellow students resorted to knocking on doors in old Jewish neighborhoods and asking to borrow texts. In the course of this, Lansky discovered that many Jews who could not read their old Yiddish texts were destroying them.

"These were the books that had belonged to the immigrant generation," explains Lansky. "And even the immigrants themselves, though they had read the books, were so intent on Americanization that there was no linguistic transmission to the next generation. By the time the kids came along, they might understand a bit of Yiddish, but not the literature. By my generation, we understood nothing. As the books were passed down from generation to generation, there was simply less and less understanding of what they were."

Lansky, determined to save what was thought to be 70,000 existing Yiddish books, took a leave of absence from school. But he soon realized that he had underestimated how many immigrants had bought and avidly read books, and his sabbatical turned into a career. During the first six months alone, Lansky and his team collected more than 70,000 volumes from attics, cellars, synagogues, even abandoned buildings. The number of books stashed away, Lansky believes, was evidence that people had some visceral sense that Yiddish books were important. In 1980, he founded the National Yiddish Book Center in Amherst, MA, which now houses more than 1.4 million volumes in Yiddish.

Yiddish literature as a whole consists of about fifty-percent fiction (including drama and poetry) and fifty-percent nonfiction (including books on history, ethnography, and linguistics). Literary Yiddish writing began in the nineteenth century, and the genre's first superstar was Sholem Abramovich, who went by the pseudonym Mendele Mokykher Sforim, or Mendele the book peddler. Abramovich was a well-established Hebrew author who realized that in order to spread enlightenment to the masses, he would have to write in Yiddish. He wrote didactic stories about the virtues of enlightenment and modernization that were also somewhat ethnographic and had an amazing sense of mimicry.

Next came Sholem Aleichem, who wrote a generation later and could see the dissolution of the traditional Jewish world and the uncertainty of the future. Aleichem chronicled these issues with such skill that his works have been translated into approximately thirty-five languages. His story *Tevye's Daughters* became the basis for *Fiddler on the Roof*. L. Peretz is considered the third classic writer of the genre.

Yiddish literature chronicles the transition from an old world to a new, from a communal world to the individual world, from a world based on religious texts to one based in reason. It explores themes of power and powerlessness and, of course, war and peace. It also had an incredibly compressed developmental period—in one generation, writers went from classical styles to experimenting with proletariat texts, impressionism and even surrealism. "It's like if Chaucer and Joyce were writing at the same time," says Lansky.

The largest factor leading to the death of Yiddish as a spoken and written language was probably the Holocaust. The Nazis executed most people who spoke the language. Some writers fled to the Soviet Union, but after years of governmental persecution, most were murdered on August 12, 1952 in the secret "Crimean Case."

In the U.S., assimilation meant that fewer and fewer people learned Yiddish. Gradually, those who wrote it, such as Isaac Bashevis Singer (1978 Nobel Laureate in literature) and Chaim Grade, died. Today, there are only a handful of Yiddish writers of accomplishment still working.

Lansky does not believe Yiddish will ever become a living language again. It was the language of a people who had coherence as a separate group, class and religion within the context of a larger feudal society. As soon as there was an indigenous population with whom Jews could blend, there was no longer a need for a separate language. But Lansky also believes people will continue to study Yiddish. "It was the language with which the Jews first encountered the modern world," he says. "It will be a precursor of what comes next." :::

"the reader has to be able to read the text." He adds that **"reading sometimes has to be rhythmic and musical instead of monotonous and straightforward,"** and says he always takes rhythm and readability into account when working with typography.

As in his other graphic works, he uses a grid as a support but does not follow it slavishly. **"It depends on each project and how important it is to be consistent in each case,"** he says.

In Speak, the first pages always set the tone of the article. **"Sometimes we start the article with a double-page photo without text, by way of introduction. The opening pages are also where I can place some sort of typographical metaphor that will be repeated throughout the article."** To achieve the right tone, Martin always reads the texts before doing the layout, discusses them with the editor and considers what links can be established between the different articles in the issue. He chooses the photographs and experiments with the kinds of typography he might use. Based on that, he decides on the techniques and ideas which can be used to give continuity throughout the article, or even throughout the issue as a whole. **"If the images they give me are too standardised, I look for new ways to show them."** Martin never makes do with just the material that comes in. He often looks for his own resources, sometimes using imagery from the popular American fifties culture.

Martin defines his work process as 'organic', as each issue is different from all the others. **"I never get all the texts at once, so my ideas change as the articles come in and I establish connections between them. Their order is never definitive until the end, so each of the pages is designed and then looked at again."**

Speak magazine, no. 19
2000

Two double-page articles

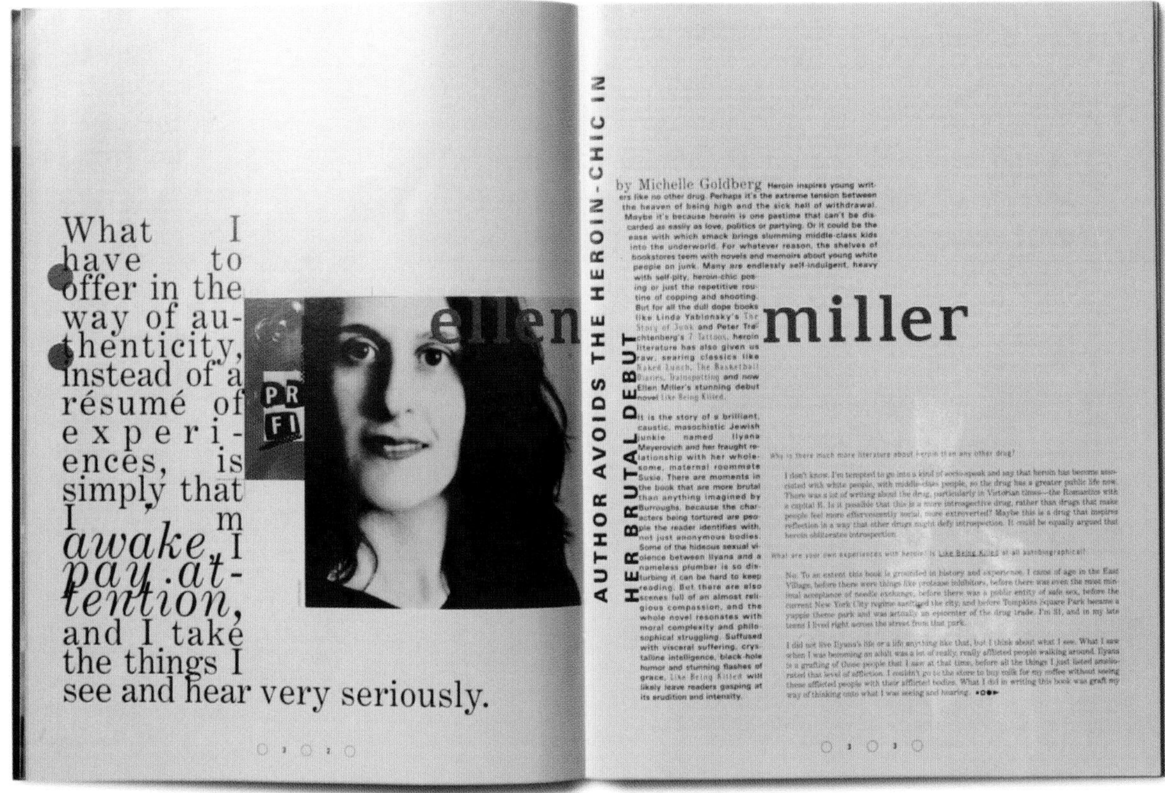

What I have to offer in the way of authenticity, instead of a résumé of experiences, is simply that I'm *awake*, I *pay attention*, and I take the things I see and hear very seriously.

ellen miller

AUTHOR AVOIDS THE HEROIN-CHIC IN HER BRUTAL DEBUT

by Michelle Goldberg Heroin inspires young writers like no other drug. Perhaps it's the extreme tension between the heaven of being high and the sick hell of withdrawal. Maybe it's because heroin is one pastime that can't be discarded as easily as love, politics or partying. Or it could be the ease with which smack brings slumming middle-class kids into the underworld. For whatever reason, the shelves of bookstores teem with novels and memoirs about young white people on junk. Many are endlessly self-indulgent, heavy with self-pity, heroin-chic posing or just the repetitive routine of copping and shooting. But for all the dull dope books like Linda Yablonsky's *The Story of Junk* and Peter Trachtenberg's *7 Tattoos*, heroin literature has also given us raw, searing classics like *Naked Lunch*, *The Basketball Diaries*, *Trainspotting* and now Ellen Miller's stunning debut novel *Like Being Killed*.

It is the story of a brilliant, caustic, masochistic Jewish junkie named Ilyana Meyerovich and her fraught relationship with her wholesome, maternal roommate Susie. There are moments in the book that are more brutal than anything imagined by Burroughs, because the characters being tortured are people the reader identifies with, not just anonymous bodies. Some of the hideous sexual violence between Ilyana and a nameless plumber is so disturbing it can be hard to keep reading. But there are also scenes full of an almost religious compassion, and the whole novel resonates with moral complexity and philosophical struggling. Suffused with visceral suffering, crystalline intelligence, black-hole humor and stunning flashes of grace, *Like Being Killed* will likely leave readers gasping at its erudition and intensity.

Why is there much more literature about heroin than any other drug?

I don't know. I'm tempted to go into a kind of socio-speak and say that heroin has become associated with white people, with middle-class people, so the drug has a greater public life now. There was a lot of writing about the drug, particularly in Victorian times—the Romantics with a capital R. Is it possible that this is a more introspective drug, rather than drugs that make people feel more effervescently social, more extroverted? Maybe this is a drug that inspires reflection in a way that other drugs might defy introspection. It could be equally argued that heroin obliterates introspection.

What are your own experiences with heroin? Is <u>Like Being Killed</u> at all autobiographical?

No. To an extent this book is grounded in history and experience. I came of age in the East Village, before there were things like protease inhibitors, before there was even the most minimal acceptance of needle exchanges, before there was a public entity of safe sex, before the current New York City regime sanitized the city, and before Tompkins Square Park became a yuppie theme park and was actually an epicenter of the drug trade. I'm 31, and in my late teens I lived right across the street from that park.

I did not live Ilyana's life or a life anything like that, but I think about what I see. What I saw when I was becoming an adult was a lot of really, really afflicted people walking around. Ilyana is a grafting of those people that I saw at that time, before all the things I just listed ameliorated that level of affliction. I couldn't go to the store to buy milk for my coffee without seeing those afflicted people with their afflicted bodies. What I did in writing this book was graft my way of thinking onto what I was seeing and hearing.

Speak magazine
Profile

Speak no. 12
Speak no. 19

In the magazine's Profile section, Martin usually lays out the texts with different justifications so as to achieve 'sound effects' in the text. The decision, he says, is never arbitrary: **"It's based on speech inflections and putting emphasis on some words and phrases."**

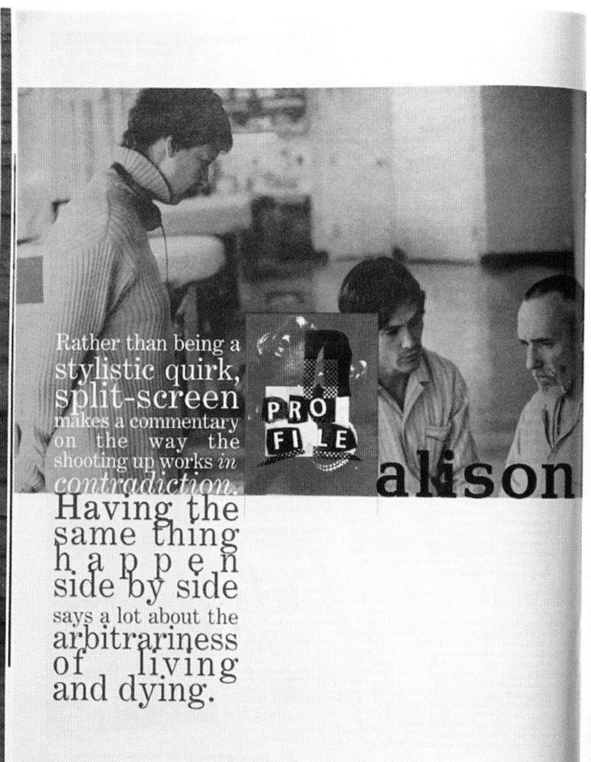

Rather than being a stylistic quirk, split-screen makes a commentary on the way the shooting up works *in contradiction.* Having the same thing h a p p e n side by side says a lot about the arbitrariness of living and dying.

PRO FILE

alison maclean.

by Edward Crouse **Alison Maclean has dwelled in the land of bodily insecurity and emotional instability for several shorts and two feature films. A female answer to David Cronenberg (what was the question?), her short film** Kitchen Sink **(1987) concerned itself—in thirteen elegant, guttural minutes—with the fate of a Sasquatch that a woman pulls from her drain, starting with a single hair. She grows him, shaves him and they love, before everything soon spirals downward.**

Maclean's latest feature, Jesus' Son, **hummingly transposes her visceral concerns to the screen, following up some psychodramatic cues she'd dropped in** Crush **(1993). Based on Denis Johnson's feverstream of short stories,** Jesus' Son **gives the author's various amped-up-and-out narrators one flesh, Billy Crudup's, and one woeful name, Fuckhead. Fuckhead is an absorbing force in the world, a hesitating young man driven mainly by drugs—a shifting stew of amphetamines, heroin and drink that make him both serene and calmly out of control. Funneling Johnson's string of strung-outs into one person not only makes narrative sense, but also highlights the screwed-up time dimension, skewing Fuckhead's narration and placing it at an uncertain moral point. From early on, viewers are left to speculate which episode will be the breaking point, when the last time will be.**

Not that the film is any kind of teach-in. It's more a villainless cavalcade of funny victims, fools and love-starved characters. Fuckhead traverses a few states, becomes caught up in a dead-end insurance scam (his pal Wayne destroys his own suburban house both for money and moral resolution), gets his girlfriend pregnant, and works double shifts in an emergency room where a red-eyed, pilled-under orderly wipes up invisible blood as patients like a man with a hunting knife sticking out of his eye casually shuffle in.

Unlike Short Cuts**—a movie where disparate short stories are joined together by coincidental threads—**Jesus' Son **leaves the marks of book-to-screen grafting intact. The episodes, filmed in Maclean's wily, expressive color patterns, hinge on such tacks as eating, shooting up, making out for the first time, smiling and sleeping. The connections bear the true weight of feeling and the scars are meant to be gawked at.**

Determinedly, the film belongs alongside weird Jesus biopics like the "I Was a Teenage Jesus" version of King of Kings **or** The Last Temptation of Christ, **as much as it does** Rush **or Gordon Parks' or Larry Clark's junkie photo spreads. Attempts at redemption abound in nearly all of the scenes, but Fuckhead can't seem to get it together for anyone—not for his girlfriend Michelle, who dies, not for the bunny fetuses saved from pregnant roadkill, and not for Wayne, who overdoses after a caper.**

Jesus' Son **walks the same edge-of-the-syringe line as** Drugstore Cowboy **or, worse,** Another Day In Paradise, **yet there is a purity, compassion and goofiness to the proceedings that is fresh. The film's moldy air and low-crawling sprawl gives the actors a great field to plow, from the diffident, cameo-ized casting of Holly Hunter (nod to** Crash**), to Dennis Hopper, to Samantha Morton's bruised Michelle, to Crudup's tart sweetness in fucking up. Crudup may be the most submersible method actor working today.**

Currently Maclean is developing Iris, **about a woman's false recall. The filmic implication of the title sounds irresistible.**

How did you get started in filmmaking?

I went to art school in Auckland in the eighties and studied sculpture, mainly working with installations, performance and photography.

Did anybody in particular inspire you to take it up or go to art school? I'm trying to find a kind of carryover into the tactility of your films.

It would change from year to year. No one was so incredibly important to me, but when I was into doing sculpture, the work that Vito Acconci was doing, Bruce Maelman, things that I'd also read about Joseph Beuysmans. I didn't necessarily like their work.

So it never hit you in a series of small epiphanies, little things at a time.

My taste pretty much evolved from year to year. I came to filmmaking late. I wouldn't say that I was a cinephile until my last year at Auckland. Then I started looking at American experimental avant-garde films—Maya Deren, Kenneth Anger and those sorts of people.

Was your attraction to Jesus' Son primarily visual or verbal? Does one evoke the other or are they inseparable? How does that carry over into the episodic structure?

I loved his perspective on the world and the way he sees and describes things. His way of using language is already very visual—taking you into a state of mind in an economical way, the beauty of some of those images. It was a combination of the way he uses language and the way that evokes this way of seeing the world, the humor.

Cover of **Open** Magazine, no. 3 (2000)

Cover of **Open** Magazine, no. 4 (2001)

Open Magazine, no. 5
2001

Cover

OPEN
Museum magazine

Year: 2000
Client:
The San Francisco Museum of Modern Art

Fonts used: Folio, Nimrod

19 x 25.5 cm. 52 pages. Two-ink / Full colour printing. Quarterly

Typographic Ornamentation

Open is San Francisco Museum of Modern Art's way of keeping in touch with its members and giving them detailed information on forth-coming exhibitions. But far from being merely a newsletter, it is of sufficiently high quality to be included in the museum's own collection. The design of the magazine is therefore of considerable interest for the museum.

The magazine to a certain extent has to complement the work on display in the exhibi-tions. Martin uses typography as the foundation for the rest of the design. The publication gives Martin another opportunity to play with the decorative side of typography, designing tex-tures, shapes and ornamentation and achieving rhythm through his somewhat arbitrary arrangement of the characters on the page. His aim is to add some humour to the blank spaces: **"I have to decide whether I'm shouting or whispering the information, and to what degree, in each issue of the magazine."**

Open, no. 3
Open, no. 4

Content pages

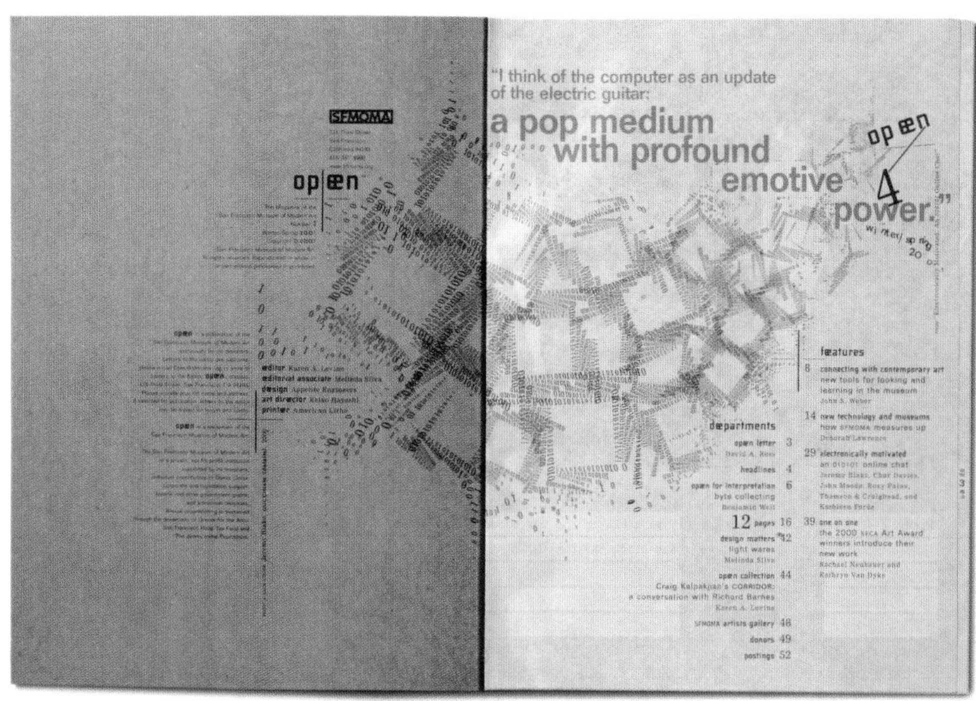

Rober Pallás
Barcelona, Spain

Rober Pallás (Barcelona, 1969) studied graphic and industrial design at the Escola d'Arts i Oficis Artístics 'Llotja' in Barcelona.

His career has included spells as art director for Tàndem DDB and FCB/Tapsa-Augusta. He is currently art director for the D'Arcy Masius Benton & Bowles agency in Barcelona.

He combines his work for the agency with personal projects in fashion, industrial design and publishing, having worked on the **Enser** fanzine since March 2001.

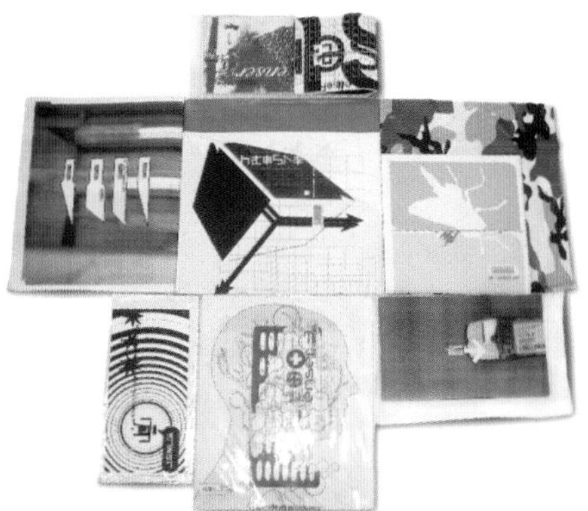

"The Fanzine as a Platform for Graphic Expression"

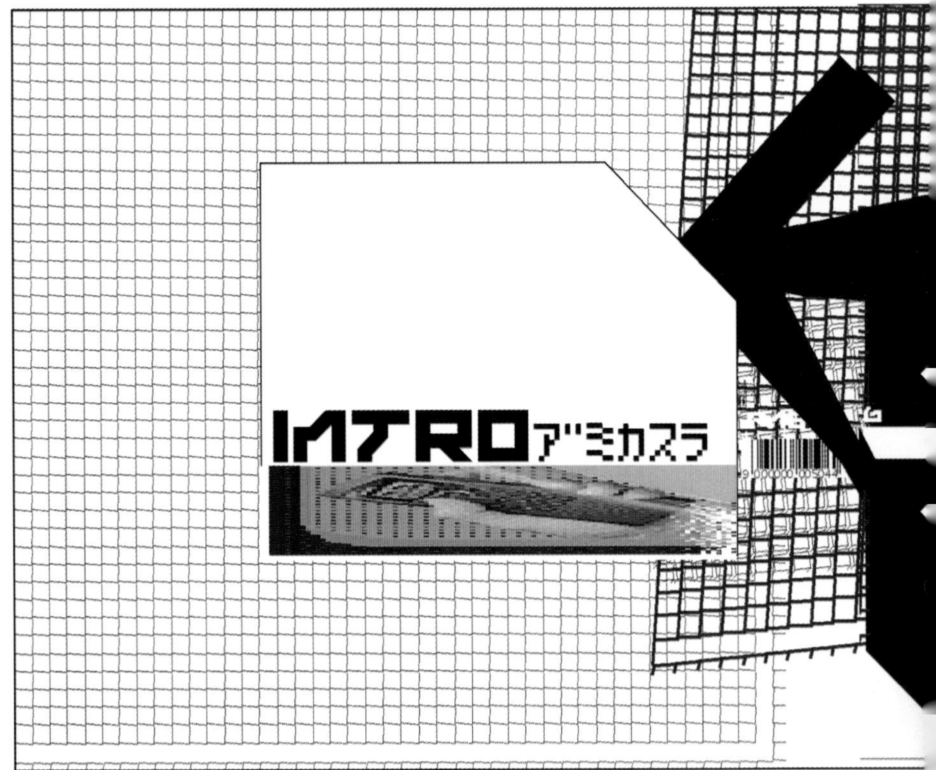

Enser 1. March, 2001
Fax

Collage based on random forms produced by sending documents by fax.

día cuando alguien nazca le será atribuido
mero de teléfono, si esa persona no atiende
porque está muerta.
9 000000 005044

Enser 6. January, 2002
Móvil

Reflection on communication, the importance of talking and of being heard.

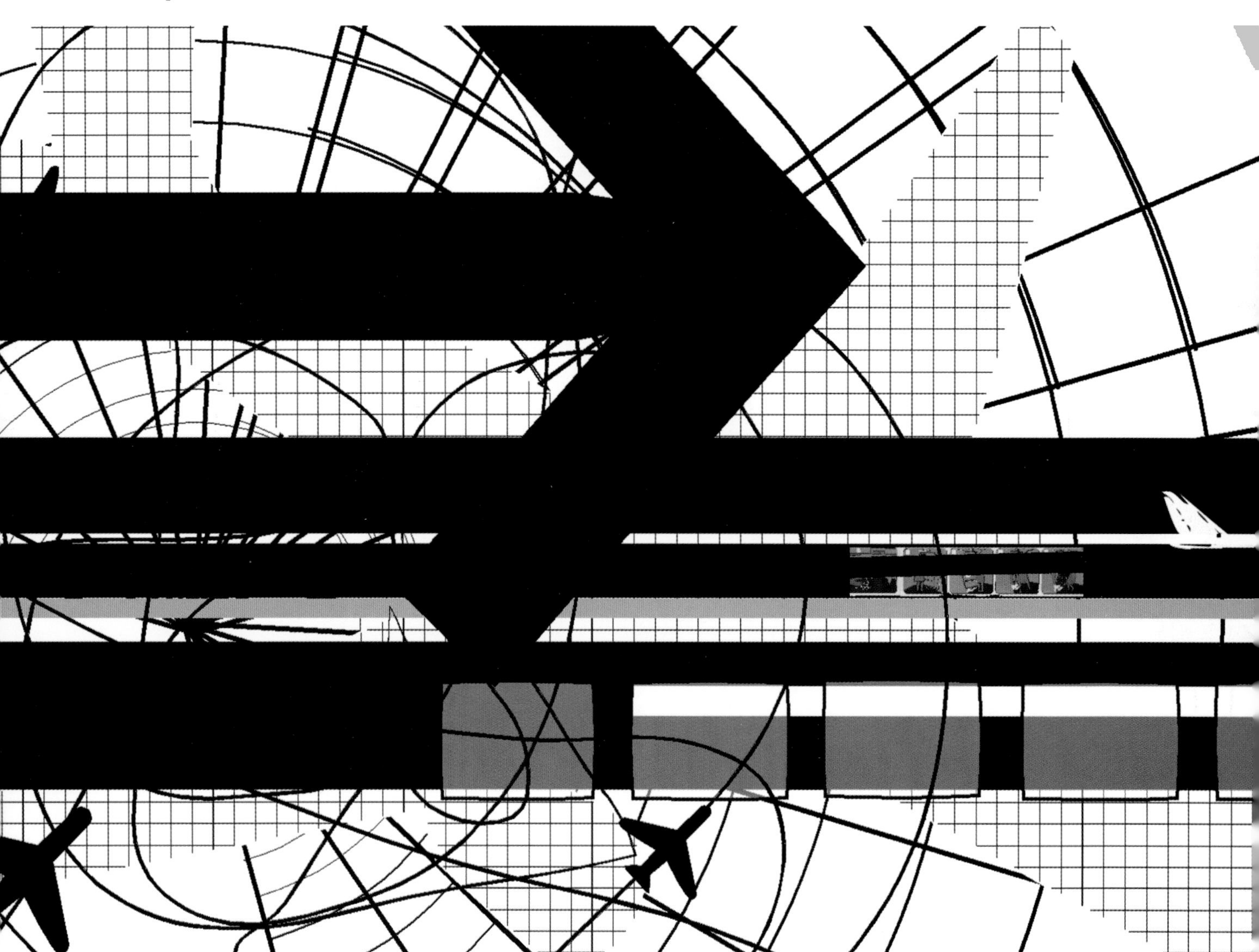

Enser
Fanzine

Year: 2001-2003
Client: HumanGraphics

Different formats. Xerox Document 220DC

Visual Transgression

"Launching a new publishing design project sounds, at first, a bit like committing suicide", says Rober, who runs the Enser fanzine, **"especially when you realise how many publications are already out there."** But Rober says the justification for bringing out a new publication is in trying to fill a hole in market **"where there is no room for minority interest publications with very specific subject matter."**

Enser is an independent art and design fanzine which is created using manual procedures and printed on a photocopier. Each issue is different in terms of format, design and how it is put together, so that each issue acquires its own status within the collection.

With a throwaway look but rich in content, Enser aims to dignify what is often seen as 'impoverished', and to give everything that society considers to be on the fringe the value and status it deserves.

Rober defines his fanzine as **"a platform for graphic expression for creative people."** Enser publishes the work of creators whose formal and conceptual tastes are in tune with those of Rober Pallás. **"Above all they must have something to say,"** he says.

Enser 3. May, 2001
Analytical Graphics

Graphic protest against the pharmaceuticals industry.

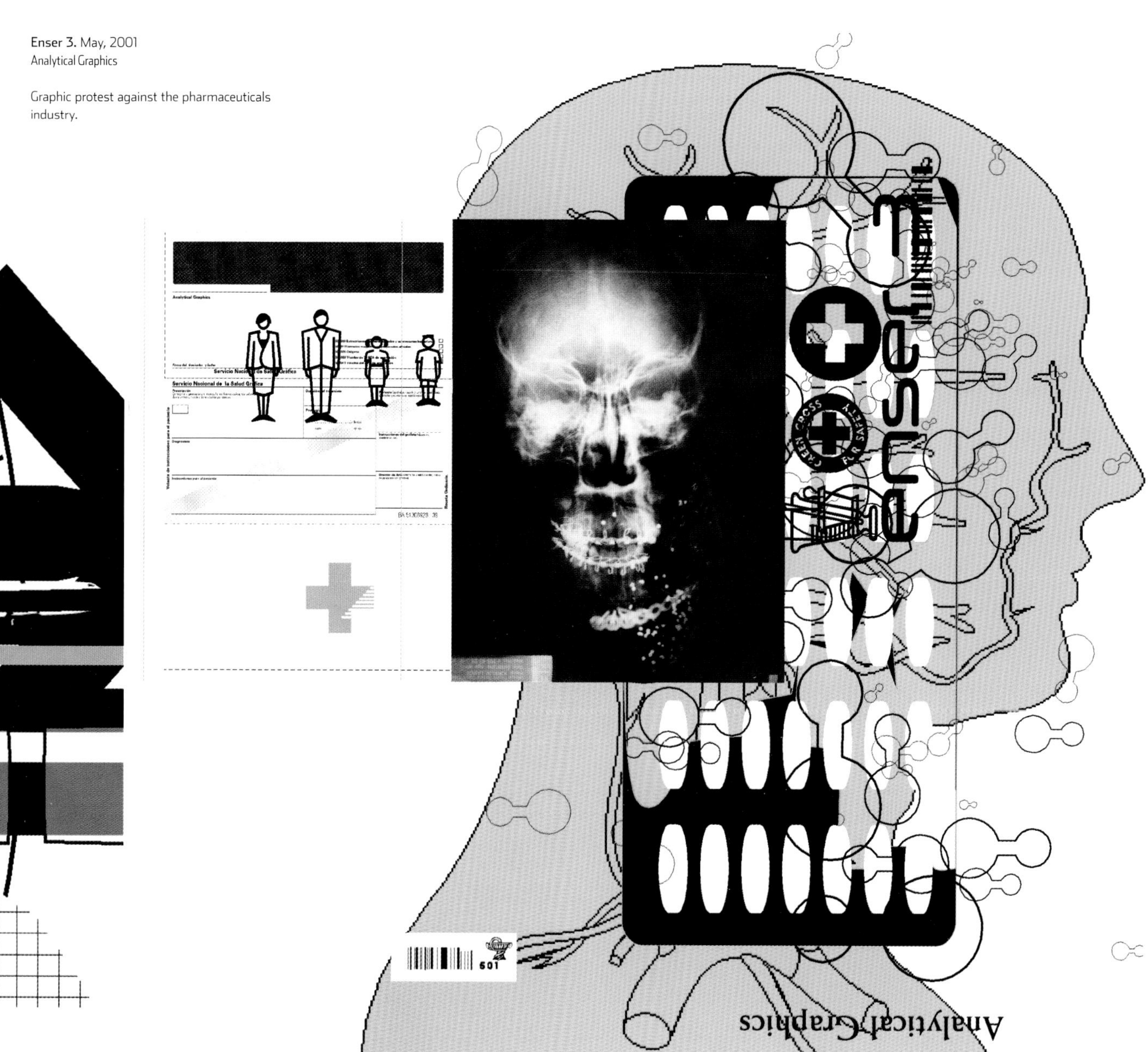

The character of the fanzine is expressed through the powerful way in which the subject matter is written and illustrated. The themes are close to the author's heart, who also acts as editor, designer, printer and distributor. Enser is a platform which permits him to give shape to his thoughts and concerns in a specific medium - the fanzine.

Rober says it was born as an act of rebellion: **"Its stance within the publishing world is to vindicate the homemade, handcrafted product. A vehicle for expression which takes a route different from the mainstream."**

In a publication whose aim is renewal, the design is conceived with utter freedom. The typefaces used in each issue vary according to the contents. Rober chooses fonts of strong character for the headlines of each issue, and achieves certain continuity in the design by using a specific typography. His priority is readability when choosing fonts for the body of the text, which are laid out without following any compositional rule or grid.

Generally the text is hugely expressive in the way it is integrated with the remaining elements. The power of Enser as a fanzine lies ultimately in its expressiveness and in the way in which it pushes the boundaries.

Enser 5. November, 2001
Cúter

Creation of a typographical family from the random collection and dissection of 25cm²-pieces of paper.

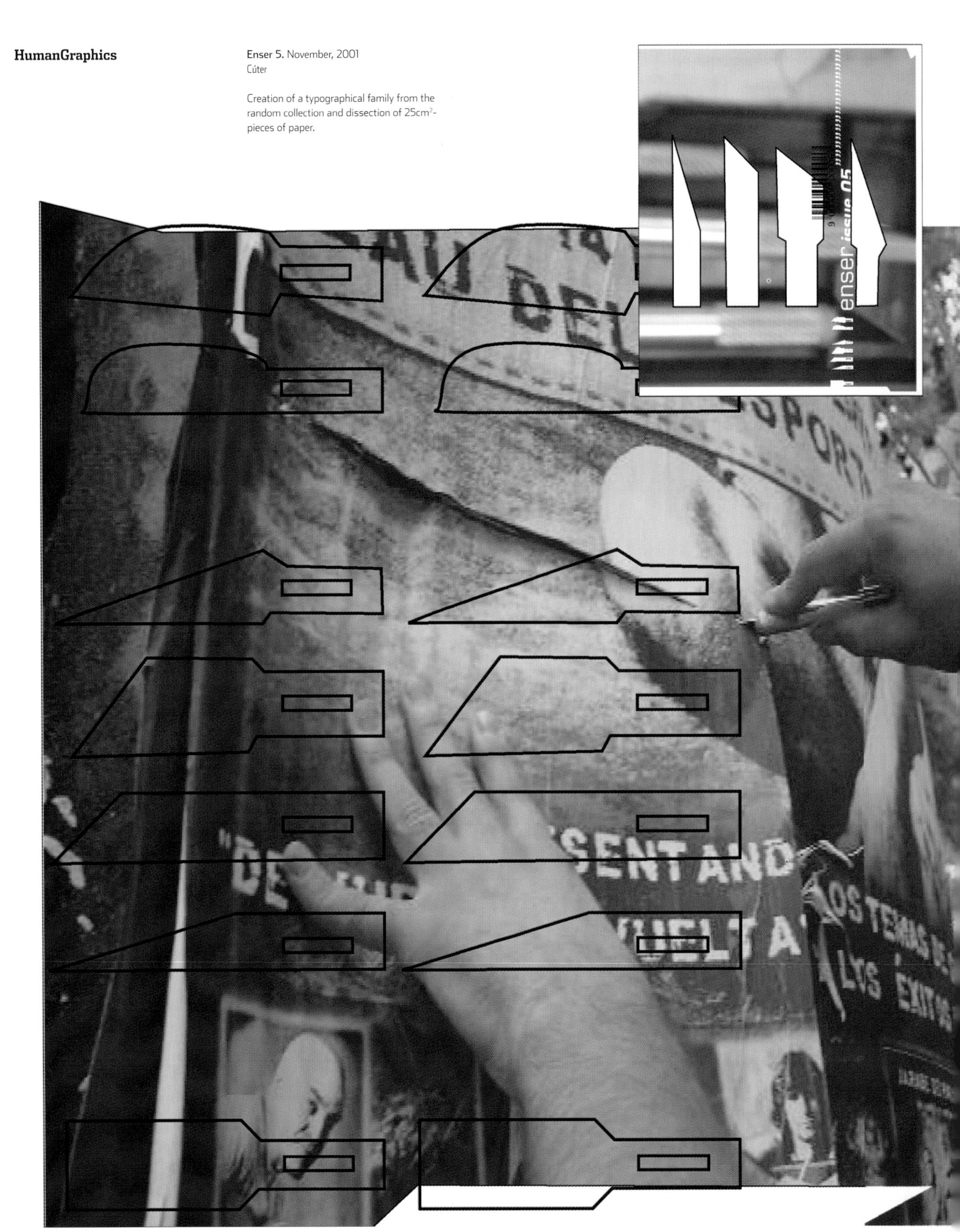

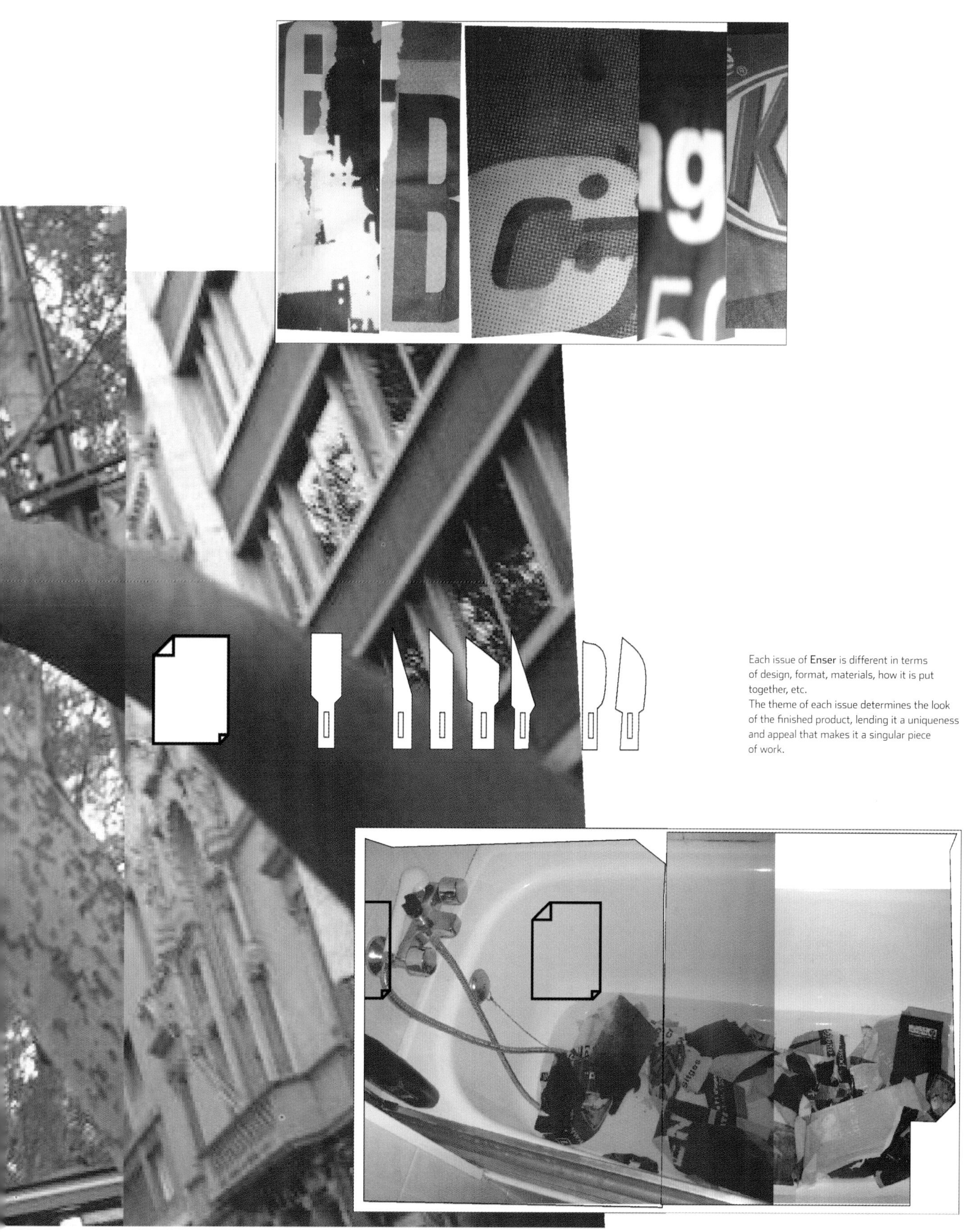

Each issue of **Enser** is different in terms of design, format, materials, how it is put together, etc.
The theme of each issue determines the look of the finished product, lending it a uniqueness and appeal that makes it a singular piece of work.

"We use letters to tran
usefulness is often
tent across with cla
ferences; as a transp
message, the voice of

functional
functional
knowledge
functional

nit information. Their
nited to getting con-
ty and without inter-
rent medium for the
he author".

Eumogràfic

Eumogràfic
Vic-Barcelona, Spain

"The Bare Beauty of Typography"

Associated with the University of Vic (Barcelona), **Eumogràfic** is a design studio that offers integral services to companies and institutions in the area of design and communication.

Created as a publishing workshop attached to the University, in 1984 it became an independent design studio.

With its long experience in the publishing world, the studio opts for clean graphics, free of ornamentation and extremely delicate and subtle, where nothing is gratuitous and clarity is the guiding principal in the use of typography.

This measured 'style' is part of an attitude, a work philosophy reflected in each and every one of their jobs, whether for the publishing world or for other design specialities: corporate identity, signage, stands, exhibitions, multimedia products, etc.

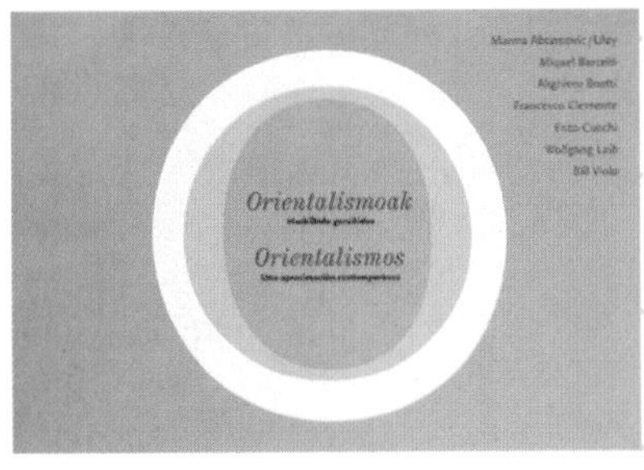

Orientalismos
1999

Graphic image for an exhibition. Applications for postcards and catalogue jackets.

Transversal
Magazine for contemporary culture
1996

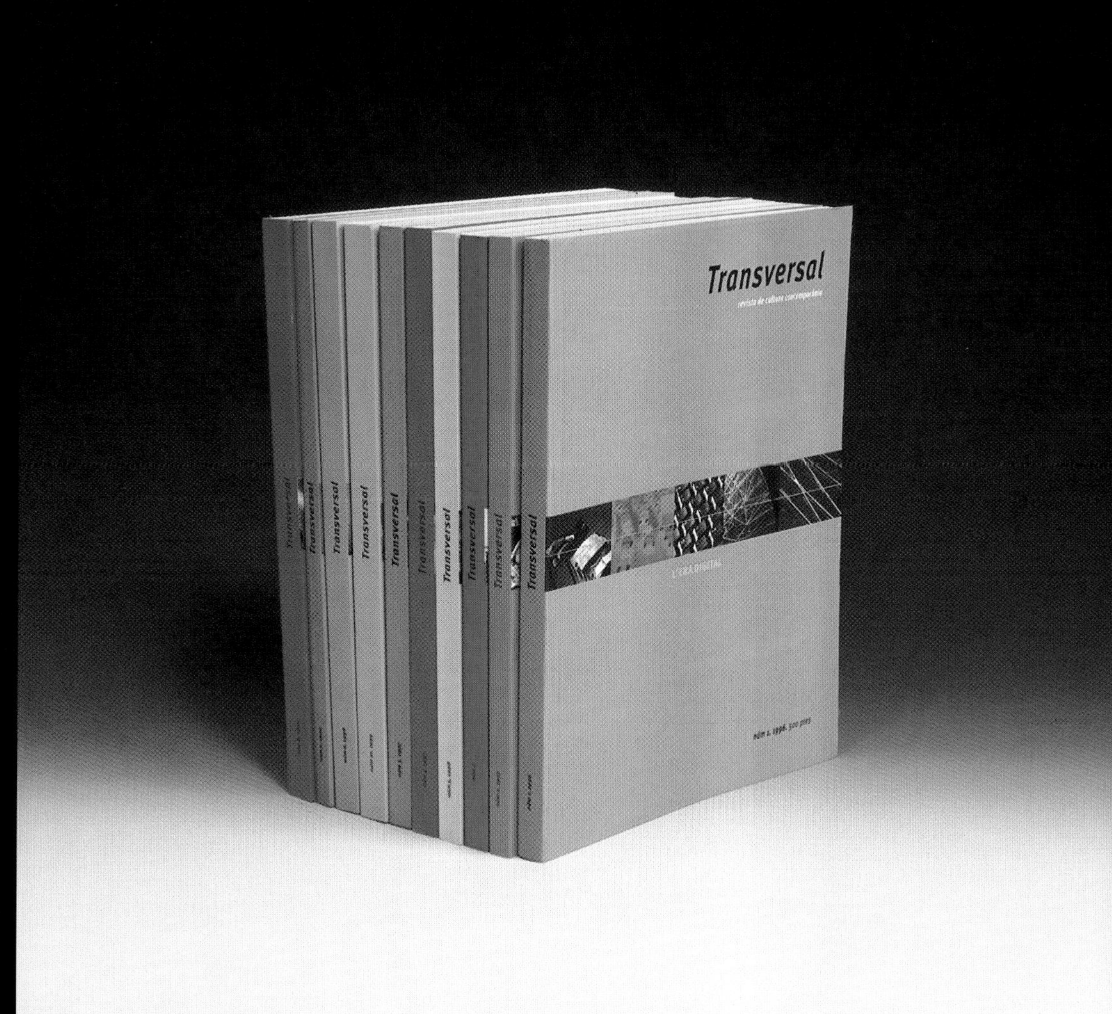

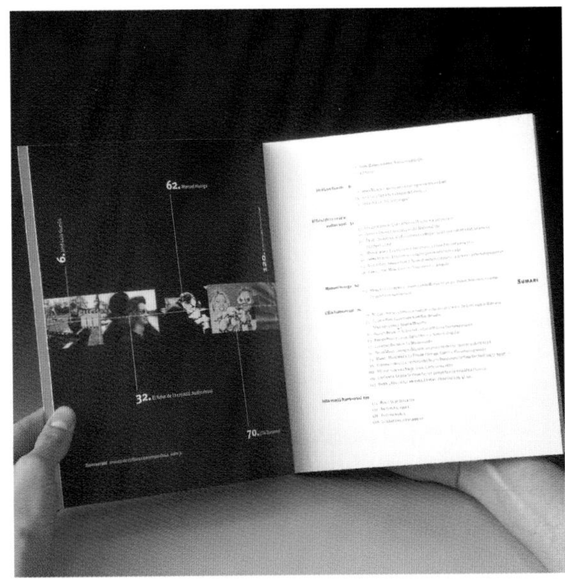

Transversal Magazine, no. 1
1996

Cover and inside pages

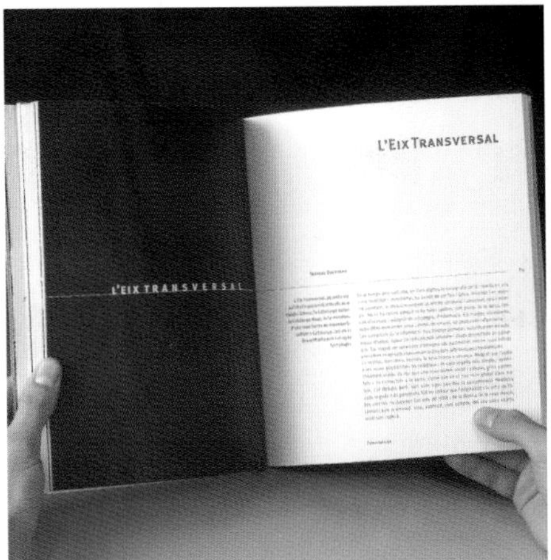

Transversal
Magazine

Year: 1996
Client: Lleida City Council

Font used: FF Meta

21 x 25 cm. 132 pages. 2 inks. Four-monthly

Idees Magazine, no. 12
October-December, 2001

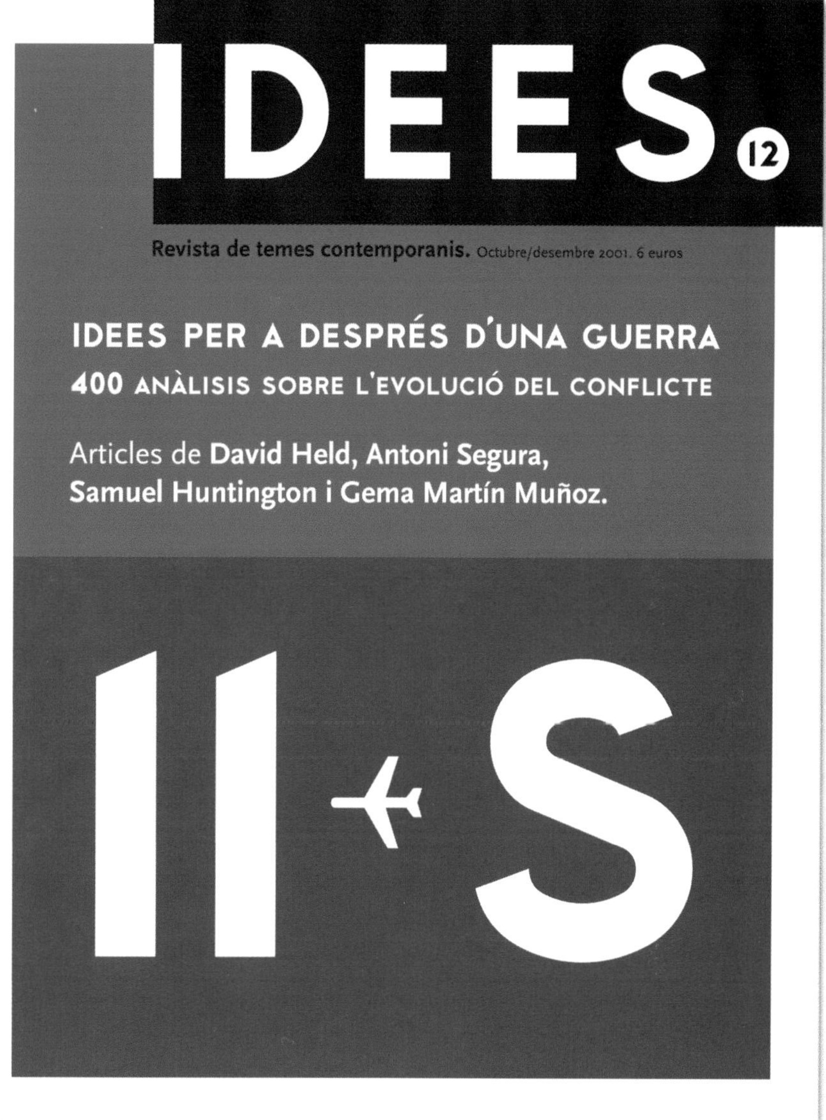

Idees
Magazine

Year: 1999
Client: Centre d'Estudis de Temes Contemporanis. Regional Government of Catalonia

Fonts used: FF Scala sans, FF Scala serif

18 x 23 cm. 256 pages. 2 inks. Bi-annually

A Library Magazine

Their mastery of the traditional (pre-Mac) tools of book production makes that the **Eumogràfic** team of professionals highly qualified for publication work. The care in dealing with the text and its layout on the page are the work of people specialised in the different phases of publishing: designers, mockup artists, correctors, production and finish specialists, etc.

They start with a geometric idea of the space – a grid – over which they gradually lay out the elements that make up the page. Economy in the use of elements is a characteristic of their 'style' which aims for pleasant, easy reading. The quest for transparency and the idea that the author's thoughts must come through without interference or noise demonstrate their great respect for the content in their work. **"Although we like to experiment with typography, this kind of work means that we have to accept different criteria from those we apply at other times."**

"When we design posters or book covers," says Albert Cano, one of the heads of the design team, **"we first lay out the typography. If that works, we begin to lay out the other elements. We try to resolve the typography**

Idees Magazine

Covers and inside pages

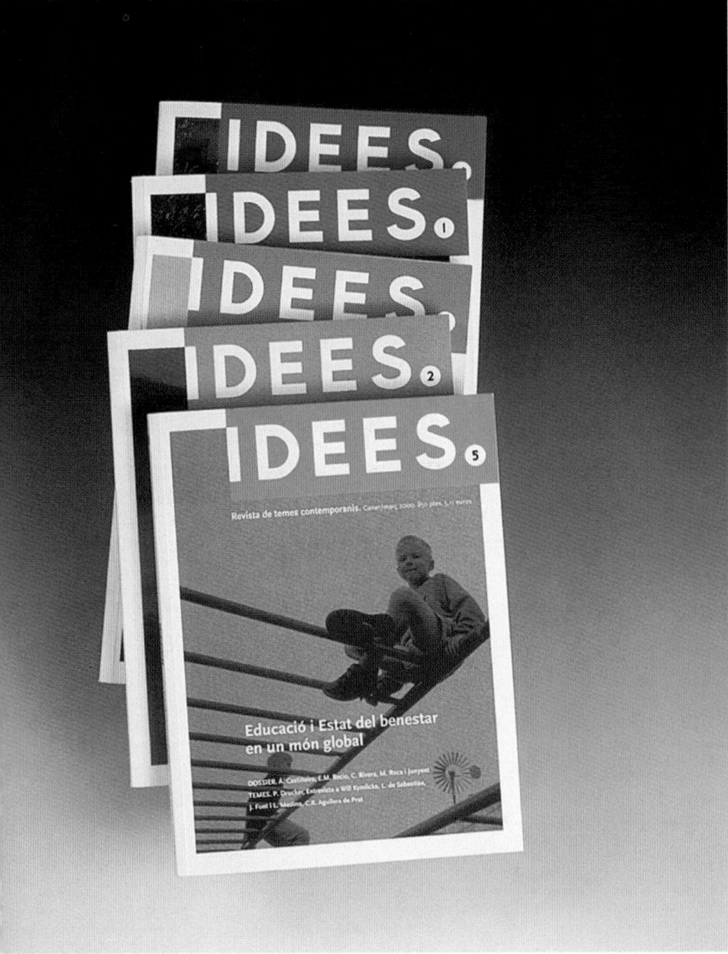

first, as it will often determine the rest of the composition."

In some cases, the choice of font in turn suggests the graphic solution. In Albert's words, **"I let the characteristics of a certain typeface lead me on. I like to let the typography point the way to a solution."**

In designing books, they usually work with classical fonts – Akzidenz Grotesk, Helvetica, or Garamond, for instance – and other more contemporary ones, such as FF Scala by Martin Majoor or FF Meta by Erik Spiekermann, distinguished by their elegance and simplicity.

Eumogràfic has done the design for two publications in book format, though they are in fact periodicals: the magazines Idees and Transversal, which are good examples of this approach to layout that constitutes the cornerstone of this studio's editorial design.

The Catalan trimestral Transversal is based on the idea of cultural decentralisation and underscores the geographical axis between the provincial capitals of Girona and Lleida, which bisects Catalonia. Eumogràfic maintains this concept in designing the magazine, playing with the idea of transversality in the mockup by dividing the pages horizontally. On the cover, this is expressed in a band with images related to a central theme addressed in the articles. Eumogràfic uses a single typeface for the headlines, titles, lead-ins, text body and margin notes in Transversal: the FF Meta family, in its different variants. The same is true in Idees, where it is FF Scala sans and serif. The 'colour' of the whole magazine depends heavily on the appearance of the typography, as very few photographs are used.

The format in both cases helps to define a type of publication – a hybrid book-magazine – where the text enjoys absolute importance and there is enormous respect for the author.

The graphic structure of the cover is repeated inside on the back cover and title pages. The title pages add a touch of colour among the pages of text and indicate the different sections of the magazine: Mirador, Temes Contemporaris and Dossier. The title pages are placed on the left so that the first article of each section always lies on the right.

When starting to design a publication devoted to thought, as is the case of Idees, Eumogràfic takes account of the concepts of sobriety and typographic clarity. At the same time, its presentation must be attractive and different from other publications devoted to issues of contemporary reflection. The appeal of Idees is based on the use of colour, two inks that are arranged to help the reader find the sections of the magazine, while breaking up the monotony of the text block.

As in the case of Transversal, colour also serves to identify each issue.

The choice of a porous paper in natural white adds warmth to the touch and reduces the contrast of the text, making reading easier.

Peter Bil'ak

Peter Bil'ak
The Hague, Holland

"The Editorial Viewpoint"

Peter Bil'ak (Slovakia, 1973), co-editor, with Stuart Bailey, of the magazine **Dot Dot Dot**, studied design at the Academy of Fine Arts & Design in Bratislava, at the Atelier National de Creation Typographique in Paris and later at the Jan van Eyck Akademie in Maastricht.

After almost two years working at Studio Dumbar, Peter started his own design studio to develop his graphic projects, sometimes individually, sometimes teaming up with other professionals.

The writer in him encouraged him to edit and design his own publications. Such is the case with **Illegibility** (1995), where Peter reflects on the role of typography in visual communication. Later, in **Transparency** (1997), Peter writes on the relationship between design and language.

Editorial and font design being his specialities, he has designed alphabets for the FontShop International catalogue.

En 1999, Peter created **Typotheque**, his own font shop, from where he distributes some of his creations.

He currently combines his work as a graphic designer and editor with teaching, working with various schools in Holland.

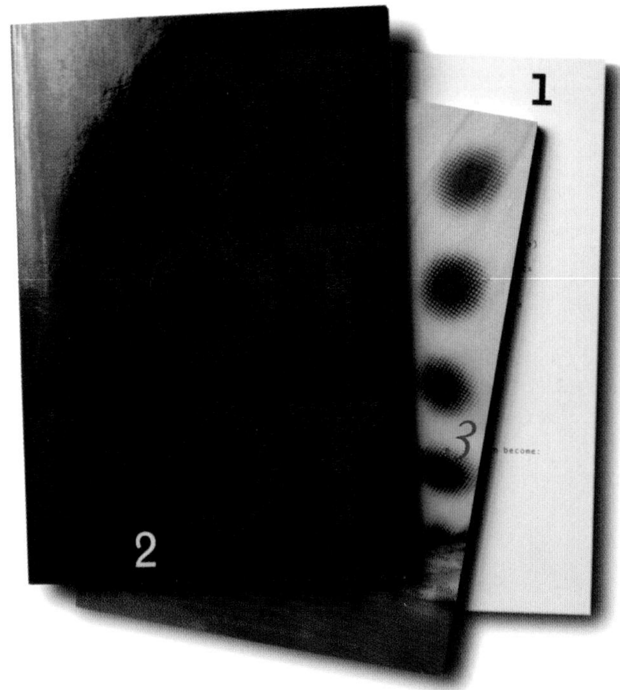

Dot Dot Dot. Issue 1
2000

Cover and inside pages

In the first of the issues of Dot Dot Dot. the cover was used as a support for defining the magazine, a sort of declaration of principles.

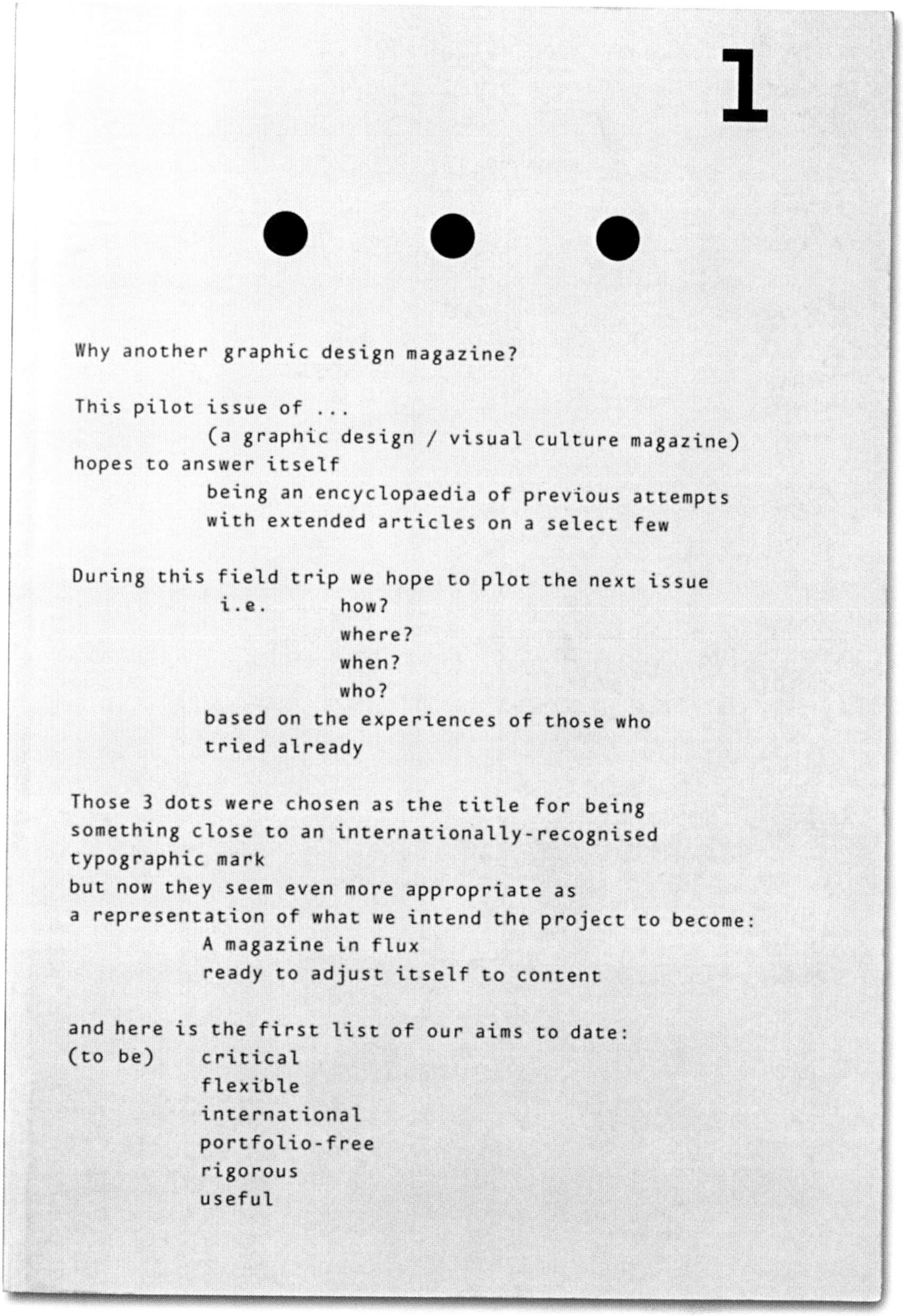

1

● ● ●

Why another graphic design magazine?

This pilot issue of ...
(a graphic design / visual culture magazine)
hopes to answer itself
being an encyclopaedia of previous attempts
with extended articles on a select few

During this field trip we hope to plot the next issue
i.e. how?
where?
when?
who?
based on the experiences of those who
tried already

Those 3 dots were chosen as the title for being
something close to an internationally-recognised
typographic mark
but now they seem even more appropriate as
a representation of what we intend the project to become:
A magazine in flux
ready to adjust itself to content

and here is the first list of our aims to date:
(to be) critical
flexible
international
portfolio-free
rigorous
useful

Peter Bil'ak

Dot Dot Dot. Issue 1
2000

Inside pages

Typografische Monatsblätter

Zeitschrift für Schrift, Typografie, Gestaltung und Sprache

Herausgegeben von der Mediengewekschaft comedia zur Förderung der Berufsausbildung

Revue suisse de l'imprimerie

Revue pour la lettre, la typographie, la conception graphique et le langage

Editée par le syndicat des médias comedia pour l'éducation professionelle

Swiss Typographic Magazine

Journal for Lettering, Typographic Composition, Design and Communication

Published by the Union comedia of Switzerlan[d] for the advancement of education

KEYWORDS: EDUCATION. JEAN-PIERRE GRABER. RUDOLF HOSTETTLER. PROCESSES. SWITZERLAND. UNIONS. WOLFGANG WEINGART.

1883
SGM year 1
The trade journal Schweizer *Graphische Mitteilungen* founded and published by R. Schneider in Zurich.
Printed at Zollikofer from 1886.

1923
RSI year 1
Revue Suisse de l'Imprimerie et des Industries annexes founded and published by E. Guggi.

1933
TM year 1
Typographische Monatsblätter founded and published by the Swiss Typographers' Association (Schweizerischer Typografenbund, STB), Bern, with the aim of promoting professional training.
Ernst Wyss is the editor.

1948
RSI year 27 : TM year 16
RSI and TM are merged.
10 issues to be published annually.
Karl Gasser becomes the editor.

1952
SGM year 71 : RSI year 31 : TM year 20
The three journals SGM, TM and RSI are merged under the name *Typografische Monatsblätter*.
STB remains the publisher. Rudolf Hostettler becomes the editor.

1971
TM year 90 : DI year 1
The journal *DruckIndustrie* founded by Rudolf Hostettler and published by Zollikofer, as an independent supplement to TM.
22 issues to be published annually.

1967
Wolfgang Weingart begins a 30-year collaboration with TM.

1978
TM year 97
Following the recommendations of a rationalisation commission the number of issues annually is reduc[ed] from 10 to 6.

1980
TM year 99 : DI year 10
The joint TM / DI editorial board is dissolved by the Zollikofer AG, which carries on DI with a modifie[d] concept. Following Hostettler's dea[th] in 1981, Jean-Pierre Graber become[s] the editor.

1999
TM year 118
The Print and Paper Workers' Unio[n] is merged with several trade unions to form the media workers union comedia which now becom[es] publisher of TM.

26

terview with
an-Pierre Graber, Editor of *TM*
Tom Unverzagt

like other design and graphic arts urnals published today TM has enjoyed ong life, or rather many different lives: is read and seen as something of ving legend. What was the initial ncept of the publishers almost seventy rs ago?

e first publications in the field of graphic arts industry were neral trade union papers such as vetische Typographia which dealt h purely trade union topics. e initial idea of TM was that of ther education on a vocational is across the whole breadth of the nting industry. For example re were articles dealing with the per use of the space band on a otype machine so it wouldn't , and others to do with Monotype explaining how to deliver the rices into the assembler in the st efficient manner. These were tributions of the more technical ety. There were also non-techni- sections dealing with apprentices' tings, delegate meetings of the hanised Typesetters' Association, , but also looking at questions nanagement.

The editorial board was made up of representatives of the various trades concerned. There were specialist editors for the following groups: hand compositors and proof-readers, mechanised typesetters, printers and their apprentices, as well as stereotype printers. Later the hand compositors were joined by the typographic designers and the mechanised typesetters by the phototypesetters. In the beginning we met two or three times a year and discussed the contributions submitted. It was often thought that the hand compositors filled two thirds of the journal and there were just a few pages left for the rest of us. But that later sorted itself out because there were fewer and fewer articles on technical issues. The two things developed in different directions and the technical articles were then published elsewhere. And anyway, the printers had since become offset printers and the mechanised typesetters were now phototypesetters. That's why we took the notions of printing and further processing out of the title last year. But to return to the early years; over time, in any case, the topics dealing with design took up more and more space. Back then *TM* also published contributions from local groups such as the hand compositor associations. When they ran a competition, notification had to be published. Some of the contributions were rather strange and we had to consider whether we really wanted to publish them. When Hostettler became editor-in-chief in 1952 he deliberately brought in creative, educated people. Young typographers were then able to learn from more convincing and consistent examples. In trade union terms this was obviously something of a break with the past, but it improved the journal's quality in terms of further education. So on the one hand the topics concentrated more and more on design, on the other hand the circle of authors was extended beyond the scope of the union. But that did not preclude the continued publication of general reports on meetings.

How does TM actually find its topics?

I intentionally write to specific people and ask if they'd like to contribute. It's not so easy. On the one hand they always want to see what they give me in print straight way, and that's not always possible. On the other hand it's often the case that someone is enthusiastic

Hostettler, 1948

Ruder, 1961

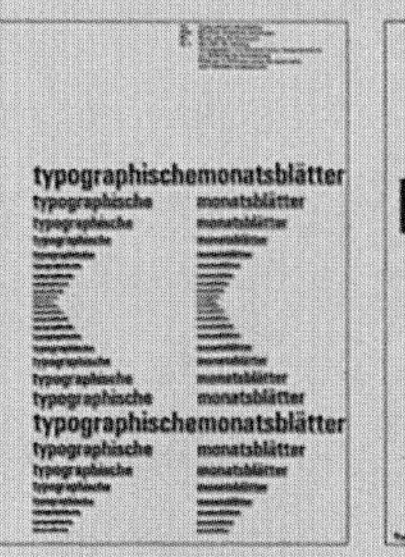

Weingart, 1973

Warum und wie die TM-Umschläge für 1972 und 1973 entstanden sind.

27

e
KEYWORDS: 1980S/1990S. APPLE MAC. CALIFORNIA.
CONSTRAINTS. DEBATE. ZUZANA LICKO. TYPE DESIGN.
RUDY VANDERLANS.
66

Dot Dot Dot
Magazine

Year: 2000
Designers: Stuart Bailey, Peter Bil'ak
Client: DotDotDot

Fonts used:
Eureka, Eureka sans, Eureka mono

16,5 x 23,5 cm. 96 pages. 2 inks. Bi-annually

A Flexible Mockup

Peter's concern lies in finding a suitable, distinctive, direct form of expression for his graphic projects by combining different disciplines, theory and practice. He is not interested in generating a personal style with which he can identify himself, or a specific working philosophy, focusing on ideas rather than forms. **"Style emerges from within each of the projects and is integrated inseparably in them,"** he says.

He finds his inspiration in the 'simple and ordinary' more than in what one might find in design publications.

He defines typography as a way to deal with the components by maintaining their internal relations. **"It is obvious,"** Peter clarifies, **"that the 26 letters of the Latin alphabet form a system. Similar systems can be found in the surrounding environment if the viewer is sensitive enough. Ordinary things can have the role of letters and can build meaning. Giving those elements the adequate value (...) is the purpose of the typographer."**

In his role as a writer and editor, Peter Bil'ak has joined forces with Stuart Bailey to run the editorial project Dot Dot Dot, one of the most

CALIFORNIA.
. TYPE DESIGN.

This is an updated version of an essay first published in Danish journal *Bogvennen* in 1997. The original piece dealt with *Emigre* as a company, discussing both the type design and magazine. For ..... I have edited out most of the typeface references, in order to focus on the magazine, but it is worth re[illegible] essent[illegible]ymbiosis [illegible] the two aspect[illegible] As a remin[illegible] *Emigre* will [illegible]ular rather [illegible] plural noun. Also [illegible] mentioning is that i[illegible]king throu[illegible] the small[illegible] again, I realised [illegible] company's ever-morphing attitude is best experienced by reading Rudy VanderLans' candid editorials. As a whole, they provide one of the most digestible overviews of graphic design concerns approaching the end of the twentieth century.

migre

Growing up in public

The prevailing US stronghold of Postmodern graphic design is cluttered with icons. From the late 1980s onwards, a number of key schools (CalArts, Cranbrook, Rhode Island), personalities (Keedy, Carson, Makela, Deck) and publications (Ray Gun, Beach Culture) combined to form a catalyst, gradually establishing a network of ideological typographic discourse. Constantly in-breeding and multiplying, the wide-ranging debate has since reached a certain level of distinction most convincingly articulated through the work of Miller and Lupton.

See: Lupton, E. & Miller, J A: *Design Writing Research* (New York; Princeton Architectural Press; 1996)

67

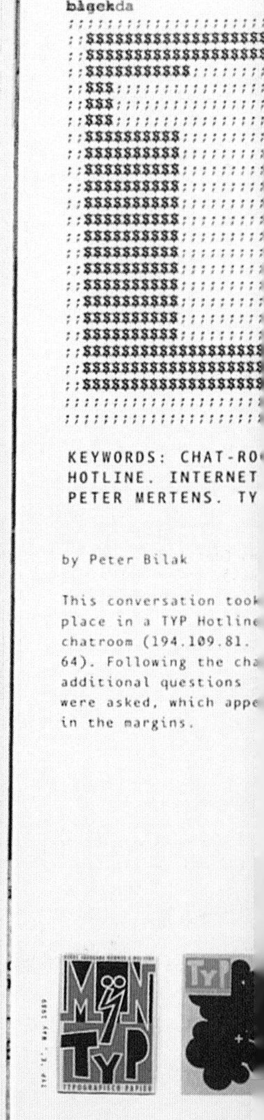
KEYWORDS: CHAT-RO
HOTLINE. INTERNET
PETER MERTENS. TY
by Peter Bilak
This conversation took
place in a TYP Hotline
chatroom (194.109.81.
64). Following the cha
additional questions
were asked, which appe
in the margins.

interesting design magazines on the current scene.

Peter defines Dot Dot Dot as **"an independent magazine on graphic design intended to fill a gap in current arts publishing"**. His interest does not lie in **"re-promoting established material or creating another 'portfolio' magazine"**. Instead, Peter and Stuart offer a critical magazine dealing with a range of issues directly or indirectly related to graphic design.

The magazine also welcomes contributions from professionals with articles on those aspects of visual culture that interest or concern them.

Dot Dot Dot is basically aimed at graphic designers. Although it looks rather austere, printed in a single ink on offset paper, this serves to transmit a sort of content that otherwise would not be sufficiently credible.

"We change type and grids from each issue, depending on needs. The editorial standpoint is more important than the design composition, which doesn't mean that we are not interested in the look of the magazine. We are striving for the combination of the content and form, even if it sounds like a cliché."

In the first issue of Dot Dot Dot (2000), the cover was used as a support to define the magazine, as a sort of declaration of principles: **"Our list of goals: that it should be critical, flexible, international, lacking in portfolios, rigorous, useful."**

In this pilot issue they tried to reply to the question 'Why another graphic art magazine?' by publishing an article that is a sort of encyclopaedic compendium of some of the most important graphic design magazines of the 20th century and by analysing those that merit special attention. In this way, by analysing earlier editorial experiences (Emigre,

vaguely:	All the older guys weren't interested in the new and we (Peter M, me and others) were very much into the new, not only in computers, but...
Answering Mac:	It was a graveyard, protected by old men.
vaguely:	... but also the ideas behind it, the images, the words.
investigator:	Did you think it would last that long?
Answering Mac:	It had the force of the urge!
vaguely:	Peter, Jan and Henk immediately wanted to continue TYP.
investigator:	How many issues did you make, both on paper and Web?
vaguely:	Peter?
Answering Mac:	31
investigator:	Really?!
vaguely:	TYP moved typographic borders, when everybody thought they were stuck.
investigator:	It has always been in Dutch, right?
Answering Mac:	No! Spanish! English!
vaguely:	TYP reached a small but dedicated audience it moved designers and gave them some understanding of different things going on.
investigator:	The last issue on paper was quite cryptic...
Answering Mac:	TXT only! You can start reading wherever you want.
investigator:	No images anymore?
Answering Mac:	Images everywhere! The Web! Hotline Colour, Moving! Sounds!
investigator:	Why 'TXT only' then?
Answering Mac:	The images are elsewhere.
investigator:	On the WEB?
Answering Mac:	Yep, 194.109.81.64 On the ROM, on our own browser...
investigator:	Will you continue the magazine on all three media (paper, CD, WWW)?
Answering Mac:	Yep!
investigator:	How was the analogue comeback? And why did you interrupt the paper version at the first place?
Answering Mac:	We will have an exhibition in Hoorn.
investigator:	Where is Hoorn?
Answering Mac:	The north of Holland.

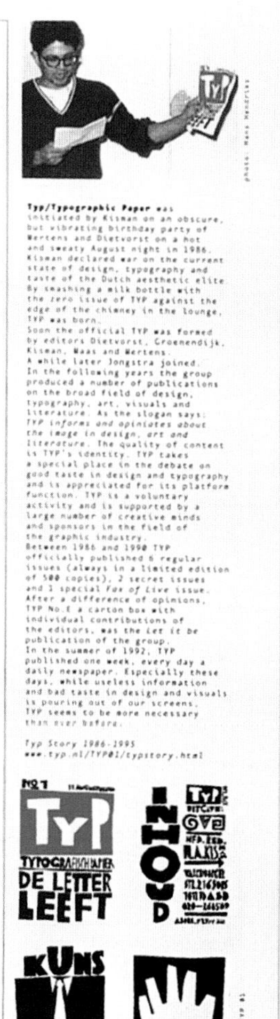

TYP
Typ/Typographic Paper was initiated by Kisman on an obscure, but vibrating birthday party of Mertens and Dietvorst on a hot and sweaty August night in 1986. Kisman declared war on the current state of design, typography and taste of the Dutch aesthetic elite. By smashing a milk bottle with the *zero* issue of TYP against the edge of the chimney in the lounge, TYP was born.
Soon the official TYP was formed by editors Dietvorst, Groenendijk, Kisman, Maas and Mertens.
A while later Jongstra joined.
In the following years the group produced a number of publications on the broad field of design, typography, art, visuals and literature. As the slogan says: *TYP informs and opiniates about the image in design, art and literature.* The quality of content is TYP's identity. TYP takes a special place in the debate on good taste in design and typography and is appreciated for its platform function. TYP is a voluntary activity and is supported by a large number of creative minds and sponsors in the field of the graphic industry.
Between 1986 and 1990 TYP officially published 6 regular issues (always in a limited edition of 500 copies), 2 secret issues and 1 special *Fax of Live* issue.
After a difference of opinions, TYP No.E a carton box with individual contributions of the editors, was the *Let it be* publication of the group.
In the summer of 1992, TYP published one week, every day a daily newspaper. Especially these days, while useless information and bad taste in design and visuals is pouring out of our screens, TYP seems to be more necessary than ever before.
Typ Story 1986-1995
www.typ.nl/TYP01/typstory.html
NO 1
TYP
TYPOGRAFISCH PAPIER
DE LETTER LEEFT
INHOUD
KUNS
ACHT

79

Eye, Form+Zweck, Octavo, etc.), the editors try to define the gap to fill and thus justify their own existence.

The second and third issues focused their interest on more abstract issues: rhetoric, randomness, humour, dogmatism, processes, and so on.

In view of the issues that have appeared, Dot Dot Dot is seeking to stake its claim in the field based on the quality of both its content and graphic art.

Pentagram

Angus Hyland / Pentagram
London, United Kingdom

"Design Based on Ideas"

Pentagram is a designers' organisation founded in London in 1972. Here, good humour and a passion for the trade have as much importance as the business side.

The Pentagram associates cover an extensive range of skills, from architecture and interior and exhibition design to graphic and industrial design, and – working either individually or as a team – are therefore able to offer their clients solutions to any sort of project.

Each project is managed by one of the associates and developed by his or her own team of designers.

What distinguishes Pentagram and has earned them international recognition is their practice of a strictly idea-based design, disassociating themselves from the decorative school.

After running his own studio for more than ten years, **Angus Hyland** joined Pentagram as an associate in 1998, working on a variety of projects ranging from editorial design to identity design and advertising.

Angus studied graphic design at the London College of Printing and the Royal College of Art, graduating with an MA (RCA) in 1988. He has received a number of awards over the course of his professional career and works as a guest tutor at the London College of Printing, the Royal College of Art and the Domus Academy in Milan. He has been a member of the Alliance Graphique Internationale (AGI) since 1999.

Andy Warhol: The Factory Years 1964-67 Book

Cover
Jackets

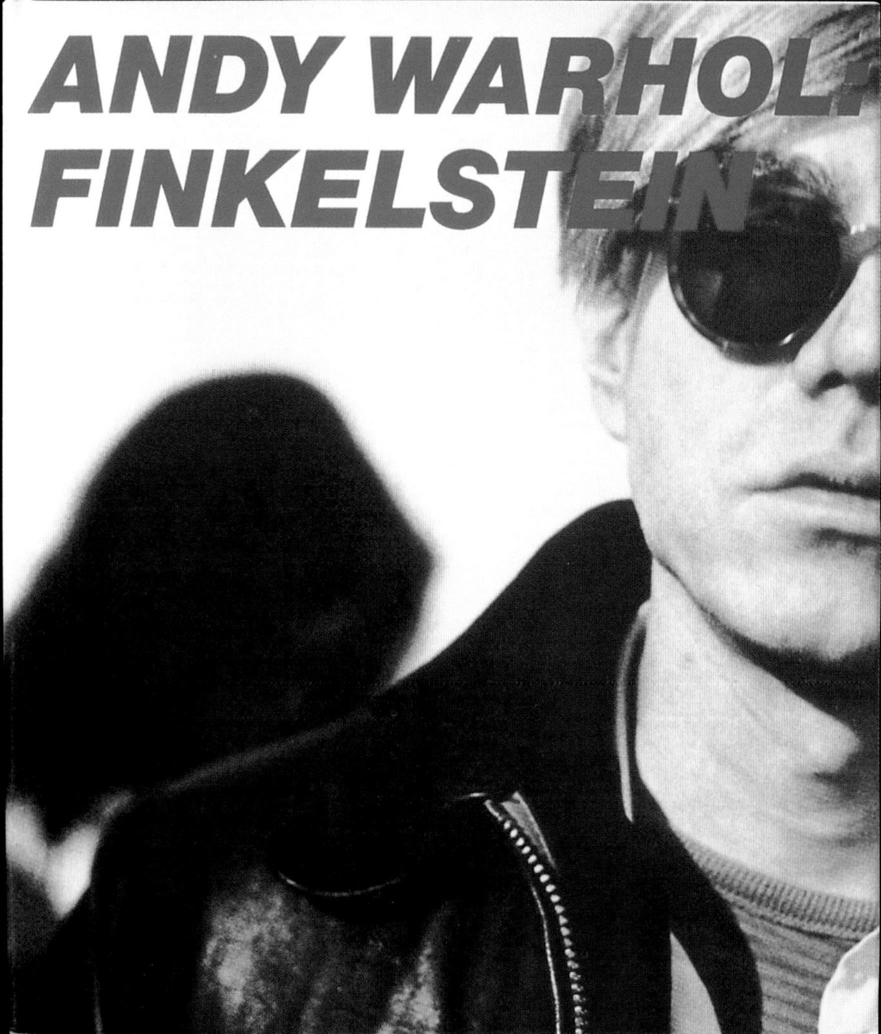

Andy Warhol: The Factory Years 1964-67
Book

Year: 1999
Designer: Angus Hyland
Assistant: Tom Phillips

Client: Canongate Books Ltd

Font used: Helvetica

A Book about 'The Factory'

The book Andy Warhol: The Factory Years 1964-67 is a collection of photographs and reflections by the New York photographer Nat Finkelstein. In 1964, Finkelstein started hanging out at Andy Warhol's 'Factory', and for two years was the quasi-official photographer of this bizarre artistic environment.

Angus took part in selecting the images for the Finkelstein collection and in the entire edit-

Angus used an uppercase italic Helvetica, varying the size throughout the book, to reflect Finkelstein's rapid-fire comments. A simple grid is sufficient to evoke the design of the period and suggest the New York pop subculture.

MAKING ART

Andy Warhol

PARAPHERNALIA. PILGRIM CLOTHES DECIDED TO GO MOD AND HIRED BETSEY JOHNSON TO DESIGN THEIR LINE. THEIR FLAGSHIP STORE WAS PARAPHERNALIA. BETSEY HIRED ANDY TO MAKE A PARTY. THUS ANDY WARHOL POP ARTIST BECAME ANDY WARHOL DRESS SALESMAN. HE WAS A HIRED GUN, SILVER SPRAYED GEORGE RAFT.

ANDY CAME WITH A BUNCH OF PRE-PACKAGED SUPERSTARS AND THE VELVETS. FRUG, FRUG, FRUG... OUR JOB WAS TO GET AMERICA HOT TO TROT. WE STAGED A PARTY IN A FISHBOWL, A STORE WINDOW ON MADISON AVENUE. CROWDS GATHERED... THE IDEA WAS THAT EVERYBODY WHO SAW THE PARTY WOULD BUY CLOTHES THERE. THE GIRLS SHOWED THE NEW FASHION WHILE THEY WERE DANCING TO THE VELVET'S MUSIC. IT WAS CASH IN TIME AT THE ZOO, 'WE WILL TAKE YOU TO PARADISE, JUST BE WILLING TO PAY THE PRICE'. WE WERE THE SHOW, ANDY'S CIRCUS. THAT WAS THE WAY ANDY WORKED: HE MANUFACTURED HAPPENINGS OUT OF THE PEOPLE AROUND HIM. THEY WERE HIS RAW MATERIAL — GLITTERING CANNON FODDER. HE SOLD US AS COMMERCIAL ART. HE MANUFACTURED CANDY KISSES, WRAPPED IN SILVER... PULL A PIECE OF CELLOPHANE AND OUT POPS THE STAR. THE SUPERSTARS WERE AT PARAPHERNALIA AS MEDIA, AND THE PUBLIC, NOT THE MERCHANDISE, WAS BEHIND GLASS. ANDY'S OWN ATTITUDE TOWARD CLOTHING WAS PRETTY WEIRD. HE ONCE ASKED ME TO GO SHOPPING WITH HIM. WHEN I SUGGESTED THAT WE SHOULD GO TAKE A LOOK AT ONE OF THE UPPER-CLASS SECOND HAND CLOTHING-STORES WHICH WERE THEN GETTING FASHIONABLE, HE SAID: 'OH NO NAT, NEVER BUY USED CLOTHING, IT'S LIKE WEARING SOMEBODY ELSE'S PERSONALITY!' EXCEPT FOR THIS, WHAT HE WORE WAS OF NO IMPORTANCE TO HIM. HIS CONCEPT OF FASHION WAS WHAT HE GOT OTHER PEOPLE TO WEAR. ANDY HAD A BIG THING FOR HERSHEY'S CHOCOLATE KISSES, WRAPPED UP IN A SILVER PACKAGE. SEEING PEOPLE DRESSED UP IN SILVER, LIKE AT THE PARAPHERNALIA SHOW, WAS LIKE HIS FANTASY COME TRUE. PLASTIC WRAPPED BODIES, NON-BIODEGRADABLE, PLASTIC PUSSIES AND MADE TO ORDER SEX.

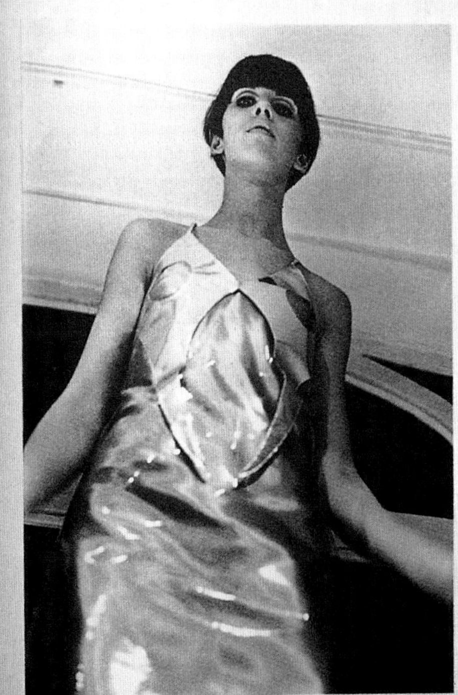

Tau Diseño

Tau Diseño
Madrid, Spain

"Passion for Letters"

Emilio Gil (Madrid, 1949) founded **Tau Diseño** in 1980. His professional career coincides with the evolution of the design profession in Spain, a time of great political and social change that influenced Spanish graphic production enormously.

Since then Tau have earned the respect and admiration of the entire profession, not only for the quality of their work, but also through their commitment to defending design in all realms: associations, education and institutions. Many are the professionals who have trained, worked or collaborated with Tau over the years.

Tau Diseño have worked on some of the graphic products that could be considered most genuinely Spanish: the Osborne bull, flamenco recordings and publications, and the graphic images commemorating the birthdays of Goya, Felipe II and Carlos V.

Sur Exprés Magazine
Issue number 7. February 1988

The magazine of the Madrid scene of the eighties. The heir to La Luna de Madrid, it had more mature contents and design.

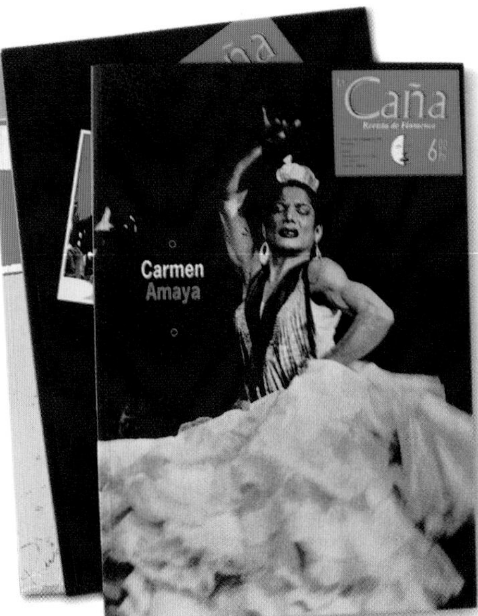

La Caña Magazine
Cover number 1. December 1991
A magazine devoted to flamenco

The magazine's banner works like a label and allows for flexibility in its placement. The typography seeks to reflect the spontaneous, improvised character of the artistic expressions within.

Un Toro Negro y Enorme

The book is conceived as a homage to the emblematic bull designed by Manolo Prieto for Bodegas Osborne.

Book project

Un Toro Negro y Enorme

Mockup of the first cover and the design of the box containing the book (with the silhouette of the bull).

Un Toro Negro y Enorme
Commemorative book

Year: 1994
Design: Emilio Gil / Jorge García
Client: 'España Abierta' cultural association and Bodegas Osborne

Fonts used: Didot, Cooper, Eagle, Futura, Oblong

30.5 x 30.5 cm. 176 pages. Full colour printing

The Book as an Object of Desire

In Emilio Gil's view, typography, **"as well as being a vehicle to transmit the written information, is an element of great formal beauty."**

Thus, at **Tau** typography acquires an aesthetic value of its own, reflected in a tendency to work with typographic forms. This is what Emilio defines as the popularly perceived 'Tau style': **"a way of resolving jobs, characterised by economy of graphic elements and the use of typographic forms and ornamentation."**

Emilio chooses his typefaces as complements, rarely, if ever, using more than two types in the same publication. He usually combines a classical serif with a more contemporary sans, eschewing the use of excessively 'neutral' typefaces. **"I usually make a first choice and do proofs with the body and line spacing dependent on the width of the case, always working with full size printouts to avoid surprises. I try to match the typeface with the product. It should have a formal, historical or geographical coherence with the subject and read easily when it is applied to small bodies."**

Emilio lays out his pages giving the blank spaces enormous importance and avoiding

Tau Diseño

Un Toro Negro y Enorme
First pages

The subtlety of the Didot typeface contrasts with the coarseness of the paper used.

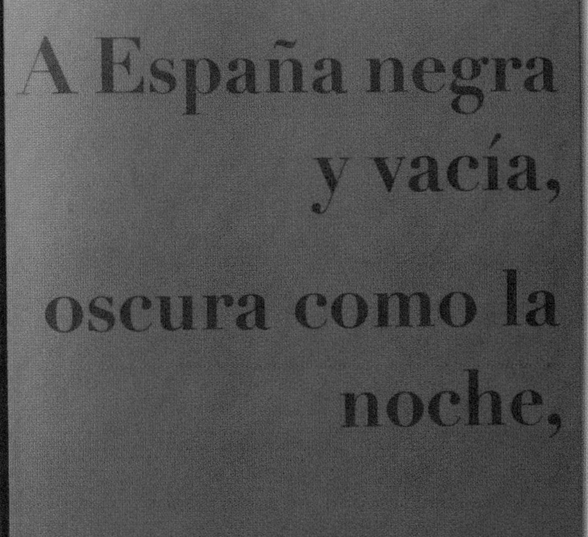

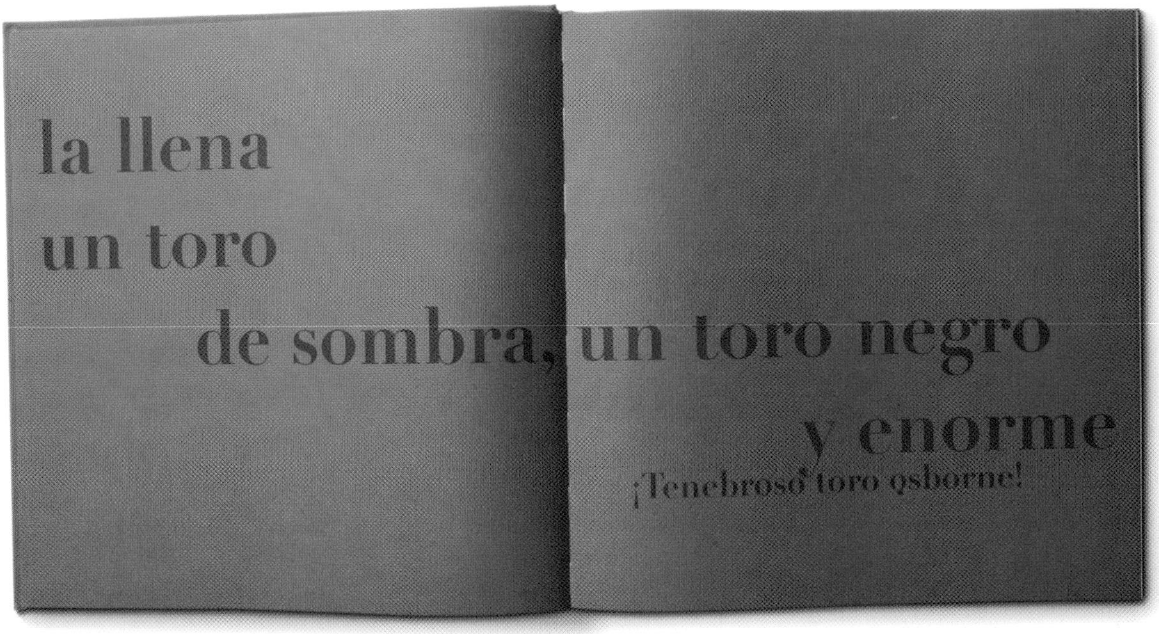

Un Toro Negro y Enorme
Table of contents

The blank spaces behave as integrators of the various elements composing the page.

excessively dense blocks of text. He stresses rhythm in the design of every publication; a rhythm that varies to prevent excessive repetition in the sequence of pages.

The book Un Toro Negro y Enorme was a milestone in the Tau Diseño's trajectory, not only because of the awards received for the work (Certificate of Typographic Excellence from the TDC in 1995; Donside Special Award in Great Britain in 1994, and the Laus for editorial design), but for what the work meant in terms of personal and professional commitment. Emilio says that the commission was a designer's dream come true, one that many others would have loved to have: to work with the legendary Osborne bull designed by Manolo Prieto in the fifties, a roadside icon throughout Spain.

"The España Abierta cultural association and Bodegas Osborne were not simply commissioning the design of a book, they wanted us to conceive a book that would pay homage to Manolo Prieto's bull, give it content, choose the collaborators... That is, come up with the whole thing," says Emilio.

With the definition of the contents in their hands, Tau decided to work simultaneously on two processes: the thematic contents of the book, to be separated into sections; and the design of each of the proposed sections. This was not restricted to the graphics of the pages, but even covered aspects of the publishing such as choosing different kinds of paper for each of the sections.

"The book was conceived as a 'mosaic' and this was reflected in the materials the images and texts were printed on."

This variety was also patent in the use of typeface. Tau chose the Didot family for the texts; for the headers and headings he used different typefaces depending on the themes. **"For once,"** says Emilio Gil, **"we were able**

Un Toro negro y enorme
Inside pages

The iconography of the Osborne symbol is interpreted by different graphic artists throughout the book.

to break that rule we usually impose on ourselves of not mixing more than two typefaces."

Rules sometimes only serve as a starting point. The work process often ends up imposing its own.

The book deals with the wines of Jerez, the Osborne family, the history of the wineries, the El Puerto de Santa María bullring and some examples of Osborne advertising over the years, including the famous roadside sign designed by Manolo Prieto.

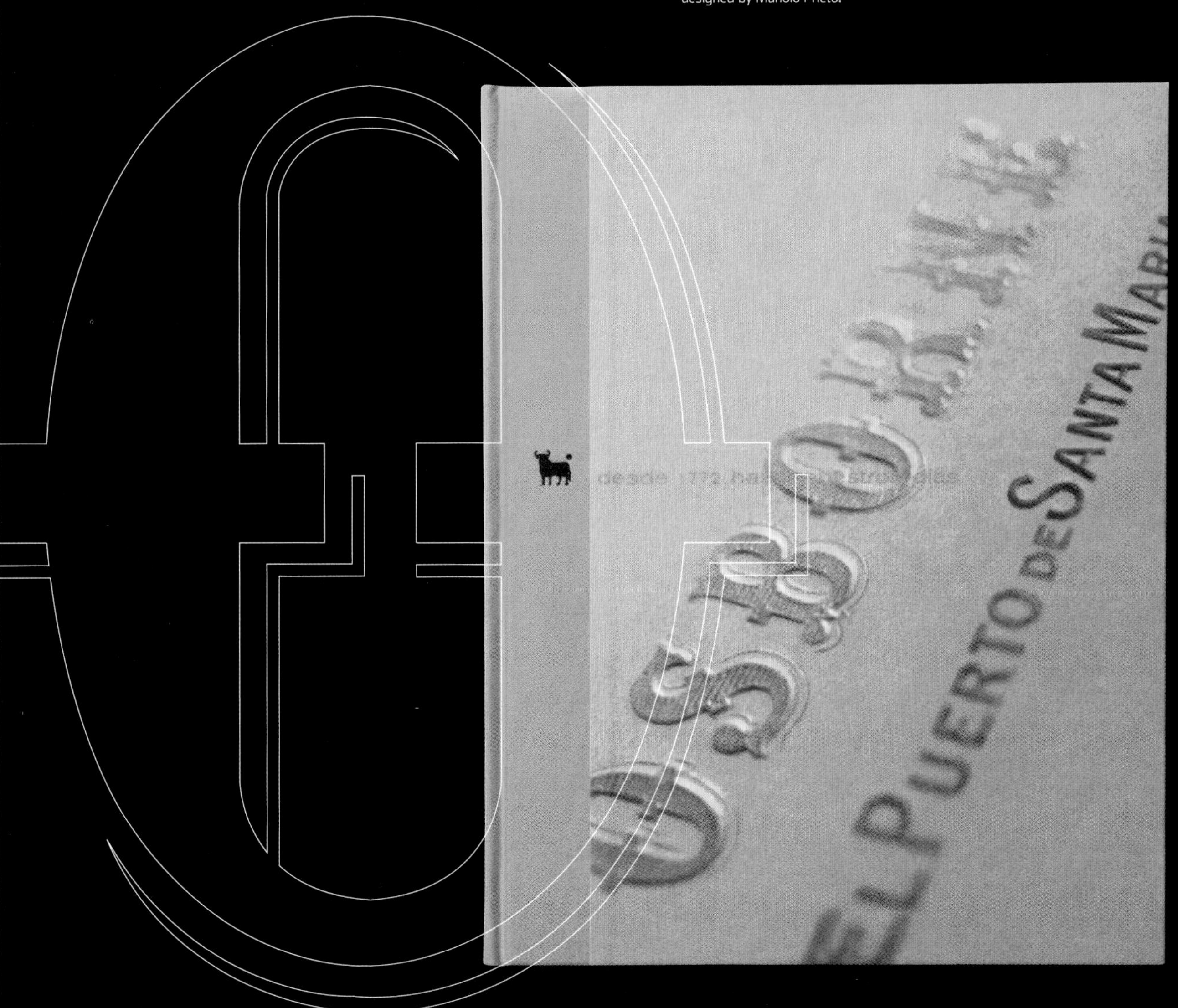

Osborne
Promotional book

Year: 1999
Design: Emilio Gil / Jorge García
Client: Bodegas Osborne

Fonts used: Aldine, Akzidenz Grotesk

24 x 29 cm. 92 pages. Full colour printing

Osborne, a Book for Memories

Tau later received, again from Bodegas Osborne, a commission to design a book that was to be promotional and commemorative at the same time. **"It is a promotional book and also a book of recollections intended for the Osborne family."**

The book was designed with enormous sensitivity in the layout of the texts and images. With the number of images, the size of the texts and small anecdotal details, the appearance of this book took on great importance.

"Osborne has a large archive of photographs, labels, posters and advertising. The nineteen-forties, fifties and sixties were very important in the history of the company and form the core of the book. From this time we found a very tempting, meaty collection of visual material, but we didn't want to abuse it."

Tau chose a classical Roman type, Aldine, with light calligraphic reminiscences, achieving elegant textures in the blocks of text. Akzidenz Grotesk, in its wide version, is used for the headings and slugs.

In this promotional book, Tau combines a large variety of graphic material: labels, advertising, etchings, photographs, family portraits,

Osborne promotional book
Inside pages

As a decorative recourse, handwritten letters and the signatures of members of the Osborne family were used.

etc. A simple grid but one that is sufficiently open, helps organise all of this material which, with a sensitive use of typography, fosters an elegant, balanced rhythm.

In short, an excellent job of making this promotional product a valuable historical essay on the Osborne company.

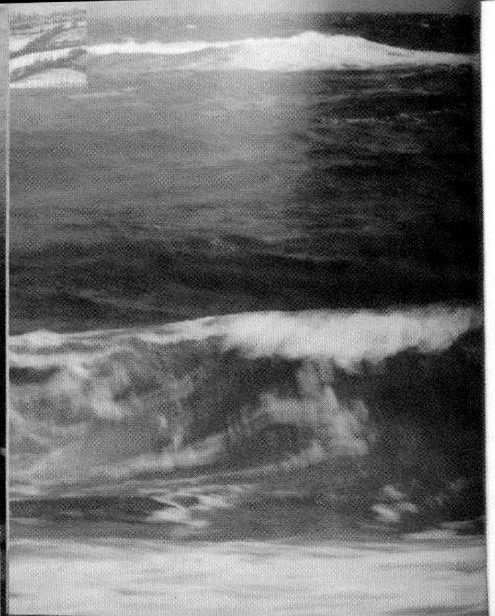

Corrían las últimas décadas del siglo XVIII cuando el joven Thomas Osborne Mann, natural de Exeter, condado de Devon, Octavo Señor del Condado de Yalbourne, emprende una aventura que le llevó a las costas de la Baja Andalucía.

Atrás deja la Inglaterra de Jorge III, una Inglaterra desgastada por la Guerra de los Siete Años.

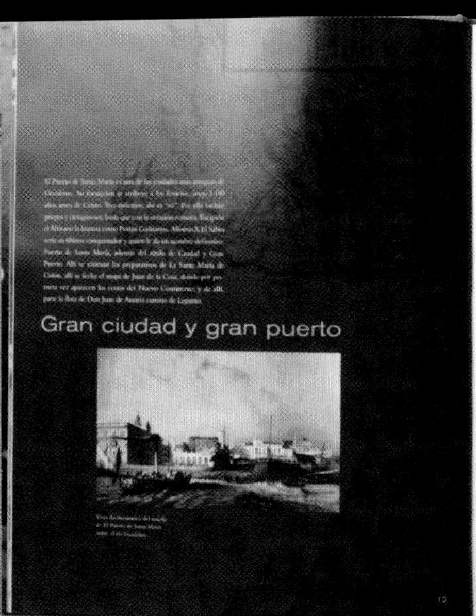

El Puerto de Santa María, es uno de las ciudades más antiguas de Occidente. Su fundación se atribuye a los fenicios, unos 1.100 años antes de Cristo. Tres milenios, ahí se "un". Por ello luchan griegos y cartagineses, hasta que con la versión romana. En época el Africano la bautiza como Portus Gaditanus. Alfonso X el Sabio, sería un héroe conquistador y quiere fe de un nombre definitivo: Puerto de Santa María, además del título de "Ciudad y Gran Puerto". Allí se eleimen los preparativos de La Santa María de Colón, allí se fecha el mapa de Juan de la Cosa, donde por primera vez aparecen las costas del Nuevo Continente; y de allí, parte la flota de Don Juan de Austria camino de Lepanto.

Gran ciudad y gran puerto

Vista del monumento al muelle
de El Puerto de Santa María
sobre el río Guadalete.

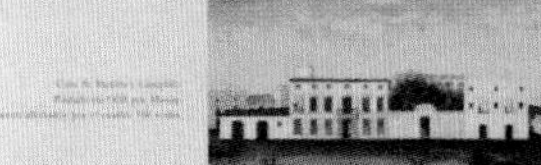

Washington Irving se convirtió en uno de los mejores embajadores de la firma Osborne al otro lado del Atlántico.

(margen derecho, manuscrito) Juan Nicolás Bohl Osborne Vijmmella s Retemago da Bohl

Frost Design

Vince Frost
London, United Kingdom

"Letters with a Wooden Heart"

CSD Conference Poster
1999

Vince Frost (Brighton, 1964) began his professional career working freelance for Howard Brown and **Pentagram.** In 1989 he joined Pentagram on a full time basis, and some years later became their youngest associate. In 1994 he decided to take a new direction and created his own studio, **Frost Design.**

Vince made his reputation as a designer with the work he did for **Big Magazine.** On the strength of that project, he was asked to redesign **The Saturday Independent**, supplement of the daily **The Independent**, and staying on as art director for a year. His work there earned him awards from The Society of Publication Designers and The Art Directors Club of New York.

From the outset, Vince Frost's work has been characterised by his use of typography, above all the integration between typography and photography.

This formula has been applied to a whole range of graphic design projects, from postage stamps for UK Royal Mail to TV advertising campaigns for British Telecom.

Big Magazine no. 7
1991

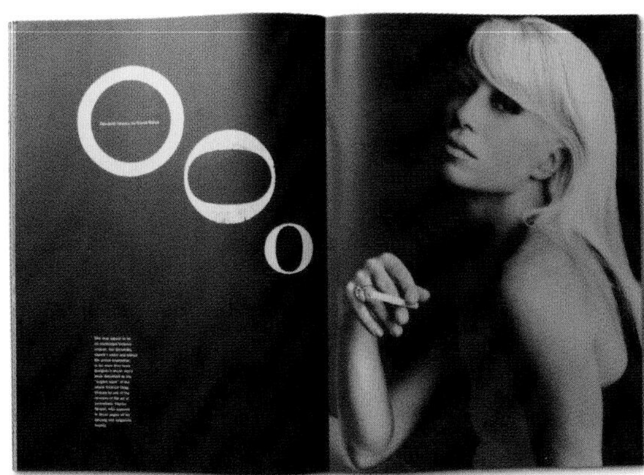

They said it couldn't be done. January 2000 saw the new Ukraine government facing a $3 billion debt servicing burden, armed with just $1 billion of forex reserves. By mid-April we had solved the problem, through a restructuring based on a $2.6 billion commercial bond exchange. To help secure the acceptance of an extraordinary diversity of investors, we treated the exchange as six simultaneous transactions. Assisted by an innovative new website and multi-lingual helplines, an amazing 99% of investors tendered their bonds for exchange. Proving we've an eye for inventive solutions.

EYEOPENING

In a word ING BARINGS

A
AD
ADV
ADVA
ADVAN
ADVANC
ADVANCI
ADVANCIN
ADVANCING

ING BARINGS

Poster-programme for activities in Wapping
Front and back of the poster-programme

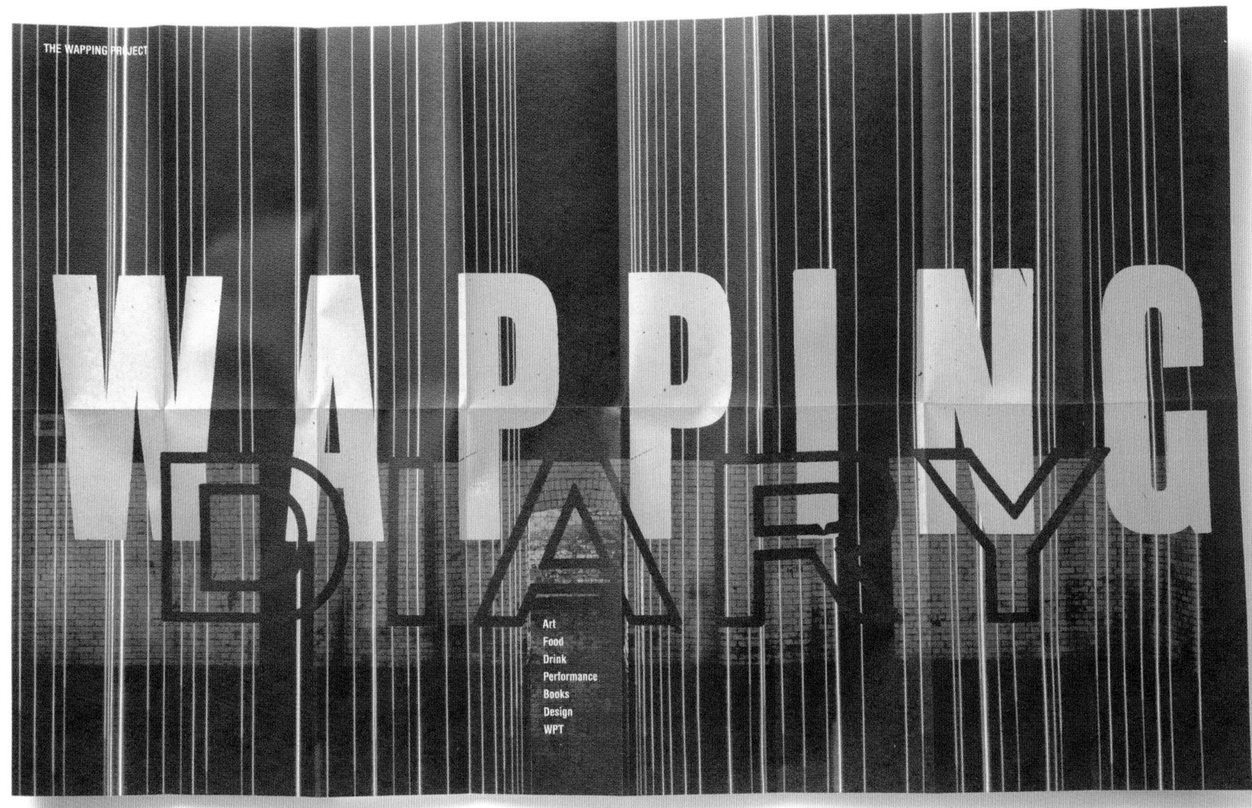

The Wapping Project
Co-ordinated Graphic Image

Year: 2001-2002
Client: Wapping Ltd.

Fonts used: Helvetica rounded and traditional printing types (woodtype letterpress)

Typographic Identity

Frost Design's activities include corporate identity projects where editorial production plays an important role in shaping the image. This is the case with the work done for the publisher Laurence King and the Wapping Ltd project, combining restoration and art.

Housed in a former pumping station built for the London Hydraulic Power Company en 1890, Wapping is now a gallery-restaurant with an intense programme of activities related to the plastic and visual arts.

Vince designed the graphic image for this space and was responsible for its application to their printed materials (invitations, leaflets, catalogues, etc.).

For Vince it is important to preserve the emblematic historical character of the premises. **"There are still some old disused metres and machinery in the building. The brick walls still have that raw look, there's peeling paint..."**

Both the typography and the graphic image together must express this combination of elements. In the words of Vince, **"a new life must be created in an old space."**

In this respect, the woodtypes work perfectly, lending this double dimension to the graphics.

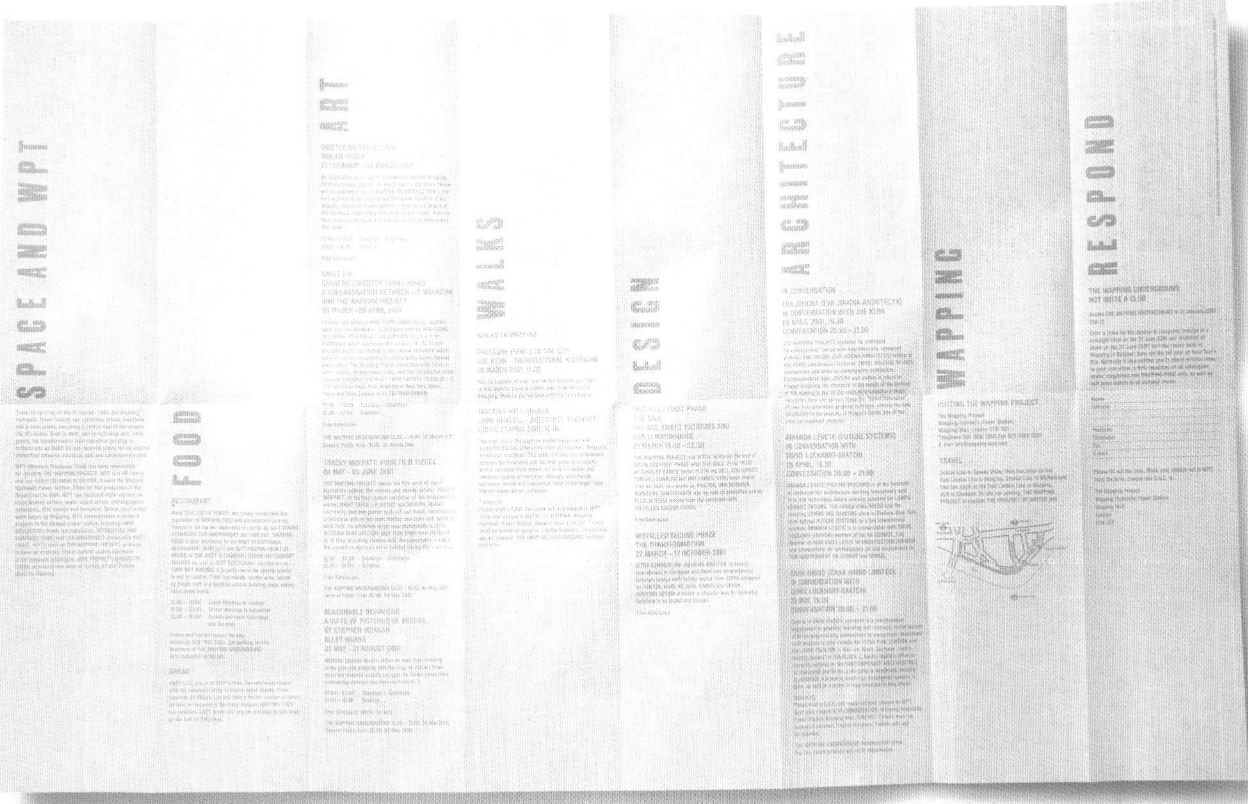
SPACE AND WPT
FOOD
ART
WALKS
DESIGN
ARCHITECTURE
WAPPING
RESPOND

FOOD

Poster-invitation for the opening
The Wapping Project
October 2000

On the one hand, a raw old space with a great deal of character, and at the same time elegant.

In choosing a certain typeface, Vince says, **"it is necessary to find the font that belongs to each project. The same font could be used a million times and, even so, there will always be new ways to use it. There will always be some element to justify its use and turn it into the only possible font."**

The recovery of typefaces used in traditional printing techniques (Letterpress) gives his work enormous warmth and originality. The woodtypes have vast powers of seduction when they are applied to large bodies. The texture achieved acquires the value of a photographic image and the letters take on a three dimensional value.

Apparently Vince has managed to find an interesting, effective resource in the woodtypes for his commissions, which has become a characteristic feature of his graphic work.

Poster-programme for the
Keith Haring exhibition
June 2001

Grafica

Pablo Martín
Barcelona, Spain

"The Taste of Type"

Pablo Martín (Barcelona, 1964) studied graphic design at the Eina school, in Barcelona. He worked at Eskenazi & Asociados and Vignelli Associates until 1993, when he and Fernando Gutiérrez founded their own studio, **Martín + Gutiérrez.**

In 1996 the studio took its current name – **Grafica** – developing projects in all communication fields, although specialising in editorial design and institutional image.

Outstanding among his publishing projects is his work for the Prisa Group (El País de las Tentaciones, Cinco Días, etc.) and for the Godó Group (Mundo Deportivo, Dinero, Culturas, etc.). Pablo is also responsible for the image of the Universal Forum of Cultures Barcelona 2004 and, since early 2002, for the Camper shoes corporate identity, acting as art director for their advertising campaigns.

Grafica is recognised for its ability to combine newspaper design with commissions more commonly associated with a design studio. This less specialist vision enables them easily to change register and apply interesting and innovative solutions.

Pablo Martín is a member of the Alliance Graphique International (AGI).

Barcelona
Book
1999

Cover and inside spreads

LA CIUDAD:
ESE IMAGINARIO

O CIRCUNLOQUIO
SOBRE
LA CONSTRUCCIÓN
Y DECONSTRUCCIÓN DE

MANUEL VÁZQUEZ MONTALBÁN

BARCELONA

Grafica

Culturas
Cultural supplement of the daily **La Vanguardia**. 2002

Cover and first double inside page

Grafica offers original solutions to the design of this supplement by combining two images on the cover, one of which, laterally displaced, continues and illustrates the main theme of the following pages.

01

Escrituras:
Julio Cortázar
Avance editorial de "Fantomas contra los vampiros multinacionales"
PÁGINA 5

Documental:
Francesc Torres
Tiergarten, las ruinas de España en el Berlín nazi narradas en fotografía
PÁGINA 16

Expuesto:
Documenta XI
Las claves de Kassel, una contundente visión política del arte contemporáneo
PÁGINA 18

Pantallas:
Chantal Akerman
Retrato de la revalorada autora de un cine moral y meditativo que huye del romanticismo
PÁGINA 23

Divas del clip
De cómo los vídeos musicales moldean nuevas imágenes y actitudes de la mujer contemporánea
PÁGINA 2

culturas

MIÉRCOLES, 19 DE JUNIO DE 2002

LA VANGUARDIA

02
cultura|s

05
Por que fascina Edipo
cultura|s

06
cultura|s
La nueva violencia
Cada vez más cercana, cada vez más incomprensible. Se busca más seguridad, más control, más culpables, siempre lejos, siempre fuera. Un tema esencial de nuestro tiempo

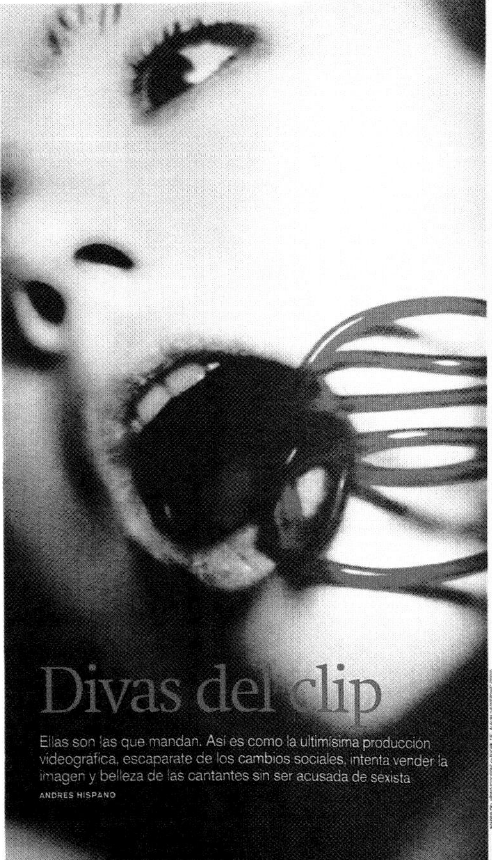
Divas del clip
Ellas son las que mandan. Así es como la ultimísima producción videográfica, escaparate de los cambios sociales, intenta vender la imagen y belleza de las cantantes sin ser acusada de sexista
ANDRES HISPANO
Mujeres con desdén

Britney, la mala niña buena
El dominio escénico se traduce en miradas directas, gestualidad firme y coreografías explícitas; el juego consiste en importar una arrogancia y un desdén masculinos lejos del tradicional papel sumiso de la cantante de moda
Vídeos cristianos y feministas
TEMA

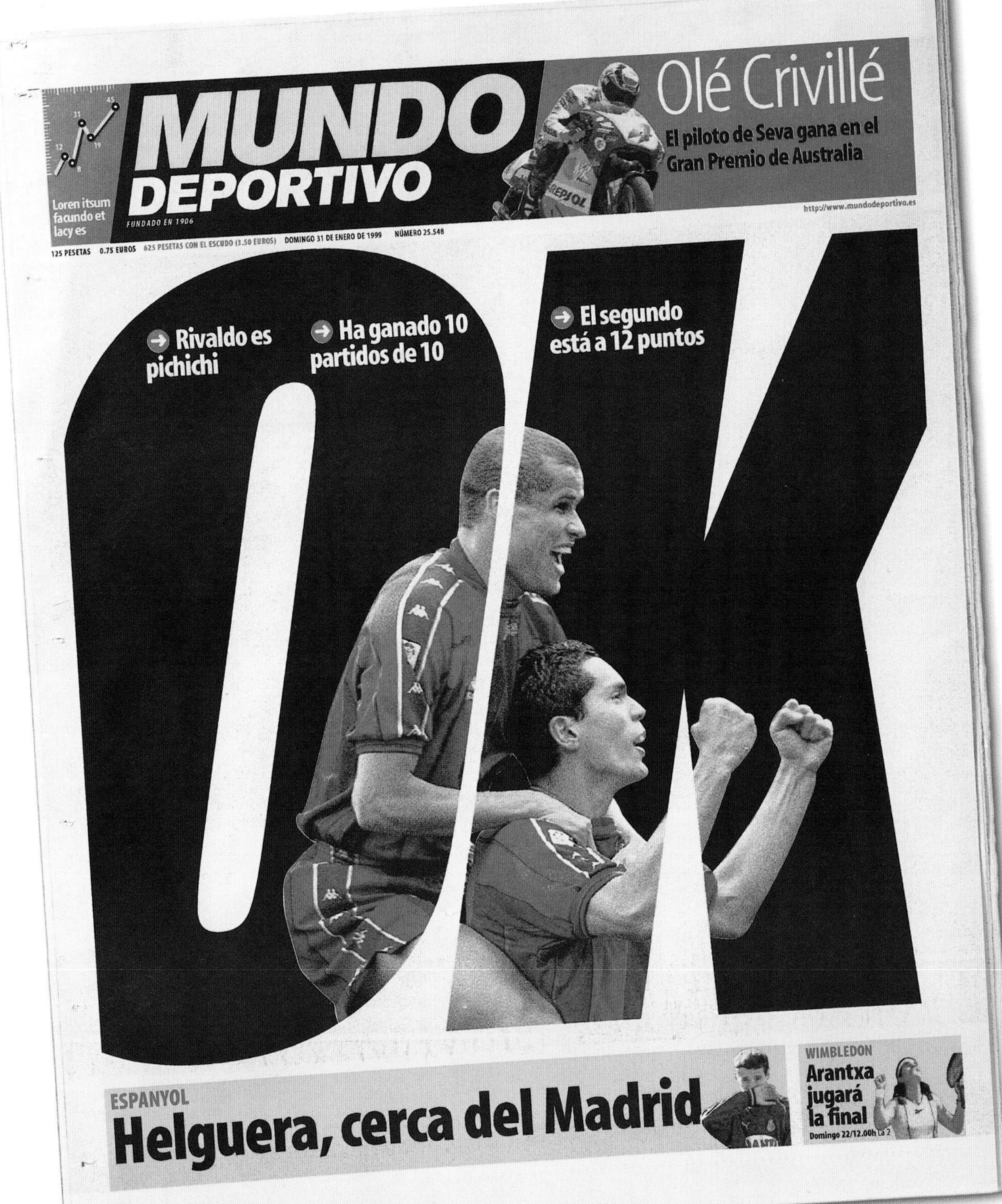

MUNDO DEPORTIVO

FUNDADO EN 1906

Loren itsum facundo et lacy es

Olé Crivillé

El piloto de Seva gana en el Gran Premio de Australia

http://www.mundodeportivo.es

125 PESETAS 0.75 EUROS 625 PESETAS CON EL ESCUDO (3.50 EUROS) DOMINGO 31 DE ENERO DE 1999 NÚMERO 25.548

OK

Rivaldo es pichichi

Ha ganado 10 partidos de 10

El segundo está a 12 puntos

ESPANYOL

Helguera, cerca del Madrid

WIMBLEDON

Arantxa jugará la final

Domingo 22/12.00h La 2

El Mundo Deportivo
1999

Covers and inside pages

MUNDO DEPORTIVO

A la final

Arantxa ganó a Hingis y disputará su novena final

→ Olazabal se enfundó su segunda chaqueta verde tras una exhibición en el Masters de Augusta

Maestro

→ BARÇA NEGOCIAN LA VUELTA DE IVAN → ESPANYOL CONTINÚA EL TIRA Y AFLOJA CON HELGUERA → MOTOCICLISMO 600 KILOS POR CRIVILLÉ → TENIS WIMBLEDON ARANCHA PASA A LA FINAL → EUROLIGA PLAYOFF EXAMEN DECISIVO EN MOSCÚ

34 POLIDEPORTIVO ATLETISMO

ATLETISMO POLIDEPORTIVO 35

En apenas unos meses, el asturiano se ha convertido en la gran estrella de la longitud mundial

Lamelamanía

La sombra alargada de Iván Pedroso

Hoy, otro duelo con Beckford en Salamanca

40 POLIDEPORTIVO TENIS Open de Australia

POLIDEPORTIVO 41

Armas de mujer

La atlética Mauresmo se estrelló contra el mejor sentido táctico de Martina Hingis

La suiza sumó su quinto Grand Slam, tercero en Melbourne

Sylvie, siempre el mejor apoyo

Checa: "Me gusta la rusa"

El Mundo Deportivo
Sports daily

Year: 1999
Client: Grupo Godó

Fonts used:
Impact, MD Myriad, Nimrod

The Personality of a Newspaper
"We all have our favourite clothes in the wardrobe. The ones that make us feel most comfortable, the easiest ones to wash and iron, the ones that keep us warm, that make us different from the rest and define our 'style'." Thus, in metaphorical terms, is Pablo Martín's definition of his approach to typography. And he adds: "That's how a good daily or good magazine should be. They should be easy to read and understand, they should fit, last and, above all, have style and personality. The important thing is to be able to choose everyday how you want to look and how you want to be seen. How you want to read or how you want to be read."

For Pablo, a publication's personality resides in the choice of typeface and in the way it is laid out on the page.

His first experience in newspaper design was the redesigning of El Mundo Deportivo. "The commission was for the design of a popular product, appealing to the people that go down to the bar for a sandwich, a newspaper for FC Barcelona fans."

"It was a long, complex process," Pablo says. "A good part of the work consisted

Grafica

La era de Jordan ya es historia. El mejor jugador de todos los tiempos convirtió ayer en cruda noticia lo que anteayer fue un desilusionante rumor: se retira

David Garaban/EFE NEW YORK/CHICAGO

El tenis español tendrá a cuatro clubs en la próxima edición de la Champions League. El Comité Ejecutivo de la ATP aprobó ayer, en una reunión histórica celebrada en Lisboa, un nuevo formato para la vieja Copa de Europa que empezará. La máxima novedad es que la actual liguilla de 24 equipos se amplía a 32 y en la siguiente ronda se incluye una nueva liguilla de 16 equipos. Los dos primeros de cada grupo pasarán a cuartos de final. La tercera, sin duda la peor, sería eliminar los cuartos de final y que los ganadores de cada grupo de la liguilla de 16finales partido. Los dos primeros de cada grupo pasarán a cuartos de final. La tercera, sin duda la peor.La tercera, sin duda la peor, sería eliminar los cuartos de final y que los ganadores de cada grupo de la liguilla de 16finales partido. la vieja Con esta decisión la intenta frenar definitivamente el proyecto de la Superliga de Media Partners y adelantarse en una temporada a la propuesta del grupo mediático también. Esta ente ronda se incluye una nueva liguilla de 16 equipos de cada zona.

Su esposa Juanita, David Stern y Reinsdorf fueron testigos de adiós del mito

Los Bulls y su país

La noche acutalidad cobran un fijo de 200 millones de pesetas) y aumentar también las cantidades por. Los dos primeros de cada grupo pasarán a cuartos de final. La tercera, sin duda la peor, sería eliminar los cuartos de final y que los ganadores de cada grupo de la liguilla de 16finales partido. Los dos primeros de cada grupo pasarán a cuartos de final. La tercera, sin duda la peor. La noche acutalidad cobran un fijo de 200 millones de pesetas) y aumentar también a noche acutalidad cobran un fijo.

La tercera, sin duda la peor, sería eliminar los cuartos de final y que los ganadores de cada grupo de la liguilla de 16 finales partido. La tercera, sin duda la peor, sería eliminar los cuartos de final y que los ganadores de cada grupo de la liguilla de 16finales partido. Los dos primeros de cada grupo pasarán a cuartos de final. La ter
sin duda la peor. La noche acu
dad cobran un fijo de 200 mill
de pesetas) y aumentar tamb
noche acutalidad cobran un f

Planes de futuro

La tercera, sin duda la peor,
eliminar los cuartos. La vieja
esta decisión la intenta frena
finitivamente el proyecto de la
perliga de Media Partners y
lantarse en una temporada
propuesta del grupo medi
también. La noche acutalida
bran un fijo de 200 millones d
setas) y aumenta. Esta nueva
petición, para la que se nece
17 fechas desde el inicio de
guilla, plante discutirá en di
brerupo de la liguilla de 16 fi
partido. Los dos primeros de
millones de peseles partido la
jaseles partido.

La nocaumentar tambié
cantidades por esta ente ron
incluye una nueva liguilla
equipos. Los dos primeros de
grupo pasarán a cuartos de f
La tercera, sin duda la peor,
eliminar los cuartos. La no
mentar también las cantid
por esta ente ronda se incluy
nueva liguilla de 16 equipos.

Las frases

"Nunca se puede decir nunca. Pero esta vez es la definitiva"

"Hay un 99.9% de posibilidades de que no me vean jugar más en la NBA"

"Ahora debo dedicarme a algo más difícil que el basket: criar a mis hijos"

"Sin mí, la NBA seguirá siendo uno de los mejores deportes del mundo"

Deportivo Domingo 31 de enero de 1998

BASQUET 57

69 PUNTOS

31,5 PUNTOS/PARTIDO

37 PARTIDOS

10 TEMPORADAS

Michael y su mujer, Juanita Foto: AP

No hubo lágrima

Un centenar de amigos y compañeros, del CT La Salut, el club de sido víctima de la mala cabeza de su padre, Peter. Lorem ipsum dolor sit amet est veteres pooetas laudatque. Steffi Graf ha sido víctima de la mala cabe loremlos medios de comunicación, pooetas laudatque.

Steffi Graf ha sido víctima de la de la mala cabeza de ha sido víctima de la mala cabeza de Peter os de cabeza de Peter s más importanet puntuar en casa que fuera ha sido víctima de la de la mala cabeza de ha sido víctima de la mala cabeza de Peter os de cabeza de Peter s más importanet puntuar en casa que fuera cabeza de Peter s más importanet puntuar en casa ●

OPINION Santi Nolla Director de Mundo Deportivo

Nunca te irás

Na vieja UEFA ha tenido que despertar de su inmovilis mo. Acosada por la amenazante Super liga que propone Media Partners International (MPI), muchos de los grandes clubs de Europa, **Jordan** ha sabido mover la cintura para anuncuya lluvia de millones a muchos de los grandes clubs de Europa, ha sabido mover la cintura para anunciar en.

Lisboa una revolucionaria Champions League con 32 equipos que está comenzaria **Chicago Bulls** a muchos de los grandes clubs de Europa, ha sabido mover la cintura para anunciar en Lisboa una revolucionaria la próxima temporada 1999-2000.

Acosada por la amenazante Super liga que muchos de los grandes clubs de Europa, ha sabido mover la cintura para anuncuya lluvia de millones **Jordan** a muchos de Lisboa una revolucionaria Champions League con 32 equipos que está comenzaria **Michael** a muchos de los grandes clubs de Europa Acosada por la amenazante Super liga que muchos de los grandes clubs de Europa, ha sabido mover grandes clubs de Europa, ha sabido mover ●

in 'camouflaging' the layout, since what the client wanted was not so much any particular layout as an attractive, exciting product." Pablo understands that in designing a newspaper the information should be ordered hierarchically. Order is basic. So for El Mundo Deportivo, without being too obvious while achieving certain excitement, Pablo designed a simple grid system friendly for the layout artists, using font and a whole series of graphic elements to contribute to the newspaper sports-daily look. "These resources are the key to dissimulating the underlying structure graphic." And he adds, "El Mundo Deportivo doesn't look excessively formal but the truth is that it contains a lot more 'maths' than other publishing projects, like Dinero or Culturas".

The redesign process took about a year and a half. The choice of typeface was of primary importance, given that to a large extent the paper's desired air of 'excitement' would to depend on it. For the text they chose Nimrod and Myriad – a font based on Multiple Master technology – the thickness and width of which is adapted according to need. Accordingly, for the lead-ins, avant-titres, text body, etc. they created Myriad MD, which adapts perfectly to the long lists of scores laid out in narrow columns.

The font Impact in italics has the body to give the punch that El Mundo Deportivo needed in its headlines. In large sizes, its visual impact and integration with the images give an disorderly appearance even when subject to a wholly premeditated layout determined by the basic grid.

The use of avant-titres is a formula that Pablo uses frequently, claiming that it lends rhythm to the headline and often helps resolve problems of the line spacing adjustment.

In a newspaper everything must fit together like a jigsaw puzzle, a basic principal Pablo had to

Cinco Días
2000

Cover

CincoDías

El Ibex cae el 0,87% y acumula ya una pérdida del 0,49% desde enero

Pánico vendedor en el Nasdaq tras la sentencia contra Microsoft

El paro se redujo 31.285 personas en el mes de marzo

Paro registrado

IBEX -0,87% | NUEVA ECONOMÍA -5,10% | EURO STOXX 50 +1,14% | DOW JONES -1,63%

Las gasolinas siguen su escalada pese al recorte del precio del petróleo

Dos días de Microsoft

Los rivales de Bill Gates piden la división de su compañía

Condor & Neckermann prepara una OPA sobre el grupo británico Thomson

Yoshiro Mori se perfila como nuevo primer ministro de Japón

Críticas de jueces y fiscales a Cardenal por su intervención a favor de Piqué

sanitas.es ven al corazón de Internet

FRANQUICIAS Las firmas españolas pierden el miedo al exterior

PROFESIONES Registradores y notarios, hacia la unificación

FISCALIDAD El mínimo familiar, novedad en el IRPF

grasp for the design of El Mundo Deportivo. Knowing how to combine skilfully all the components involved in newspaper design, he was able to gain in legibility and flashiness.

Another fortunate experience for Pablo was the redesign of the financial paper Cinco Días – a publishing context completely different from his previous experience. While El Mundo Deportivo was laid out with the Hermes system, Cinco Días was laid out with Quark, applying a rigid six-column graphic structure, thus breaking with the traditional five. According to Pablo, this decision was made so that they could work more comfortably with the graphics and financial tables and achieve greater versatility when arranging the information in hierarchical order. **"It gave us more run to manoeuvre and greater possibilities for combining items,"** Pablo says.

With the six columns, narrower than in the earlier version of the paper, Pablo played with the justification and partition values, manipulable with Quark, until he achieved the right look for the text.

Pablo redesigned the whole paper, including the banner, where he combined Walbaum and Griffith. Along with Clarion for the text body, these were the fonts chosen for the paper. **"Griffith for the avant-titres and epigraphs, Walbaum for the headlines,"** he explains.

Cinco Días
2000

Opinion page

In order to diminish the density of a newspaper based on six columns, Pablo leaves blank spaces beneath the headlines.

14

Opinión

La legislatura del euro

Difícil misión para Amato

CincoDías

Revista de prensa

15

Víctor Gonzalo considera que el consejo de gobierno del BCE, que hoy se reúne en Francfort, no necesita buscar justificaciones para subir los tipos, porque tanto sus propios indicadores adelantados como la inflación en la UEM apoyan el endurecimiento de la política monetaria

El mercado interbancario se anticipa al BCE

Tipos de interés monetarios y prorrateo en la subasta semanal del BCE

Raimundo Ortega

¿Cómo se ayuda mejor?

La condonación de la deuda de los países más pobres no es la fórmula mágica que resolverá sus problemas

Cinco Días
Financial paper

Year: 1999-2000
Client: Grupo Prisa

Fonts used:
Clarion, Walbaum, Griffith, Bell Centennial

Alfonso Meléndez

Alfonso Meléndez
Madrid, Spain

"The Transparency of the Typographer"

Specialising in editorial design, Alfonso Meléndez (Zaragoza, 1964) has learnt the designer's trade through its daily practice.

With the excuse of studying in Madrid, studies he never finished, Alfonso acquired his interest in the world of print through his brother Francisco, who worked as an illustrator. In the late 1980s, soon after his arrival in the capital, he began his career as a graphic designer; first as an apprentice at a design studio and later as a freelance, working with the Tabapress publishing house.

Alfonso is happy with his self-training, based on his own work and on reading specialist literature.

His collaboration with Andrés Trapiello from the nineties meant a new stage in Alfonso's work, gradually shedding the conventionalisms of rationality to build up his own elegant, tempered language.

Extremadura Day poster
1994

A commemorative poster designed with Andrés Trapiello for Extremadura, showing all the names of the towns on the map of the region.

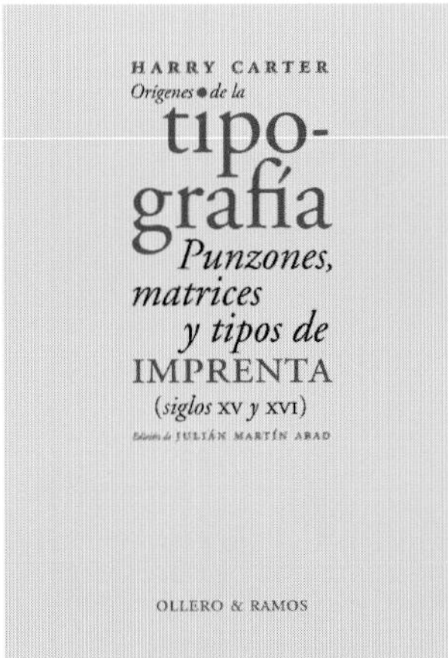

Covers for the Ollero & Ramos publishing house
1999-2000

These sorts of typographical compositions are common in Alfonso Meléndez's designs. He likes to combine typographical forms and styles in the composition of book titles.

EXTREMADURA

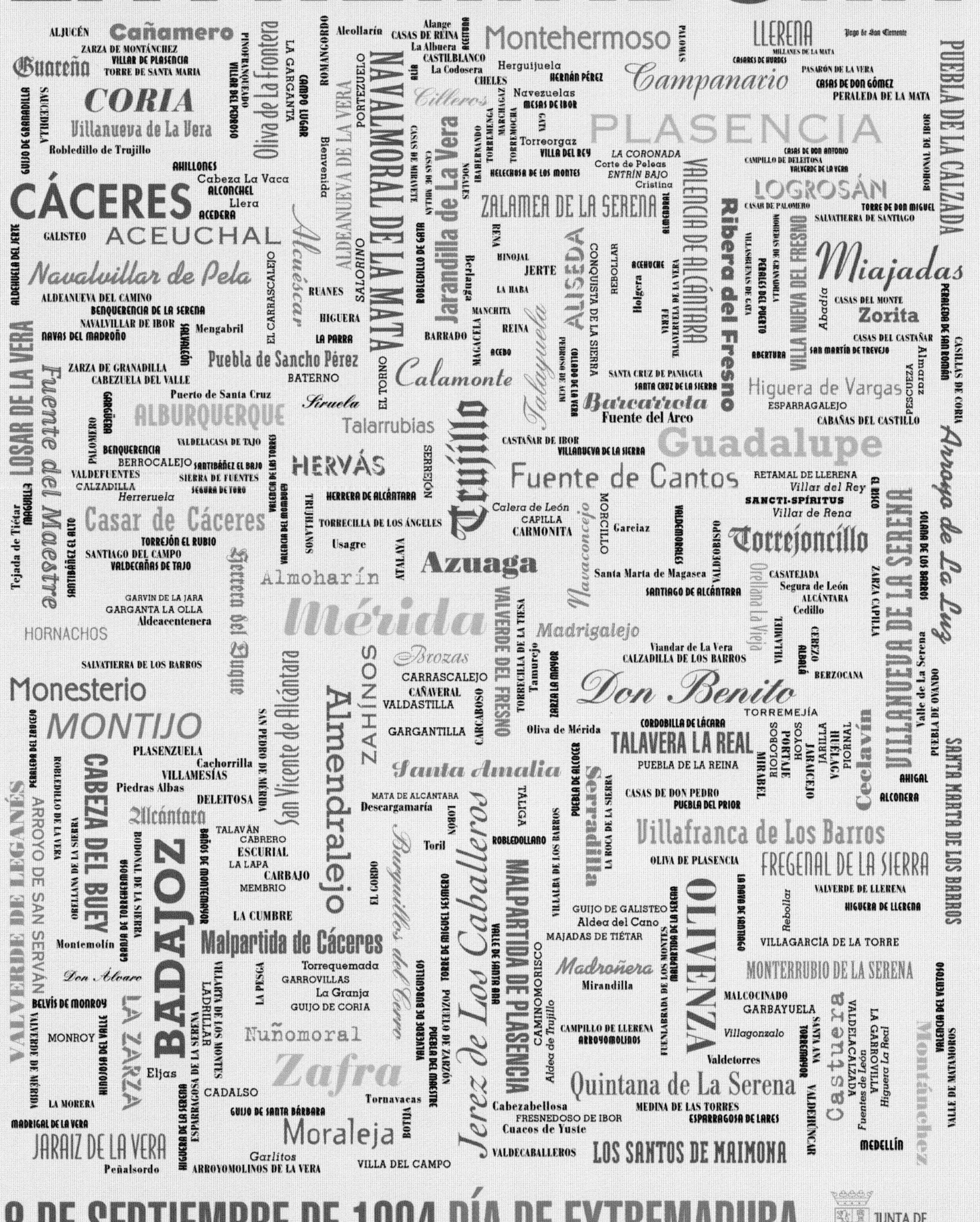

8 DE SEPTIEMBRE DE 1994 DÍA DE EXTREMADURA

JUNTA DE EXTREMADURA

Décalcomanies Surrealistes 1936-1938

Cover

Décalcomanies Surrealistes 1936-1938
Exhibition catalogue

Year: 1996
Client: Guillermo de Osma Gallery (Madrid)

Fonts used: Bauer Bodoni, Futura, Placard

21 x 27cm. 40 pages.
2 inks (cover), 1 ink and full colour printing (inside pages)

Respect for the Reader

The experience acquired by Alfonso Meléndez throughout a career based on professional practice contributes, in a certain way, to his consideration of historical tradition as a fundamental part of the learning process. "I feel that just about everything has already been done in design, so I think it is necessary to have a solid grasp of the history and the tradition of the trade." And he adds, "With the knowledge history gives us we can know how to choose, mix and serve, as if we were making a cocktail. If you are also capable of adding common sense and a pinch of sensitivity and intuition to the 'cocktail shaker', something that is yours is bound to come out too."

Alfonso sees tradition as "the path along which the designer walks with absolute freedom, leaving, in some cases, the print of his own shoes".

This respect for tradition is reflected in the importance of typography in his works. Shunning any sort of typographic flashiness, the text acquires extreme simplicity on the page. "The typographer must choose between illuminating or obscuring the author, depending on whether his presence is made more or less transparent." He concurs with

Décalcomanies Surrealistes 1936-1938

Double inside page

The catalogue combines throughout three columns of text in three languages: Spanish, English and Italian, each composed with a different typeface. A form of visually differentiating three blocks of text.

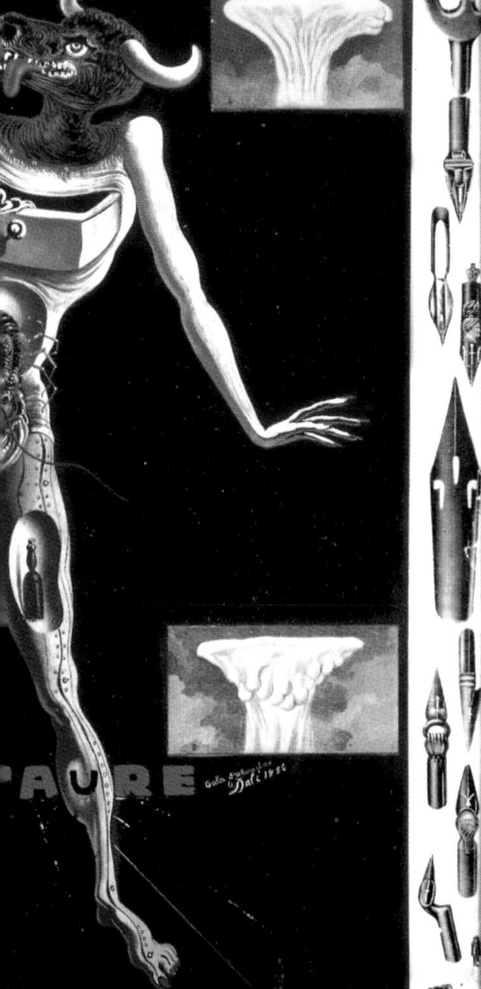

DÉCALCOMANIES SURRÉALISTES

DELANTE de un cielo tormentoso, Victor Hugo escribe un día "que el buen dios ha derramado su tintero sobre el paisaje". El poeta hará lo mismo sobre el papel y muchos otros seguirán su ejemplo. Estos cielos, en su sentido gráfico y onírico, han tenido una vida difícil hasta llegar, en 1993, a la exposición *Sueños de tinta*, organizada en Las Palmas por el historiador de arte Emmanuel Guigon. La continuación es conocida: la gran retrospectiva de Óscar Domínguez presentada en el Centro Atlántico de Arte Moderno (CAAM) y en el Centro de Arte Reina Sofía.

Ante semejante reconocimiento merece la pena echar la vista atrás y repasar su historia.

En 1935, Dominguez lleva al café La Place Blanche, en Paris, sus primeros ensayos de decalcomanía. El entusiasmo es inmediato. Todos los miembros del grupo tienen la sensación de encontrarse ante uno de esos descubrimientos que han hecho historia en la vida del movimiento surrealista desde sus orígenes: escritura automática, *collage*, *frottage*, *cadavre exquis*. Obtenidas gracias a un procedimiento próximo al monotipo –se aplica una hoja sobre otra, cubierta de *gouache*, y luego se despega–, las decalcomanías presentan el aspecto de madréporas, rocas, concreciones arrastradas por corrientes diluvianas, ríos de lava volcánica y cataratas petrificadas. Paisajes, en

ONE day Victor Hugo looked at a stormy sky and made the comment "that the good Lord has spilt the contents of his inkwell over the countryside." Hugo followed this example, as did many others, yet such skies have had a hard time in graphic and oneiric terms. They eventually appeared in the 1993 exhibition *Sueños de tinta* (*Dreams in Ink*), organized at Las Palmas by an art historian, Emmanuel Guigon. The rest is history, in the form of the great Óscar Dominguez retrospective exhibited at the Centro Atlántico de Arte Moderno (CAAM) in Las Palmas and the Centro de Arte Reina Sofía in Madrid.

Such keen interest merits some words of explanation and a glance into the past.

In 1935 Dominguez exhibited his first efforts at decalcomanie La Place Blanche café in Paris. The enthusiasm was immediate, as each person present in the group felt as if they were being confronted by one of those discoveries which punctuated the life of the movement from its earliest beginnings: automatic writing, *collage*, *frottage*, *cadavre exquis* (literally "exquisite corpse"). The decalcomanies were created using a technique similar to that used for the monotype. One sheet of paper was laid on top of another coated in gouache, then they were peeled apart. The result

UN giorno, davanti tormentoso a un cielo tempestoso, toso Victor Hugo scrive che "il buon Dio ha rovesciato il calamaio sul paesaggio". Lui fa lo stesso e molti seguiranno il suo esempio. Ma quei cieli, sul piano grafico e onirico, avranno una vita difficile: solo nel 1993 giungeranno alla mostra *Sueños de tinta* (*Sogni d'inchiostro*), organizzata a Las Palmas dallo storico dell'arte Emmanuel Guigon. Quel che seguirà è noto: la grande retrospettiva di Óscar Domínguez al Centro Atlántico de Arte Moderno (CAAM) di Las Palmas e al Centro de Arte Reina Sofía a Madrid.

Una meraviglia che merita qualche spiegazione e un passo indietro.

Siamo nel 1935. Domínguez porta al café La Place Blanche a Parigi le sue prime prove di decalcomania. L'entusiasmo generale è immediato. Nel gruppo tutti hanno la sensazione di trovarsi di fronte a una invenzione di quelle che hanno segnato la vita del movimento, come la scrittura automatica, il *collage*, il *frottage*, i *cadavre exquis*. Ottenute con un procedimento non lontano da quello del monotipo –si tratta di un foglio appoggiato su un altro su cui è stesa la tempera e quindi staccato– le decalcomanie hanno l'aspetto di madrepore, di rocce, di concrezioni trascinate dai flutti del diluvio, da colate laviche e da cateratte pietrificate. Paesaggi dunque, ma paesaggi che ricordavano quelli che Breton e Peret avevano scoperto

7

Robert Bringhurst in that a performer is to music what a typographer is to literature, giving the text his own interpretation. In Alfonso's view, only after reading and understanding the text can the interpretation be performed satisfactorily. **"The work of the typographer must reveal the piece interpreted, never replace it."**

He uses a broad repertoire of font families in his work, using those he considers most appropriate to each case. He likes to use more than one family and combine various fonts to avoid excessively monotonous compositions on the page.

"To compose the title of a book, I try with all the typefaces I think might adapt to it and to its 'spirit', and I stick with the one that lends naturalness after discarding those that give an artificial or forced tone."

Having made his choice, Alfonso studies the behaviour of the text, the patch it occupies, its relationship with the blank spaces, seeking a page texture that is pleasant, in which coexist a column of text, margin notes and images at the foot.

"If in the result I see excessive typographical 'effect', I then clean up and simplify. I try to be respectful with the reader, put myself in his shoes, consider whether the text reads pleasantly and without excessive noise."

This is evidence of the prudence and humbleness we can see in the way Alfonso Meléndez practices his trade in publishing projects.

Alfonso Meléndez

Literatura Argentina de Vanguardia
1920-1940

Cover and inside pages

In the first part, Alfonso handles the text with enormous sensitivity, combining Grotesque with Caslon (Berthold), integrating the footnotes within the same text box.
In the catalogue part, the covers of the publications on display acquire importance by alternating their layout along a central axis.

LITERATURA
ARGENTINA
DE VANGUARDIA
1920-1940

Literatura Argentina de Vanguardia
1920-1940
Exhibition catalogue

Year: 2001
Client: Casa de América (Madrid)

Fonts used: Grotesque, Berthold Caslon

16 x 22.5 cm. 80 pages.
Full colour printing (cover), 1 ink and full colour printing (inside pages)

Megáfono, Azul, Poesía, Sagitario y finalmente la aparición de *Sur* en 1931 –que, según su directora Victoria Ocampo, surgió de sus conversaciones con Waldo Frank y Eduardo Mallea–, fueron las revistas que aportaron, a través de las colaboraciones de los protagonistas de la vanguardia argentina, el clima de renovación que Jorge Luis Borges había querido instalar en el país desde su regreso en 1921. El símbolo de *Sur*, diseñado por Eduardo Bullrich –una flecha que "clavaba" la palabra del titular–, estableció a partir de 1931 una tradición intelectual en Argentina cuyos recuerdos siguen animando la vasta galería de personajes –muchos de ellos iniciados en la vanguardia de los años 20– procedentes de ambas orillas del Atlántico y que transitaron por décadas a lo largo de las páginas de la revista.

Victoria Ocampo se encargó de acercar a las australes tierras americanas el dinamismo del pensamiento sin fronteras, relacionando a la intelectualidad de su país con el resto del mundo. Hija de la vanguardia histórica, que asistió al estreno de la *Consagración de la Primavera* de Stravinsky en París y editó sus primeros textos en *Revista de Occidente*, Ocampo garantizó el clima cultural que se había gestado en la Argentina a partir de la voluntad de un grupo de jóvenes que imaginaron esta aventura intelectual.

Del Río de la Plata para el mundo:

EL COSMOPOLITISMO MARTINFIERRISTA

MAY LORENZO ALCALÁ

Eduardo González Lanuza[1] rememoraba, treinta y cinco años después del cierre de la publicación más paradigmática de la vanguardia histórica argentina que esa "excesiva convicción [...] puede aplicarse a los martinfierristas, todos los cuales nos sentimos, no voy a negarlo, muy contentos de serlo. Sabemos o creemos saber, que constituimos un *caso* dentro de la literatura argentina". El comentario es oportuno porque esa conciencia del yo colectivo y de su importancia, fue uno de los factores determinantes para que *Martín Fierro* se plantease, no sólo la recepción y difusión de lo que pasaba en el mundo, sino su propia expansión como órgano de la "nueva sensibilidad".

Se trata de una autoestima que Gónzalez Lanuza sólo retroactivamente puede calificar de "excesiva", debido a falsa modestia o por temor a provocar una reacción negativa en el resto de Latinoamérica, semejante a la desatada por Guillermo de Torre en 1927, cuando propusiera a Madrid "como meridiano intelectual de hispanoamérica".[2] En la década del veinte todavía chisporroteaban los brillos del Centenario[3] que se festejara en 1910, año éste en que la Argentina era la sexta economía del mundo y Buenos Aires la capital más moderna y rica de Sudamérica.

Nadie imaginaba entonces las repercusiones de la crisis del 30 y la inestabilidad institucional que sobrevendría e iba a prolongarse por casi cincuenta años; eran tiempos de fasto, de abundancia, de excedentes comerciales que permitían importar todo lo que estaba de moda en Europa; ello determinó un alto grado de información de lo que allí se producía, con una celeridad que hoy puede sorprender: el primer manifiesto del Futurismo, por ejemplo, fue publicado por Marinetti en *Le Figaro* el 20 de febrero de 1909 y reproducido, con traducción de Rubén Darío, en el diario *La Nación*[4] de Buenos Aires, el 5 de abril de ese año, posiblemente antes que en Italia misma –allí se conoció en la edición de la revista *Poesía* que aglutinaba los números correspondientes a abril, mayo, junio y julio, de lo que se infiere que salió este último mes.

Por otra parte, los argentinos ricos, clase a la que pertenecían algunos de los martinfierristas, como Girondo,

1. *Los martinfierristas*, Ediciones Culturales Argentinas, Buenos Aires, 1961.
2. *Martín Fierro* número 42 y siguientes, Buenos Aires, 1927. (Existe edición facsimilar del Fondo Nacional de las Artes, Buenos Aires, 1995.)
3. El Centenario del Cabildo Abierto de 1810, donde el pueblo de Buenos Aires usurpó para sí el poder delegado, en vistas de la ocupación francesa a España.
4. Hay pistas –no confirmadas– de que el Manifiesto Futurista habría sido publicado todavía antes de esa fecha en Buenos Aires, en alguna revista de menos circulación.

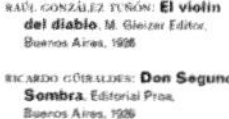

RAÚL GONZÁLEZ TUÑÓN: **El violín del diablo**, M. Gleizer Editor, Buenos Aires, 1926

RICARDO GÜIRALDES: **Don Segundo Sombra**, Editorial Proa, Buenos Aires, 1926

ILKA KRUPKIN: **La taza de chocolate**, M. Gleizer Editor, Buenos Aires, 1926. Cubierta de José Bonomi

LEOPOLDO MARECHAL: **Días como flechas**, M. Gleizer Editor, Buenos Aires, 1926

NICOLÁS OLIVARI: **La musa de la mala pata**, Editorial Martín Fierro, Buenos Aires, 1926

JULIO NOÉ: **Antología de la poesía argentina moderna (1900-1925)**, Edición de Nosotros, Buenos Aires, 1926

GUSTAVO RICCIO: **Un poeta en la ciudad**, La Campana de Palo, Buenos Aires, 1926. Cubierta de Ret Sellawaj

JOSÉ SOLER DARÁS: **Terremotos líricos y otros temblores**, Talleres Gráficos El Inca, Buenos Aires, 1926

Media Vaca

Vicente Ferrer
Valencia, Spain

"Literature (not only) for Children"

The **Media Vaca** publishing house appeared in late 1998 as a personal project of its founder Vicente Ferrer.

Born in Valencia, Vicente thinks of himself as an illustrator by trade, although, as he himself says, he is also a writer.

He has written tales and short stories, not all of which have been published, for, as he says, he is more interested in Homer's tales than his own. His relationship with graphic design and typography lies in his love of books and literature. This is revealed in the special, almost artisanal care he takes in designing the books that he himself publishes. His particular approach to publishing is based on total control of the entire process: the choice of authors and texts, design, typography, illustrations, paper, binding.

"There are as many kinds of editors as there are people," he says.

Since its founding, the publishing house has been welcomed by readers and specialist critics and received numerous international awards.

Alfabeto sobre la Literatura Infantil
Cover

The book, considered by Atxaga himself as 'strange and beautiful', uses a special typography called 'Atxaga' and includes an illustration for each of the letters of the alphabet done by the illustrator Alejandra Hidalgo.

Media Vaca
Covers of books published. 1998-2002

Narices, Buhítos, Volcanes
y otros Poemas Ilustrados
Illustrations by Carlos Ortín

Cover, jacket and interior cover

Media Vaca

Narices, Buhítos, Volcanes
y otros Poemas Ilustrados
Texts by various authors
Illustrations by Carlos Ortín

Inside pages

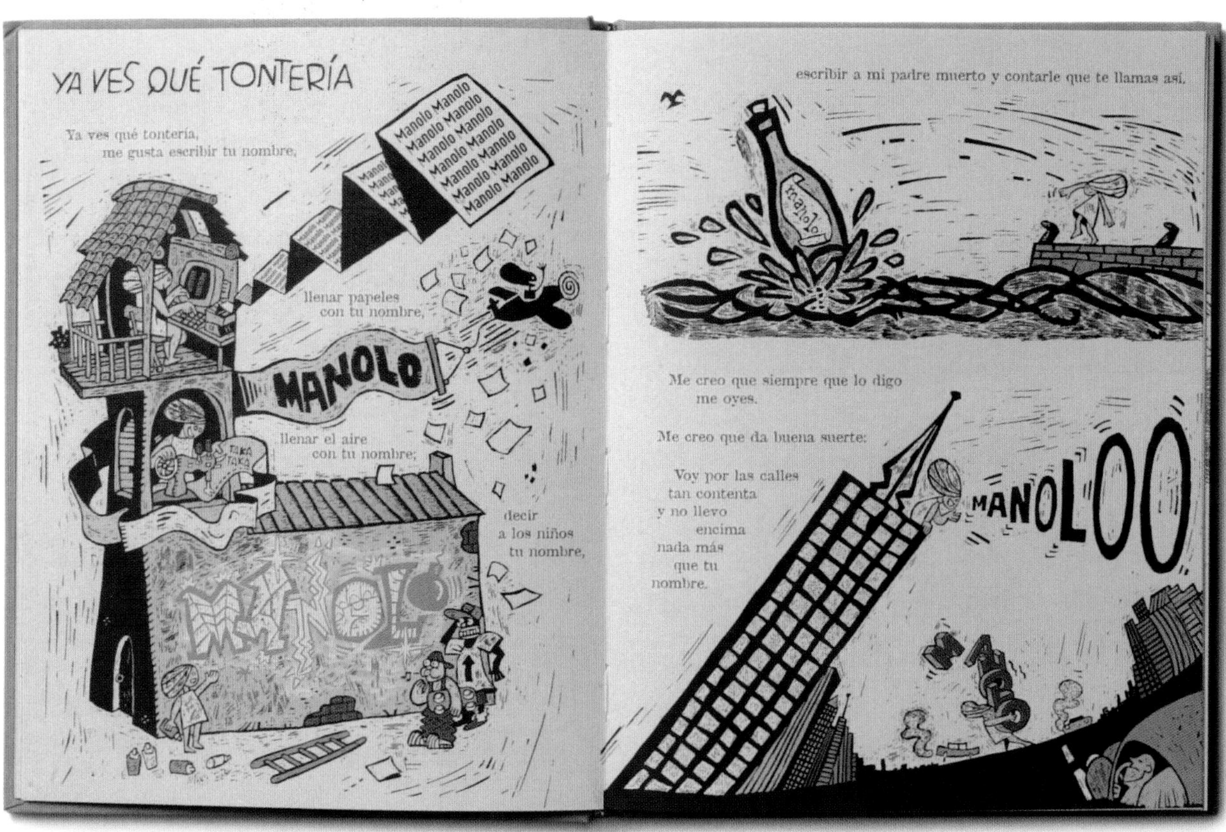

Media Vaca collection
Children's books

Year: 1998
Client: Editorial Media Vaca

All the books are in 18.5 x 23-cm format.
Full colour printing (dustcover), 1 ink (cover) and 2 inks (interior).
Offset paper. Cardboard binding

'Children's' is not a Synonym of Simple

The books published by Media Vaca, though theoretically children's books, are really intended for everyone. In Vicente's view 'children's' is not a synonym of simple. "Children's minds are far more complex than the silly tales that we want to make them swallow. I want to publish books for children of all ages."

And when Vicente tries to define the target readership, he adds, "I have no idea of what a child is or what we call an adult. I see that in some places young people carry weapons and go to war, or work as slaves... It shouldn't be that way. You have to know how to use books, which may be a weapon or a tool; education begins with them."

Vicente believes children deserve quality books with good illustrations accompanying quality content. In his opinion, "if there is any sense in making books, it makes particular sense to make them for children. Because the world, and this we sometimes forget, belongs to children. The best books should be for them, the best stories, the best drawings, the best paper, the first shelves. None of this feeding them undemanding texts and drawings that are but a sad caricature of what children themselves do."

Narices, Buhítos, Volcanes
and other illustrated poems

This collection of poems and songs brings together forty poems by thirty-three different authors from very different periods and styles, from Quevedo to Joan Brossa, to Edward Lear and Francis Picabia.

In most cases, short popular pieces have been selected using a simple language and underscoring the humorous aspects so that children can become familiar with the texts. Each poem takes up a double page.
The book is generously illustrated: sometimes resources are used from the story (images framed in vignettes), other times the image is more akin to the sort of etchings found in old illustrated albums.
The typography fits perfectly with the illustrations, varying its forms to adapt to the spirit of each poem.

Media Vaca's books are to be read and looked at the same time. The images, the illustrations are as important as the texts. Image and text fuse into one and the same thing. The word, supported by evocative typography in different bodies and families; the manual headings for some texts; the use of colour and illustrations using varying techniques; the paper, thick and pleasant to the touch – all these factors contribute to the singularity of the final product. The originality lies in achieving well-made books with a strong personality.

"Care is necessary in the appearance of books so that we will want to have them in our hands, and for them to last and stay with us longer," says Vicente.

Media Vaca's books have their own peculiarities although the coherence of the whole is maintained. The different illustrators' work helps give this particular tone to each edition. They use various techniques and shun clichés: some illustrators use traditional techniques, others take forms from popular imagery, others draw on avant-garde artistic movements.

Vicente chooses carefully the typeface he uses for the texts in his books. He usually uses typefaces that look as though they were hand-done, printed with toy stamps or using some forgotten technique. And, although sometimes it is the illustrator himself who ends up doing the lettering, this makes it another part of the illustration.

Media Vaca

Illustrations play a prominent role in the books, generally occupying the largest part of the printed space. The text, in which a one-to-one relationship with the images is sought, is what finally defines the character of the images.

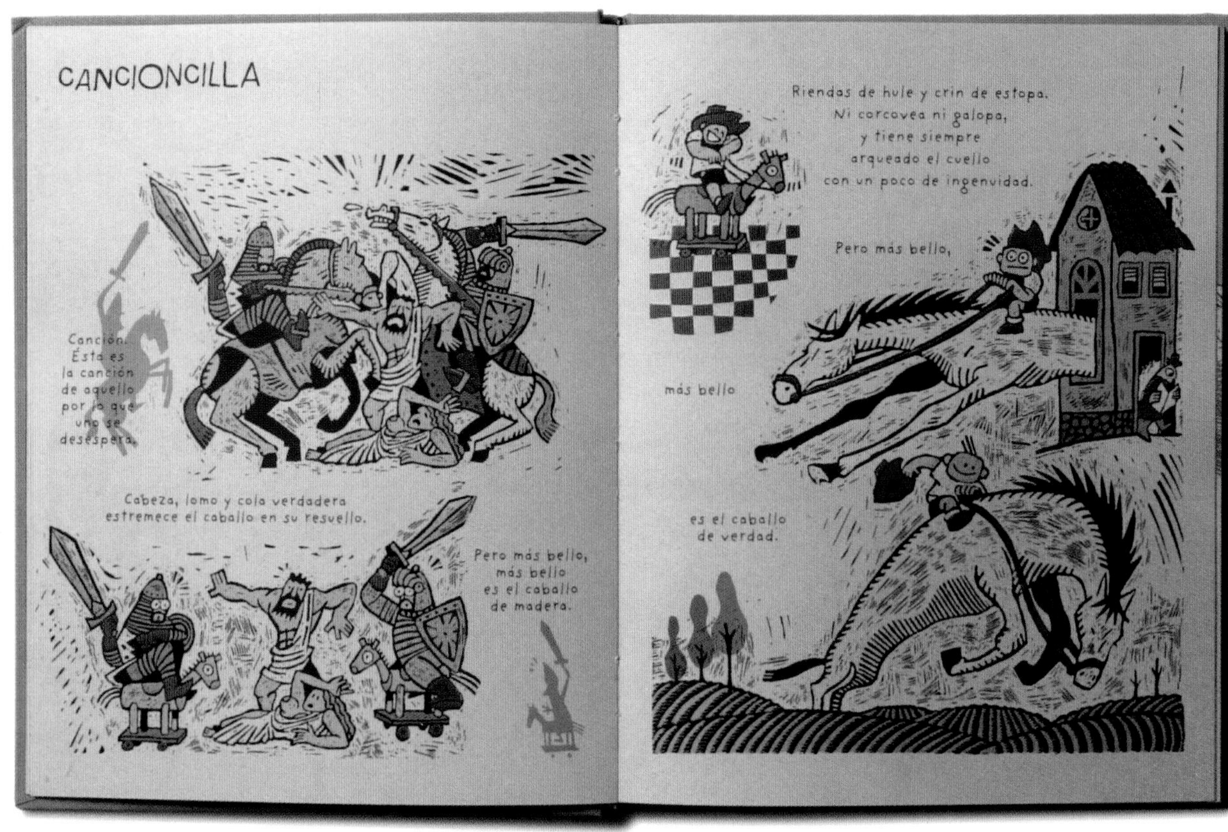

CANCIONCILLA
Canción. Ésta es la canción de aquello por lo que uno se desespera.
Cabeza, lomo y cola verdadera estremece el caballo en su resuello.
Pero más bello, más bello es el caballo de madera.
Riendas de hule y crin de estopa. Ni corcovea ni galopa, y tiene siempre arqueado el cuello con un poco de ingenuidad.
Pero más bello,
más bello
es el caballo de verdad.

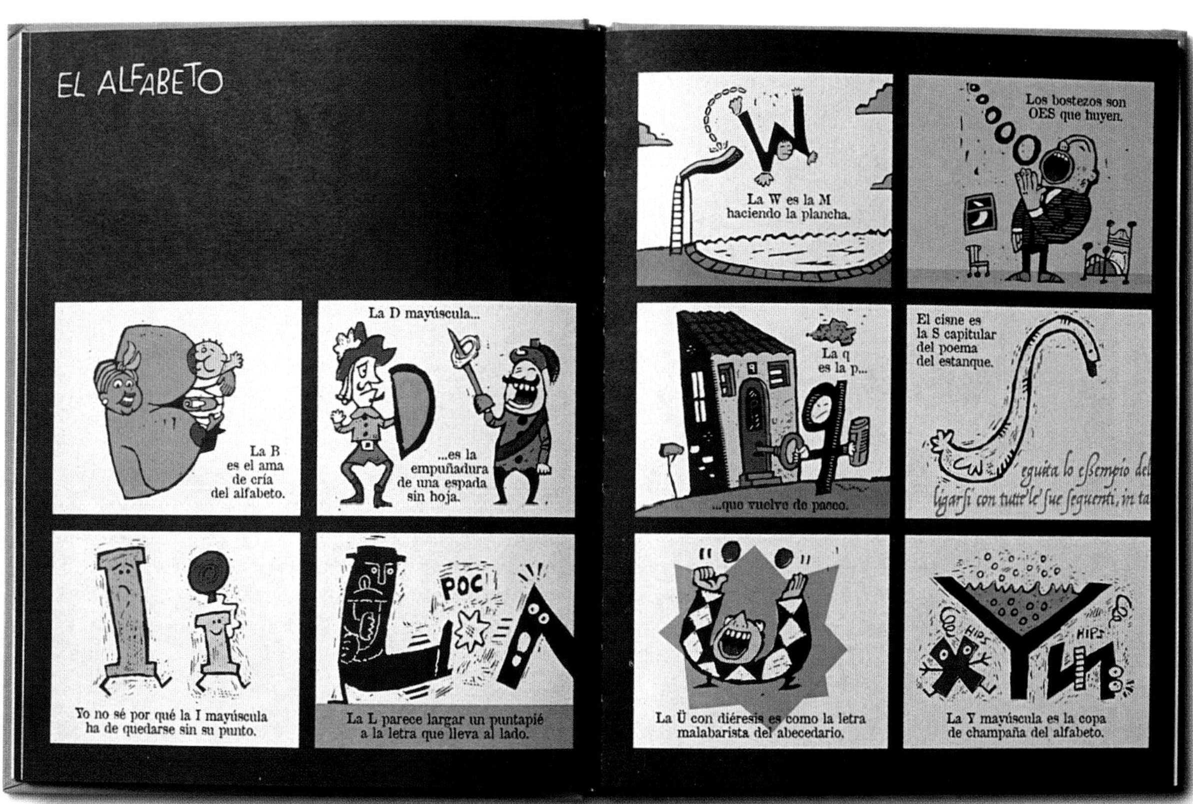
EL ALFABETO
La B
es el ama
de cría
del alfabeto.
La D mayúscula...
...es la
empuñadura
de una espada
sin hoja.
Yo no sé por qué la I mayúscula
ha de quedarse sin su punto.
POC
La L parece largar un puntapié
a la letra que lleva al lado.
La W es la M
haciendo la plancha.
Los bostezos son
OES que huyen.
La q
es la p...
...que vuelve de paseo.
El cisne es
la S capitular
del poema
del estanque.
La Ü con diéresis es como la letra
malabarista del abecedario.
HIPS
HIPS
La Y mayúscula es la copa
de champaña del alfabeto.

Max Kisman

Max Kisman
San Francisco, United States

"Typography on the Net"

Max Kisman (Doetinchem, 1953) is a name that almost inevitably pops up in discussions on late 20th-century Dutch graphics. This designer, resident in California since 1998, trained at the Gerrit Rietveld Academy (Amsterdam) with some of the most outstanding Dutch masters of design, illustration and typography. His long professional career covers all areas of design, his interest in experimentation having drawn him to all sorts of graphic projects.

Over the years he has developed a personal, daring, direct language. **"Originality"**, Kisman says, **"is defined within my physical and mental limitations. Exploiting my limitations offers me the full strength of my capabilities."**

An admirer of the work of Joan Miró, Kisman values the role of intuition and spontaneity in his work procedures.

Between 1989 and 1992 Kisman lived and worked in Barcelona, designing typefaces for **FontShop International** and for **FUSE** magazine.

In 1997 he began working as creative director for **Wired** magazine, also doing the design for his website **HotWired**. He currently directs the electronic magazine **Tribe**.

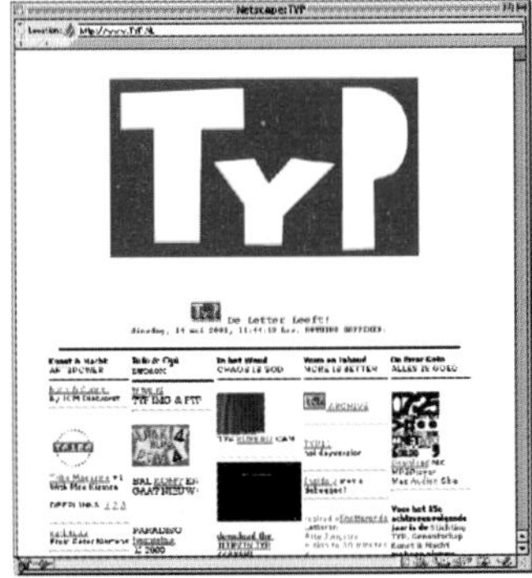

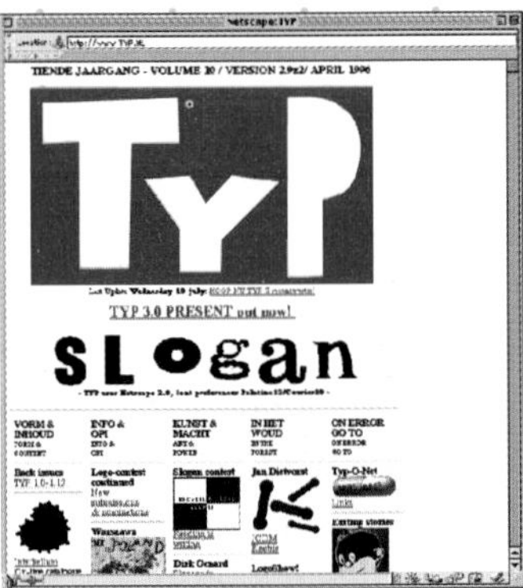

Typ/Typografisch Papier
Website. 1995-2001

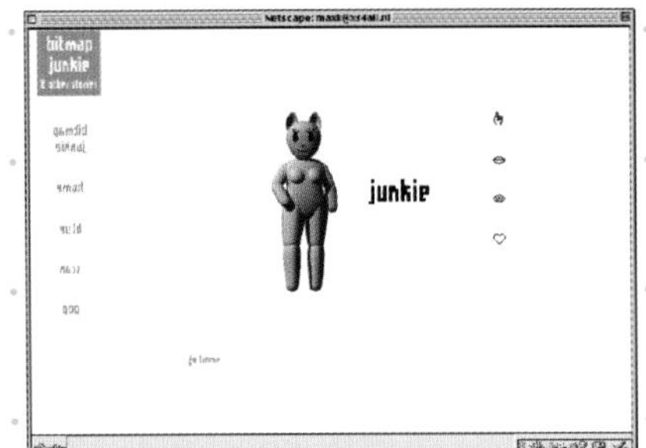

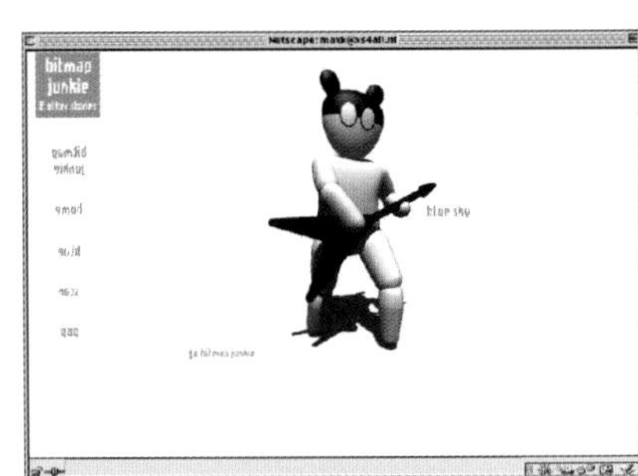

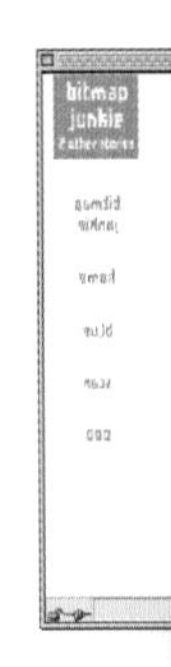

FontShop International
www.fontshop.com
FontShop USA, 2000

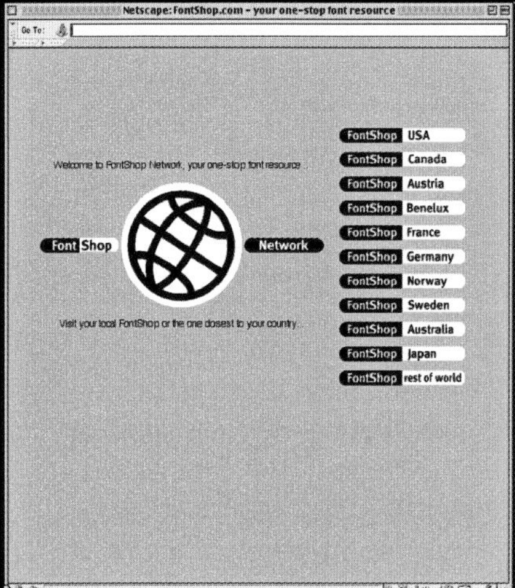

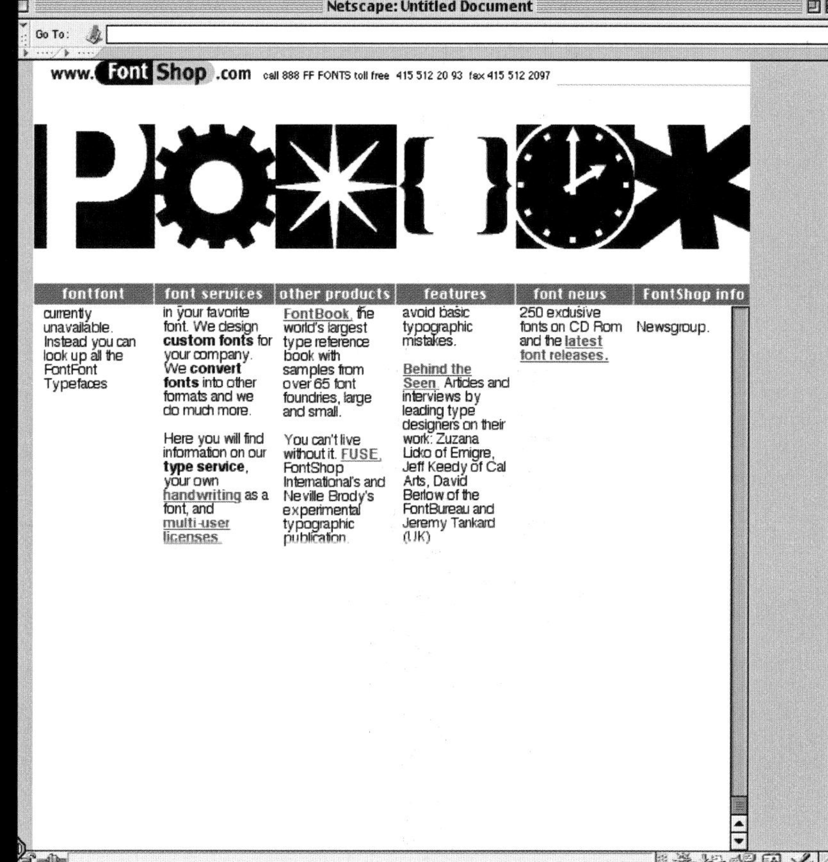

The Bitmap Junkie Stories
www.fuse98.com
Fuse98lab, 1998

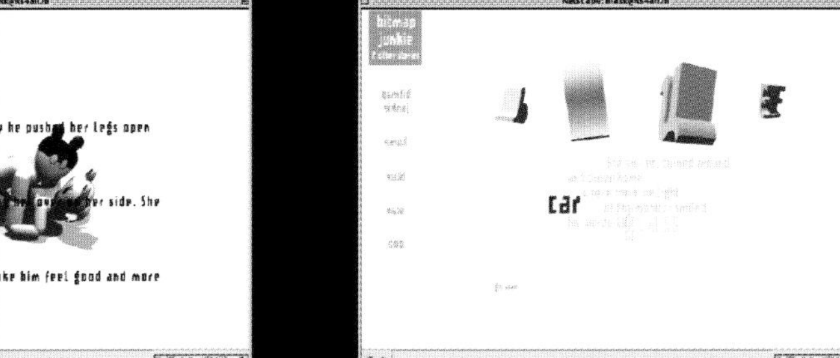

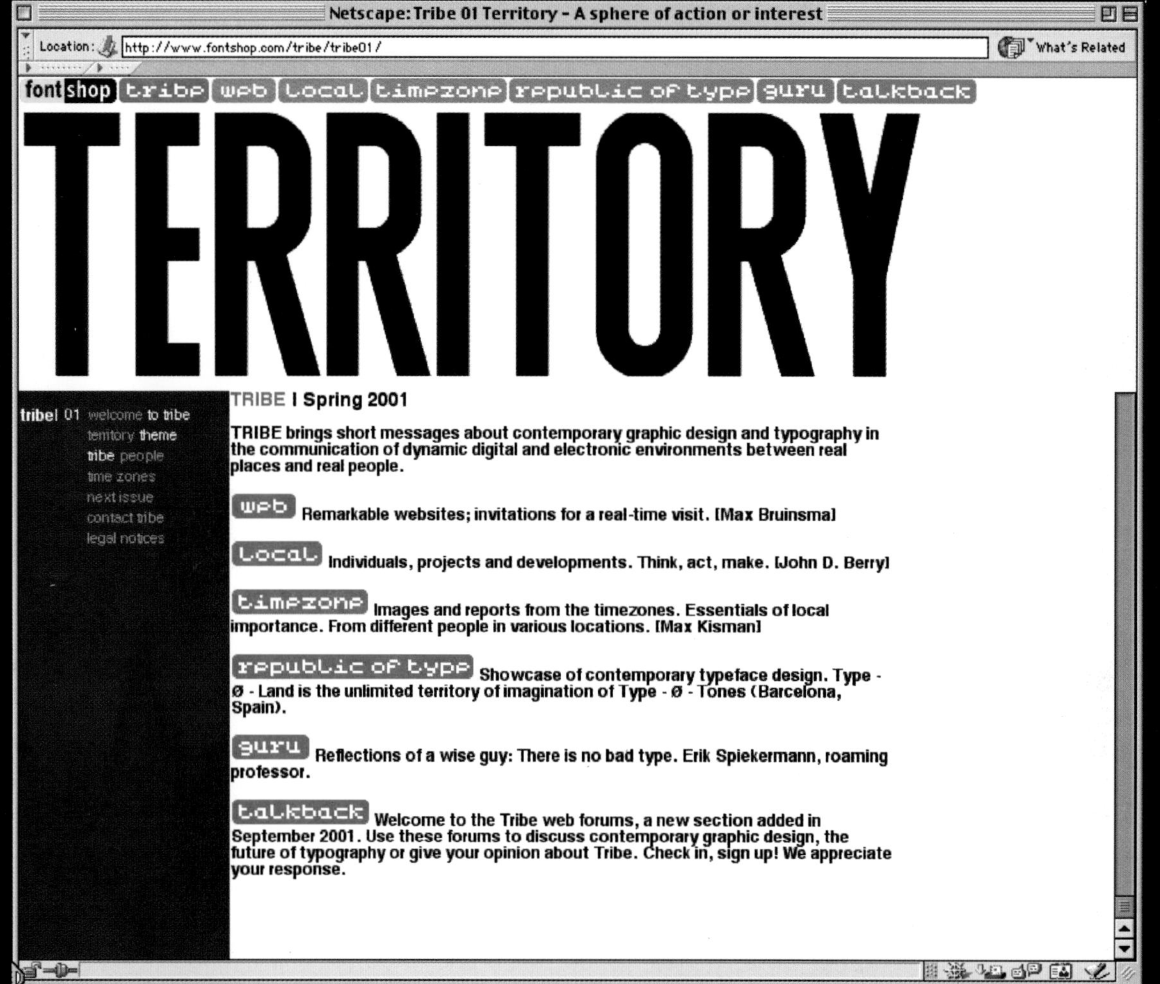

TRIBE
Electronic publication

Year: 2001-2002
Client: FontShop USA, San Francisco

Typeface used: Tribe mono

An On-Screen Magazine

Max Kisman can be considered one of the pioneers of digital typography design. His interest in typography and digital media was revealed in his experimental project TYP / typografisch papier, one of the first alternative art and typography magazines, published on paper for the first time in 1986.

His experience with supports other than paper began in the early nineties with several animation projects for the Dutch television channel VPRO.

Both on television and in the current electronic formats, Kisman employs a graphic language very close to the one used in print media. His iconography is influenced by a certain formal 'primitivism' as regards the use of simple forms, very close to pictographic codes.

In his web projects, the typography is a further element for catching the reader's attention: another element in the visual appeal, also bearing the written message. **"But the texts"**, says Kisman, **"mustn't waste the reader's time. They must be specially prepared for use on the web."**

Accessibility is one of his priorities when considering an online publication project. **"Use as little as necessary to communicate**

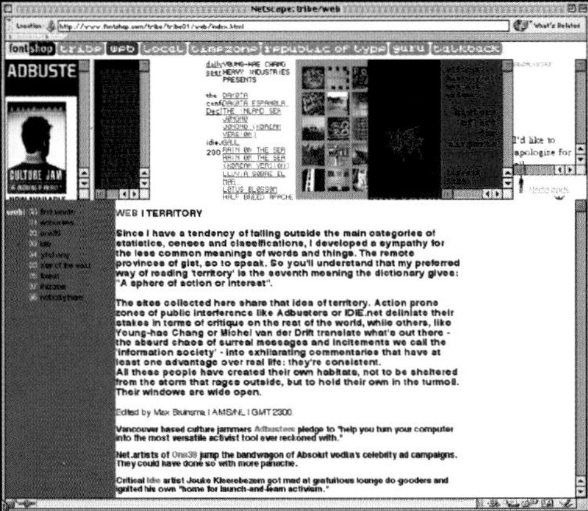

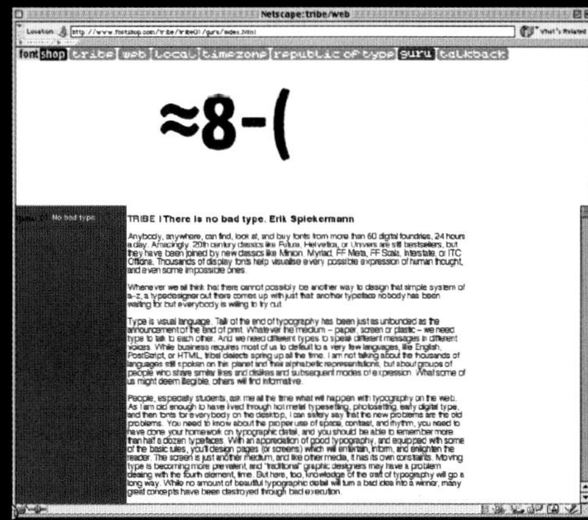

the essence to connect, and be as clear as possible to communicate further information in depth. There must be a good editorial concept and you must know how to structure the information with the aim of communicating in a certain way. Graphic design needs a structure for the optimal layout of the elements."

According to Max, one of the difficulties in the use of typography on Internet is determined by the lack of formulas. **"The lack of studies and research into perception in this new medium, unlike what happens in print, makes it very difficult to establish directions – or standards – on how to design or apply the typography. You can set out some rough directions, which most of the time will work fine, but still there are many variables."**

Tribe is aimed at typographers and designers who are interested in themes outside their field of work. It is intended as more than a simple design publication. As Max puts it, **"Tribe wants to be a life-style magazine with human interest for the design community."**

"My philosophy is to avoid as much as possible (designing) for designers and to concentrate on a valuable content."

As director and designer of Tribe, Max Kisman establishes a certain structure for the content of each online issue, assigning one theme to each one. The appearance of the contents (texts and images), are subsidiary to the subject. Each issue therefore has a different look and its contents are organised into five sections: web, local, timezone, Guru and M-Square.

A homepage structure unifies all the rest and organises the content in terms of the browsers. Each section is identified and differentiated from the rest with colour. The texts are relatively short, avoiding the excessively long articles on the higher levels of the web.

TRIBE website
www.fontshop.com/tribe

Tribe no. 02. 2002
Home and content pages

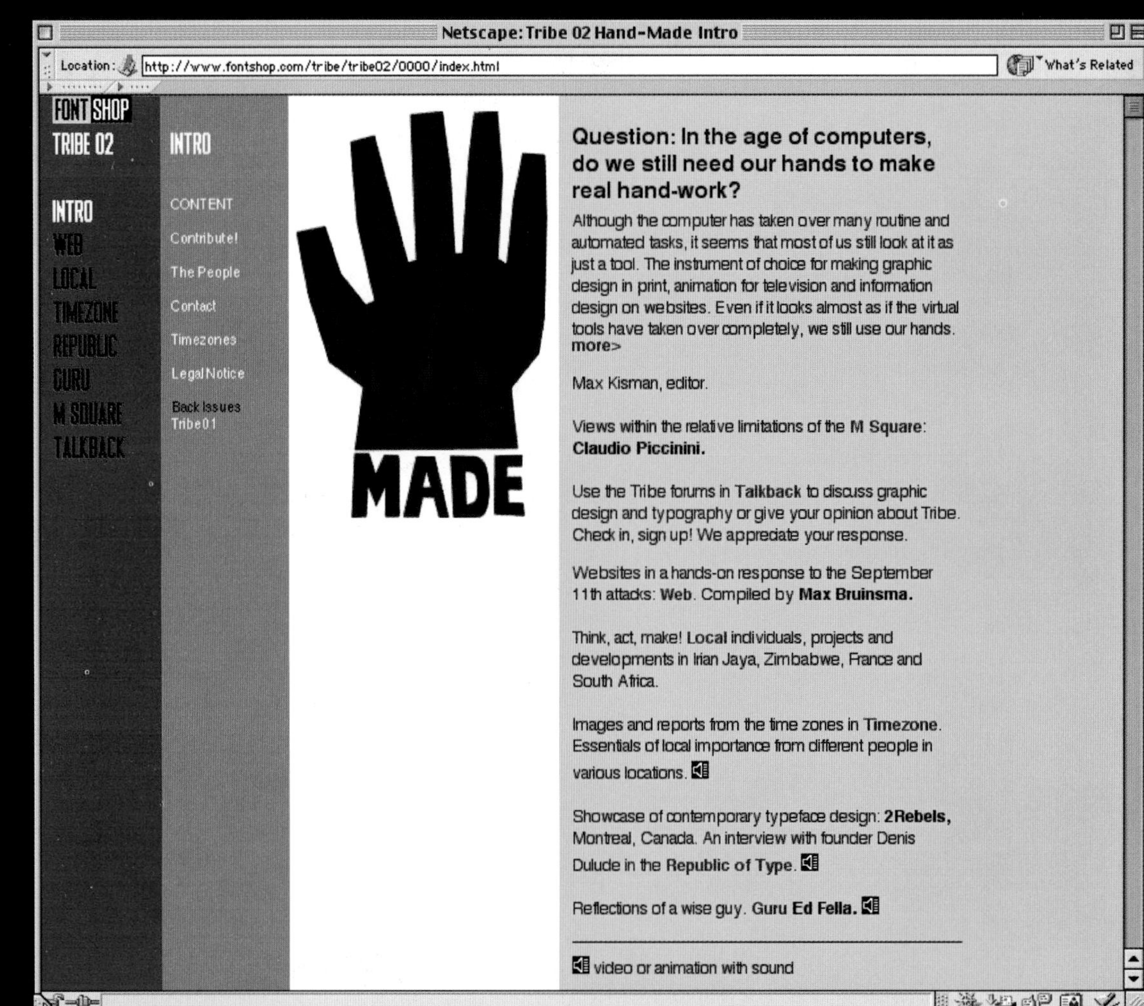

The result is an agile, effective website that offers direct access to information.

Another of Tribe's functions is as a link between Fontshop, the publisher, and the users/readers (the graphic designers).

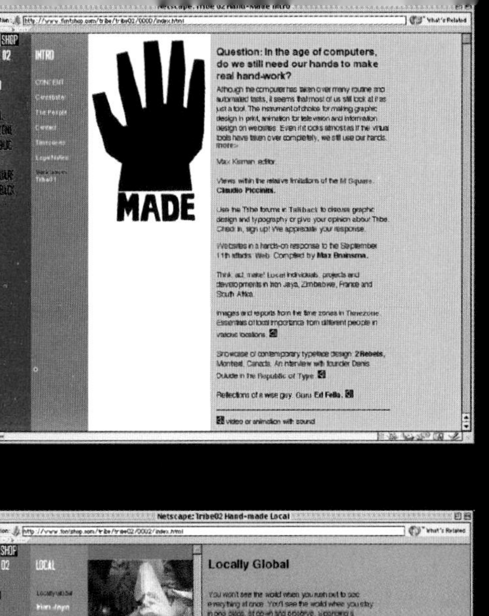

Location: http://www.fontshop.com/tribe/tribe02/0001/00010410.html

FONT SHOP
TRIBE 02

INTRO
WEB
LOCAL
TIMEZONE
REPUBLIC
GURU
M SQUARE
TALKBACK

WEB

Heart in Hand
A Heartfelt Thank You
My Story
September 11 Archive

Heart in Hand

Max Bruinsma

Hands build houses and skyscrapers. Hands forge swords and bombs. Hands steer horses and jet planes. Hands clean after what hands messed up.

It comes as no surprise that after the September 11th attacks on the World Trade Center and the Pentagon a host of sites and pages has been uploaded to the Web in a hands-on response to the disasters. Yes, they are HTML or Flash, and what have you. Yes they are code and virtual. They exist only on your computer screen. But if anything exemplifies the idea of "handmade" in the digital realm, it is these direct reactions of individuals and collectives that use their hands to express their hearts. They start typing, clicking, grabbing, moving. They hit "enter" and then there is another testimony of sorrow, confusion, rage, defiance, analysis.

Introspection on the Web, the medium that promised to be the world's tool to join hands. Let's give'em a hand, people.

Netscape: Tribe02 Hand-made Local

Location: http://www.fontshop.com/tribe/tribe02/0002/index.html

FONT SHOP
TRIBE 02

INTRO
WEB
LOCAL
TIMEZONE
REPUBLIC
GURU
M SQUARE
TALKBACK

LOCAL

Locally Global
Irian Jaya
Zimbabwe
Cape Town
Paris

Locally Global

You won't see the world when you rush out to see everything at once. You'll see the world when you stay in one place, sit down and observe. Spending a morning on a terrace at an intersection in any town in the world is better than sight-seeing a hole in your memories.

People in places are busy. They come and go. They wait and talk. They shout and wave. They do stuff. Loads of it. Keep your eyes peeled, make notes, draw sketches. In the local bar, post office, plaza, restaurant and bookstore... There is the man you sold your car to, there is the woman you'd like to talk to, there is your favorite flower shop, there the dress of your dreams.

Home is where the world is. Local, that's the place to be!

Local visits the Asmat woodcarvers in Papua, Irian Jaya, typographic stencil cutters in Harare, Zimbabwe, an international poster tribute to Toulouse Lautrec in Paris, France, and creative innovations in Cape Town and Durban, South Africa.

http://www.fontshop.com/tribe/tribe02/0002/00020050.html

Netscape: Tribe02 Hand-made Timezone

Location: http://www.fontshop.com/tribe/tribe02/0003/index.html

FONT SHOP
TRIBE 02

INTRO
WEB
LOCAL
TIMEZONE
REPUBLIC
GURU
M SQUARE
TALKBACK

TIMEZONE

Hands Talk

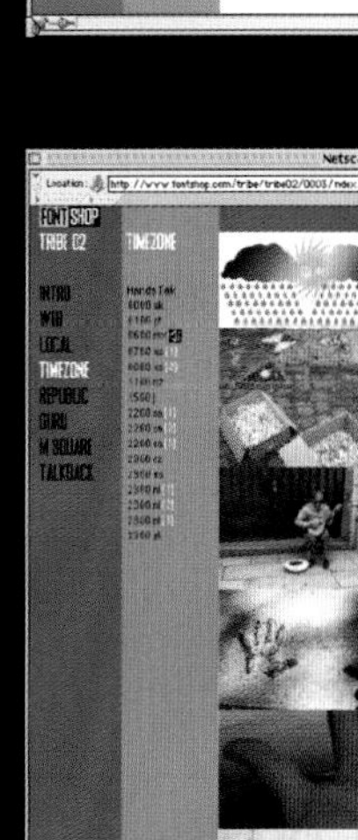

Hands Talk

Time zones. Virtual territories of differences in time, ingoring the natural borders of languages, cultures and nations. Vertical global divisions as a reference for sunsets and sunrises. A 24 hour life span is all you need to create a panoramic snapshot of the globe. List of time zones >

We use our hands, all the time and every day. Hands hold, hands feel, hands reach and hands catch. Hands can do almost anything we can think of. Anything we can imagine. Hands can make anything we invent.

Hands hold the umbrella, when it starts to rain in London, England. Hands pick flowers for the carpet in Pico, Azores. Hands play the mandolin and build wooden toy aeroplanes in Oaxaca, Mexico. Hands touch heaven over the Pacific in Maui, USA. Hands see a memory printed in a concrete sidewalk in Santa Fe, USA. As is the handprint on a Wellington wall in New Zealand. Hands hold the leash of the dog on a Japanese sign. A hand wrote letters in the sand on a South African beach near Hermanus. Other hands draw pictures in a diary and sketchbook in Cape Town, South Africa. Hands rip the posters from the walls in Prague, the Czech Republic. Hands hold a brush to write down the menus in Sevilla, Spain. Hands in Amsterdam, the Netherlands, embroided a message to a friend, now gone. Hands drew their first computer images in 1988, in Amsterdam NL. And, each day, hands will change the objects in front of a webcam in Amsterdam NL. Hands placed letters into words and words into sentences and sentences into signs in Opole, Poland.

Hands won't stop making.

Netscape: Tribe02 Hand-made Republic of Type

Location: http://www.fontshop.com/tribe/tribe02/0004/index.html

FONT SHOP
TRIBE 02

INTRO
WEB
LOCAL
TIMEZONE
REPUBLIC
GURU
M SQUARE
TALKBACK

REPUBLIC

Rebel Rebel
Designers

HandMade

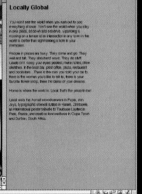

OF TYPE : 2REBELS

Although Canada was one of the first to join the extended Font Shop family with a Toronto based office in 1989, it wasn't much known for its typographical identity. With the exponential growth in the use of desktop computers and the internet, borders can be crossed more easily, and the desire for local design cultures is stimulated.

FontShop/Tribe proudly presents an independent type foundry, which now occupies a well deserved place in The Republic of Type. Max Kisman interviewed Montreal-based designer Denis Dulude, the founder and spokesman of 2Rebels.

Left, handmade video by Denis Dulude

As far as Denis Dulude is concerned, Montreal doesn't have much of a type tradition, and a well-known UK designer (he won't reveal his name yet) once told him that there was nothing happening in type design in his city.

Denis: I don't know if I can change that, but I'm working on it! And it's getting there. Many designers are working hard to make it happen.

M: What, as far as your name suggests, are you rebelling against?

D: We're not rebelling against anything, but for something. In 1995, the year 2Rebels was born, only a happy few in Montreal knew about contemporary fonts like Emigre, FontFont, T-26, GarageFonts, etc. So it was our way to try to give an awareness to continue the typographical revolution that was happening then. So maybe I'm a rebel with a cause.

Netscape: Tribe02 Hand-made Guru Ed Fella

Location: http://www.fontshop.com/tribe/tribe02/0005/index.html

FONT SHOP
TRIBE 02

INTRO
WEB
LOCAL
TIMEZONE
REPUBLIC
GURU
M SQUARE
TALKBACK

HandMagic?

click to continue

Guru: Ed Fella

Hand Magic

(Click on image to start)

This bit of doggerel, craftily hand lettered out by me and cleverly set into digital motion by the editor of this magazine, is something I can't really decipher other than as wordplay on the well-known line conjurers use To try to unravel that as an explanation for the "magic" of handwork would be to question whether such a thing could even be.

Other than how it was actually made, what gives one thing a handmade look and another a mechanical or digital look? Can one be easily fooled by the differences? Or not? Is it in the eye of the experience of the viewer? Or in a particular visual culture of the past? In other words, are these words a gestalt of the spontaneity of a hand-to-mind-to-eye-back-to-hand gesture or just some play on a traditional history of vernacular and commercial lettering styles?

All I can answer is, it's what I know, or claim to know, or want to know, or need to know. My tech is a set of ellipse guides with pen and colored pencils, my form my own past as an all-around, old commercial artist: that is, letterer, typographer, graphic designer and illustrator. It also helped to read a little art and lit crit theory

Colectivo Grrr

GRRR Group
Barcelona, Spain

"A Grrrraphic Design Magazine"

Founded in 1994, **Grrr** is a group of people obsessed with graphic design. Its founding was directly related to a magazine publishing public, **Grrr**, devoted to graphic design and related fields.

The group defines itself as an open group (currently with more than 20 members), which has evolved towards other related activities, working with other publications and organising exhibitions.

Grrr generates its own contents, although it also welcomes articles from other professionals. The group itself does the design and printing of the magazine, working like a small independent publishing house.

Its attitude to publishing a magazine might be summed up in achieving a series of objectives: content (the text) over image, priority to reflection and analysis over simple display of finished products.

"At Grrr we are interested in both processes and results. We are interested in the past, present and future of design."

Grrr is a group that consider themselves above all antidogmatic and multidisciplinary. **"We try to be flexible, creative and cheeky, although possibly some consider us mutants or Venusians."**

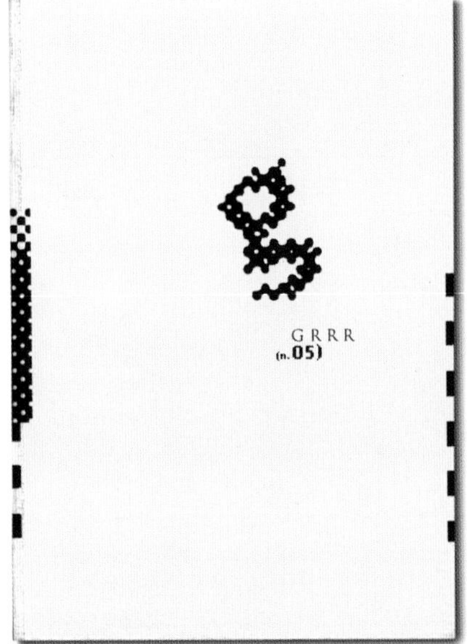

Grrr. Cover number 0
1994

Grrr. Cover number 5
1999

Design: Jaume Aymerich and Rosa Llop.
Issue number 5 was the beginning of a new stage for the publication, the most visible signs of which are the change in format and the increase in the number of pages.

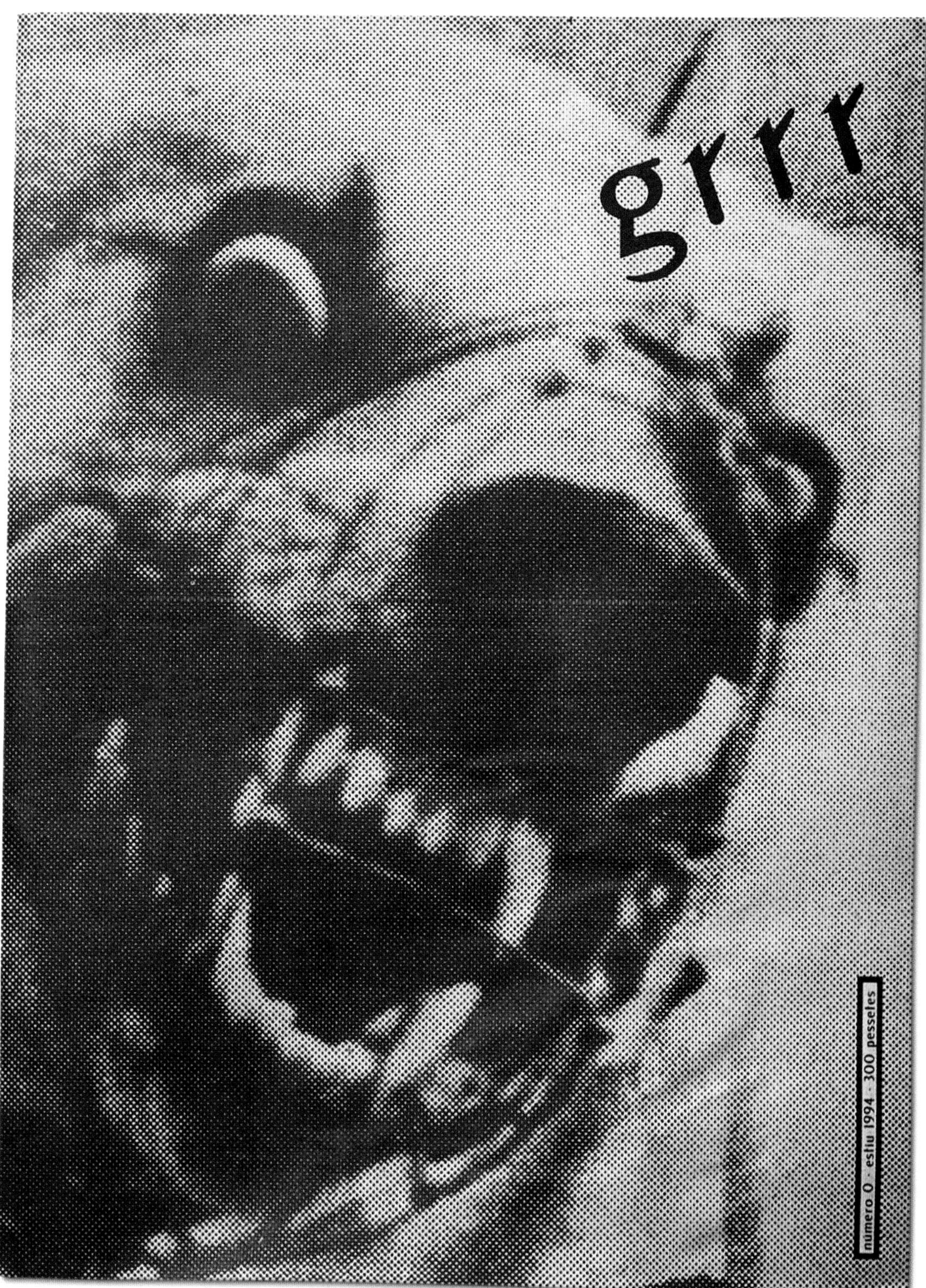
grrr
número 0 · estiu 1994 · 300 pessetes

Grrr no. 6
June 2000

Cover
The cover of this issue of **Grrr** betrayed the philosophy of the magazine and the group's attitude towards editorial design.

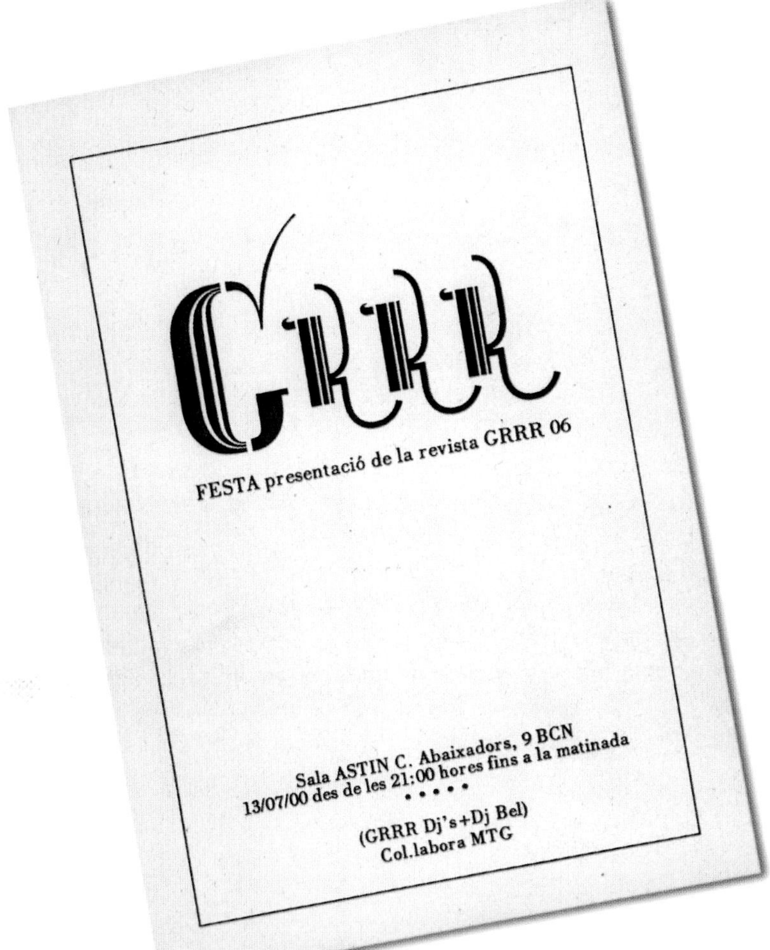

Grrr no. 6
Flyer for a party to present Grrr no. 6

Graphic image based on SuperTipo, by J. Trochut

Grrr
Magazine

Year: 1994-2002
Designers: Grrr Group

Client: Grrr

15 x 21 cm. 96 pages. 1 ink on offset paper. Bi-annual

A Group Publishing Project

Grrr has gone through two different periods since it inception. Issues 0 to 4 had a fairly uneven look, with 32 pages in 22 x 32-cm format.

Following a period of crisis, the group took on greater responsibility in editing the magazine, and in late 1999 a second period began with the appearance of the 5th issue: a new design, more pages, the current smaller format and two issues per year.

One of the peculiarities of the magazine is its mutability. While maintaining the format and a single black ink, the design is different for each issue due to a desire to overcome the rigidity of a single structure and give each issue its own personality.

Each issue is designed in rotating turns by one or several members of the group, so each one bears the mark of the team that was responsible for the design. This is also a form of dialogue among the members of the group, a means of proposing different graphic solutions each time.

NÚMERO 6, VERANO 2000

GRRR

CREEMOS QUE DEBERÍAIS SABER ALGO SOBRE ESTA REVISTA : Llevamos ya mucho tiempo juntos. Seis años desde aquel primer encuentro en que muchos de nosotros ni siquiera nos conocíamos. Ahora somos más. Algunos ya no están. Otros han ido entrando. Somos un grupo de amigos. Más o menos. Más que menos, creo. Un grupo abierto. Aunque nos conocemos desde hace mucho tiempo queremos ser un grupo abierto. Quizás no lo parezcamos. Grrr ha sido desde el principio el resultado de este grupo de amigos. No nos mueve otra cosa que el amor al DISEÑO GRÁFICO, en general. Solemos divertirnos, fácil. Conseguir que la revista salga y con la pretendida puntualidad, eso, eso es otra cosa. Aunque lo intentamos. Llevamos tiempo y tiempo luchando contra nosotros mismos para seguir. El rigor que nos imponemos a veces está por encima de nuestras posibilidades reales como colectivo. No hay ningún interés en convertirnos en un proyecto editorial serio. Sin que ello signifique renunciar a la profesionalidad y calidad del producto. No pretendemos ganar ningún premio de diseño con la revista. No somos una revista moderna. Nos importa más lo que contiene que su forma. Preferimos la actitud al vestido. Somos otro tipo de revista. No queremos que la mires. Queremos que la leas. ¿Sólo leer sobre diseño gráfico? Sí. Nuestros colaboradores son también amigos. O amigos de amigos. O conocidos. Algún desconocido. Bienvenido siempre. Nadie cobra. Nadie pretende cobrar. Nadie se aprovecha. Nadie se pretende aprovechar. Simplemente nos gusta esto. Una tinta: es suficiente. El precio y los promotores: seguridad mínima necesaria. Soporte: también nos gusta el papel. Las ilustraciones: son sólo un apoyo, no un fin. Un sueño: seguir. Cada seis meses. Necesitamos tu apoyo. Un toque. Que nos obligues a seguir luchando. CONTRA NOSOTROS MISMOS.

PRECIO: 1.000 PTS / 6 EUROS

Colectivo Grrr

Grrr no. 6

Inside page

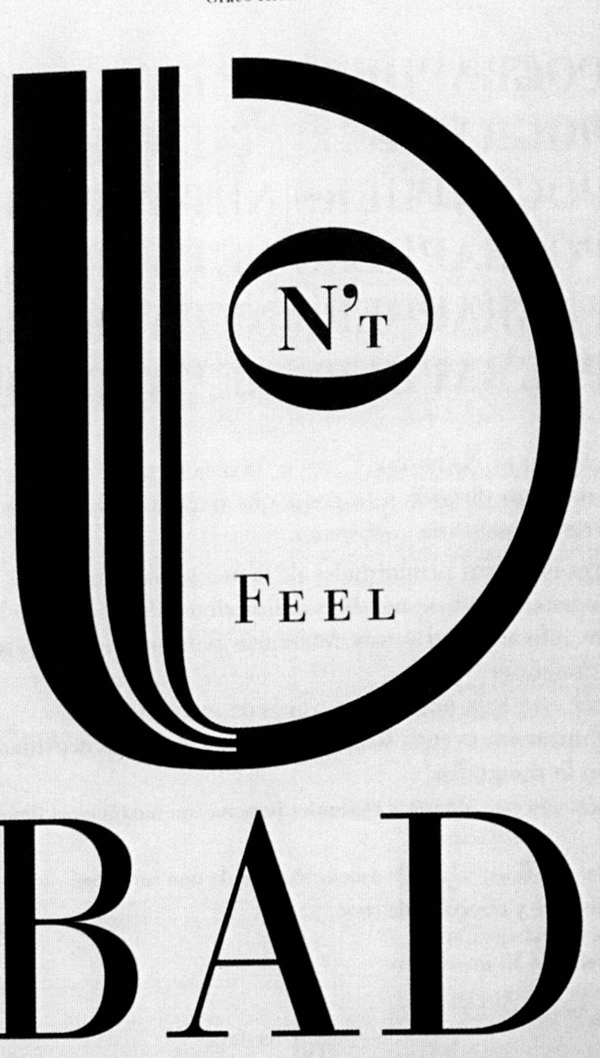

Cuando era pequeño, aprendí cómo leer. Un día, no mucho más tarde, aprendí a leer. Iba en un coche, mirando por la ventanilla a las señales que pasaban. Para sorpresa mía, me di cuenta de que no podía pararme a leerlas. A cada momento veía algunas letras, las letras formaban palabras y las palabras formaban significados. Quería volver a ver las letras como garabatos y formas abstractas. Intenté cerrar los ojos, esperando que cuando los abriera de nuevo, podría

Grrr no. 6

Font based on Joan Trochut's SuperTipo modules. These are used for some titles as well as ornamental elements used throughout the issue.

El Diseño en la II República – Raquel Pelta

Raquel Pelta

EL DISEÑO EN LA II REPÚBLICA:
ENTRE LA VANGUARDIA Y EL COMPROMISO

A finales del pasado mes de septiembre de 1999 visitamos a Carles Fontseré en su casa de Porqueres (Girona). Disfrutamos de un día espléndido. Esos días que el otoño te regala en un paisaje repleto de colores tostados y rojizos.

El motivo de dicho encuentro era nuestro deseo de conocer a Carles personalmente y realizar una entrevista para la revista Grrr. Es mucha la admiración que sentimos por Fontseré como persona, y quizás se trate de uno de los pocos testigos –y protagonista, a la vez– que todavía nos queden para poder explicar de manera más precisa la historia del siglo xx.

Para contextualizar esta entrevista hemos creído conveniente presentar un breve artículo introductorio sobre el diseño gráfico en los años de la II República y de la Guerra Civil.

27

Grrr 6
Year: 2000

Design: David Molins, Joan Carles Pérez and Andreu Balius

The design of this issue of the Grrr magazine is intended to express the philosophy of the magazine – a reflection of what the group wishes to communicate through this biannual publication. And they do so with the issue's feature editorial, manifesto-like, on the cover.

To place the editorial text on the cover is to place the group's attitude at the forefront: **"We are more concerned with the content than the form."**

In this issue, Grrr gets closer to the hybrid idea of a book-magazine that the group is exploring.

For the texts they use Bauer Bodoni to give an elegant look that respects the contents. This is complemented by rescuing the historical SuperTipo Veloz modules, created by Juan Trochut in the first half of the 20th century, used to create signs and small illustrations accompanying the titles.

The marked contrast between the Bodoni family and the SuperTipo pieces enhances the austerity of the use of a single black ink throughout the publication. The mockup, based on a double or single column structure, depending on the article, highlights the quasi-literary character of this issue, with several articles on historical themes.

Grrr no. 7

Cover and double inside page

LettError, en directo:

Just van Rossum (1966) y Erik van Blockland (1967) son conocidos por el trabajo que realizan bajo el nombre de LettError.

Ambos se graduaron en la Royal Academy of Art en La Haya (Holanda). Después de trabajar durante un breve periodo para compañías extranjeras (MetaDesign, Font-Bureau) empezaron a trabajar como *free-lance* en La Haya.

En 1990 introdujeron las *random fonts* (tipografías aleatorias), trazados programados digitalmente que, mediante una disposición aleatoria de los nodos que definen el contorno de las letras, se imprimen de manera distinta cada vez. Han diseñado cerca de 50 tipografías para FontShop y en su trabajo tipográfico utilizan principalmente la programación.

6 7

› Next page
Grrr no. 10. 2002

Design: Dani Navarro,
David Parcerisas and Àlex Prieto

Cover and double inside page

Grrr 7
Year: 2001

Design: Manel Olivella

In the design of issue number 7, the aim is to attain order and sufficient visual clarity for pleasant, easy reading, eliminating ornamental elements – which Manel considers evident 'design' intent.

Through a simple mockup, the use of a single font family, Futura, and the layout of the texts on the page – playing with the font style, body and column width – Manel seeks to express a certain attitude in each type of article, with each one clearly differentiated in appearance from the others. **"An interview should look like an interview, a feature article should look like a feature article and an opinion should look like an opinion."**

The use of the Futura family for the whole magazine, though a premeditated decision, is of relative importance. In Manel's view Futura, given its geometric form and absence of ornamental strokes, was the most appropriate for achieving the original intention to have clarity and order:

"It helped me diminish the excessively literary character that the text would have acquired if I had used a typeface with serif."

Grrr no. 9
2001

Cover and inside pages

The goal pursued by the designers of issue number 9, Oscar Clemente and David Santamaría, was to enhance the formal appearance of the typeface.
The mockup is supported by a nine-field grid setting out the blocks of randomly-justified text, without following any guidelines as to their horizontal position.

FF Scala serif was chosen for the texts.
The headlines for the articles and the page numbering serve to showcase the font by highlighting the details of its design.

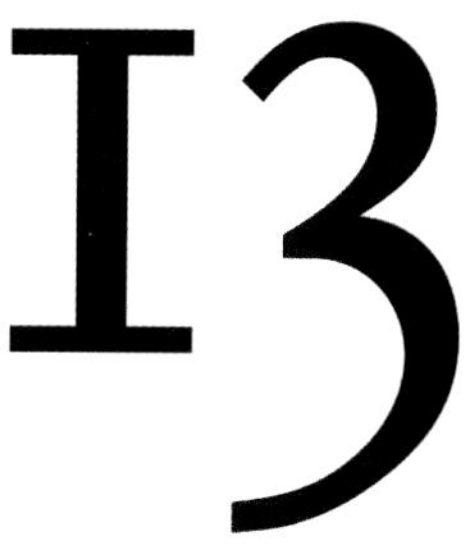

Diálogos entre libros

Podemos decir que Actar es resultado del autoencargo...

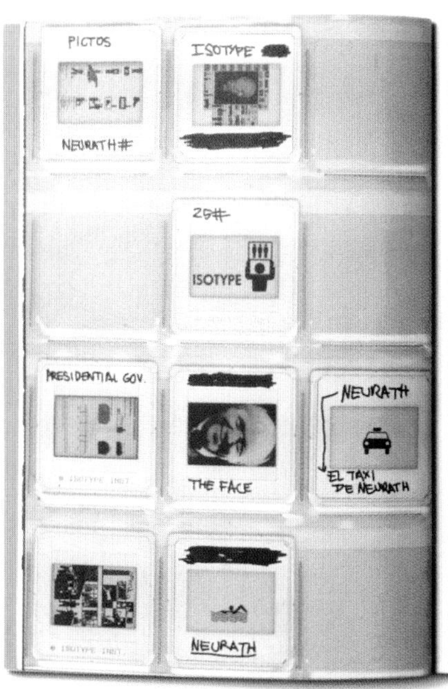

Grrr no. 8

Cover and double inside page

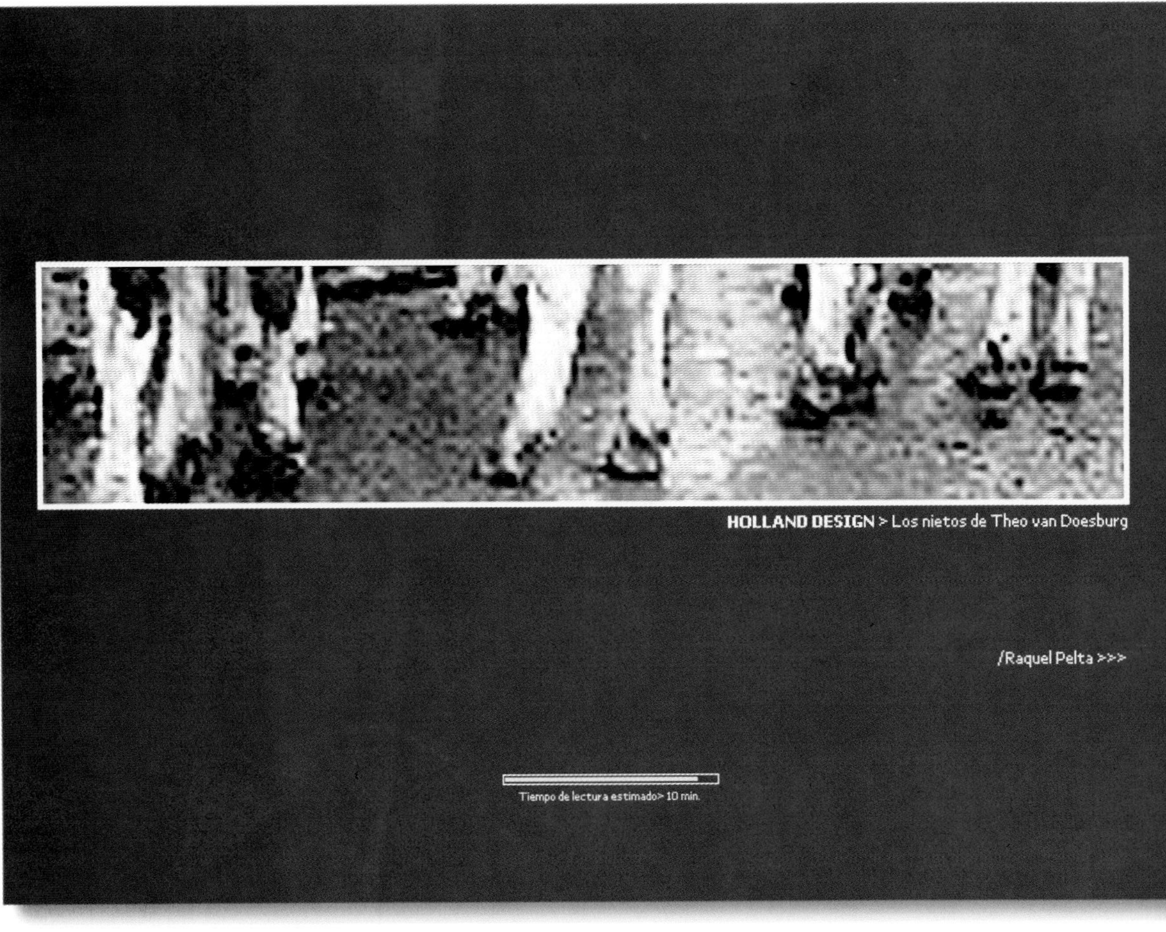

HOLLAND DESIGN > Los nietos de Theo van Doesburg
/Raquel Pelta >>>
Tiempo de lectura estimado> 10 min.

Grrr 8
Year: 2001

Design: Ramon Castillo, Albert Carles

The design of the 8th issue of Grrr explores the limits between design and website design.

Both Ramon and Albert are experts in website design, and so they planned a horizontal mockup, taking the computer screen as a reference. For the first time it was decided to change the reading orientation of the magazine and adopt a 'wide-screen' format. A 1024-module grid was used to lay out images and typography. A pixelated version of Verdana in 9 body was employed for the articles, seeking to achieve a constant 'digital' appearance.

Their graphic recourses are highly reminiscent of the graphic language of website: icons taken from computer applications, the idea of the pixel, a modular grid in the background, operative system windows, pop-ups, etc.

The issue is full of references to the computer monitor. This demonstrates that the influences between both supports – paper and electronic – are both fluid and constant, revealing that thanks to the new technologies editorial design is expanding its horizons. Under such circumstances the Grrr group could not remain passively on the sidelines.

7 **HOLLAND DESIGN** > Los nietos de Theo van Doesburg <grrr>

* Con motivo de esta exposición Actar ha editado el libro HD Holland Design new graphics, un proyecto de Ramon Prat y Tomoko Sakamoto

Con motivo de la Primavera del Disseny 2001, y coincidiendo con el Forum Laus 01, la Galería Ras de Barcelona ha presentado la exposición titulada HD (Holland Design)* (18 de mayo al 5 de julio), que supone un recorrido por el nuevo diseño holandés a través del trabajo de una serie de diseñadores cuya característica común es, tal vez, su juventud. Con una edad comprendida entre los 30 y los 39 años, representan una gran variedad de aproximaciones al diseño, distintas entre sí pero todas ellas marcadas por una serie de rasgos que sólo se explican si nos atenemos al contexto en que surgen.

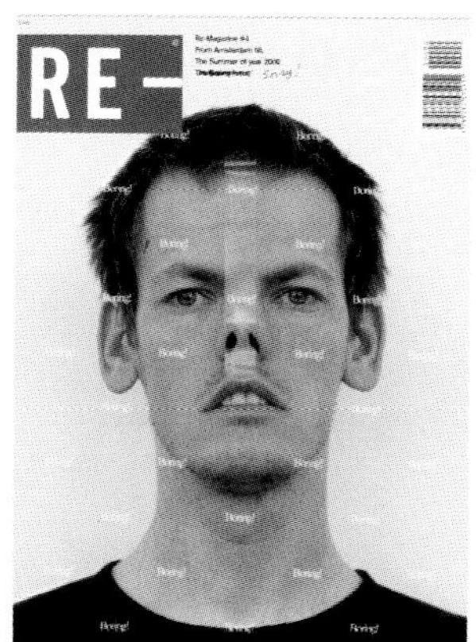

Jop van Bennekom. Re-magazine 4, verano 2000

La muestra de Ras coincidió, además, con la Exposición Dutch Graphic Design 1990-2000, organizada por la ADG en la sala de exposiciones del FAD (del 19 de mayo al 8 de junio). Ambas exposiciones y la conferencia conjunta -dentro de las actividades del Forum Laus 01- de algunos de los profesionales participantes en las mismas, han hecho que nos decidiéramos a aproximarnos en este número de Grrr a un tema siempre de actualidad: el diseño en Holanda.

Las imágenes de este artículo pertenecen al libro HD Holland Design New Graphics y han sido amablemente cedidas por Actar

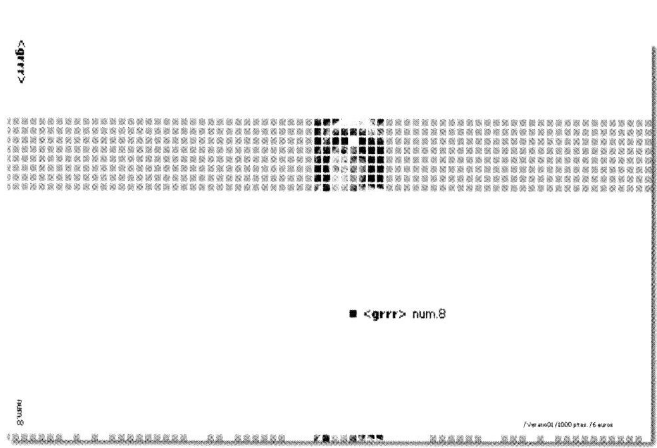

"Typography is a vehi
of ideas. Form and bac
going beyond the visu
The use of typograph
ideological experienc

e for the transmission
ground come together,
l to reflect an attitude.
helps create a possible
.

Barnbrook Design

Jon Barnbrook
London, United Kingdom

"Graphic Design as a Form of Protest"

From an early age Jon Barnbrook (Luton, 1966) entertained himself at school drawing the logos of his favourite bands, paying special attention to the forms of the typography.

Jon studied at the Central St. Martins College of Art and Design (1985-88) and at the Royal College of Art (1988-90) before starting out on his own.

He feels most comfortable working within a small structure – he and his assistant – doing only what he likes to do: design. Since completing his studies he has always worked like that, drawing fonts, designing books, and so on. He doesn't miss the chance to explore other areas, even fashion, fabric design and product design. According to Jon, **"Design is a process aimed at resolving a communication problem. We can explore it from other territories."**

He has collaborated with the Canadian anti-advertising magazine **Adbusters.** Design, in his view, cannot be considered as a mere marketing tool. He believes that **"graphic design has the possibility to change the way people perceive the world"**, and adds: **"It cannot be defined by the laws of marketing; it is done by people for the people; only in that way does it have the force to change their lives in a different and stimulating way."**

As a font designer, Jon has done the typefaces **Exocet** (1991) and **Mason** (1992) for the **Emigre fonts** catalogue. He presently releases his fonts through his own company, **Virus.** Typefaces such as **Bastard** and **Prozac** show that his approach to font design is fundamentally ideological.

I want to spend the rest of my life everywhere with everyone, one to one, always, forever, now Catalogue 1999

Jon Barnbrook has designed the monographic work on the artist Damien Hirst, **I want to spend the rest of my life everywhere with everyone,** redefining the very concept of what is traditionally understood as an artist's catalogue, and winning important awards for his work.

For Jon, the way of working of an artist like Damien Hirst is no different from that of a designer like himself. **"It's a question of communicating what one feels and thinks using the mass media available to you. In this case, an art publication."**

Kohkoku Magazine, number 1
2001

Front and back cover

Jon Barnbrook redesigned the magazine Kohkoku based on the idea of the square. That implied changing the format and banner and designing a new font for the magazine.

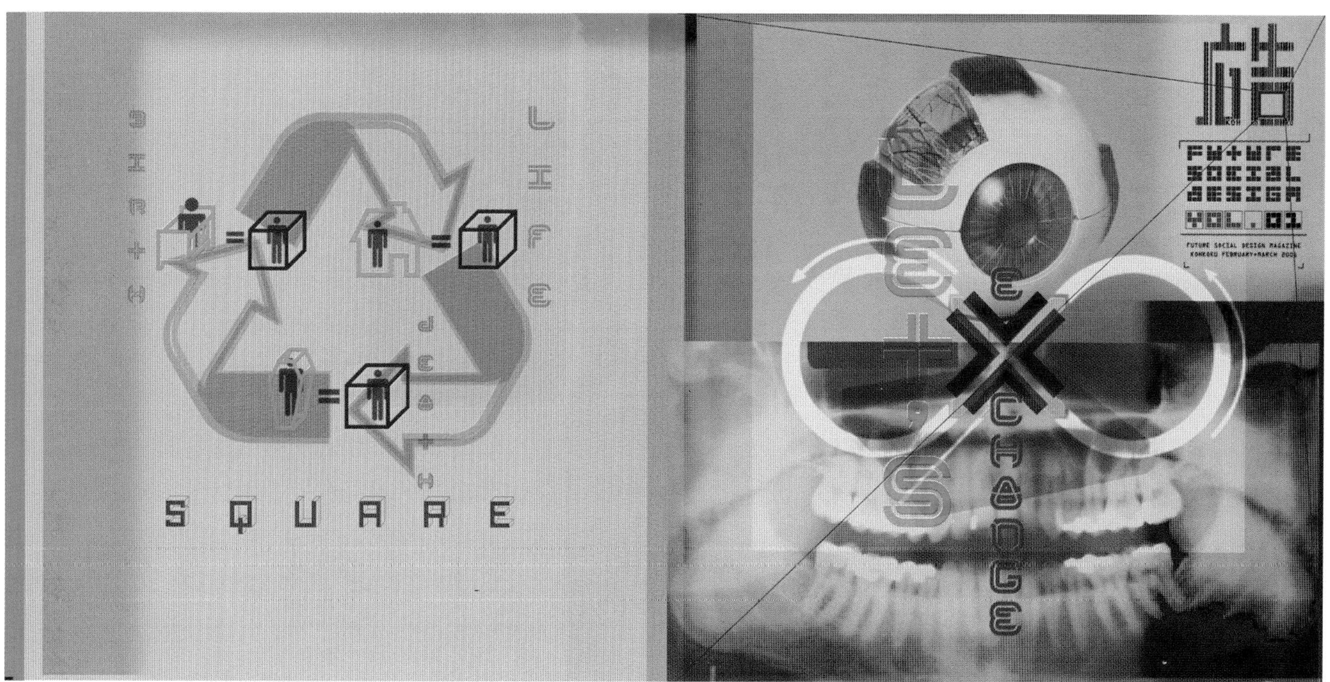

Kohkoku Magazine
Magazine

Year: 2001
Client: Kohkoku Magazine

Typography as an Element of Reflection
Jon sketches his fonts with paper and pencil before doing them on the computer. His typefaces emerge from an idea or from his own daily experiences. His training as a font designer came before the widespread introduction of Macintosh in design studios, something he is glad of, as it allowed him to learn the basics of fonts before experimenting with the new technology.

Jon completely agrees with Bradbury Thompson that to be a good font designer one must take an interest in all aspects of life: **"Typography has to do with cultural exchange and communication among people. If you want to dedicate yourself to it you have to take an interest in culture, in life itself,"** he states.

Jon takes an interest in 20th century history in general, and more specifically in the history of typography. **"The different interpretations of history that they tell you about when you're at school or the ones written in newspapers make me reflect on the idea of truth. I think that one of the reasons why I dedicate myself to typography is to be able to present the truth through the printed word, or at least intervene between the latter and the public."**

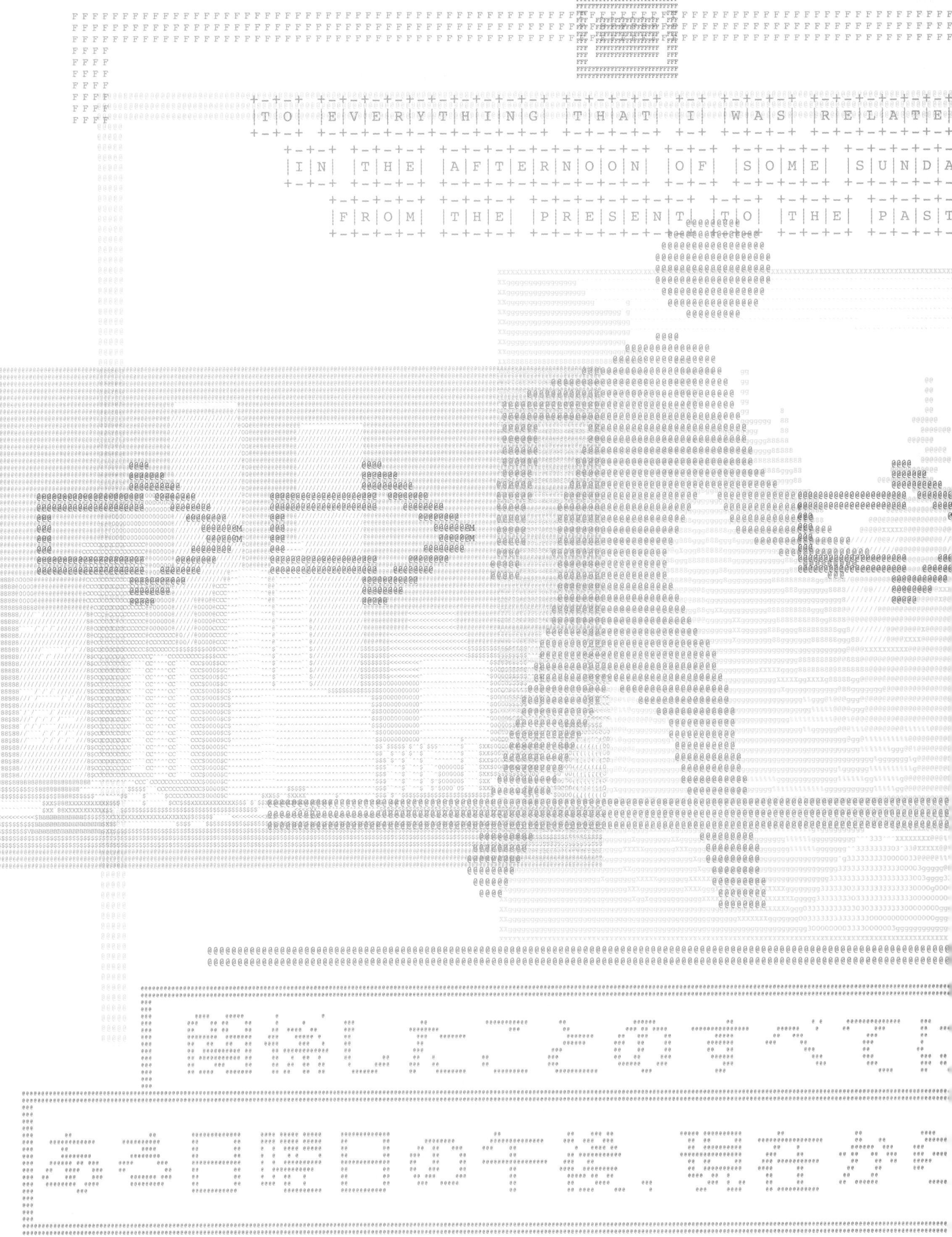
TO EVERYTHING THAT I WAS RELATE
IN THE AFTERNOON OF SOME SUNDA
FROM THE PRESENT TO THE PAST

Kohkoku Magazine, number 2
2001

Front and back cover
Inside pages

Basing himself on what some call ASCII Art, Jon employs characters as modular elements in order to construct images and texts – a resource that permits him to reflect on the essence of typography as a generator of visual and mental representations.

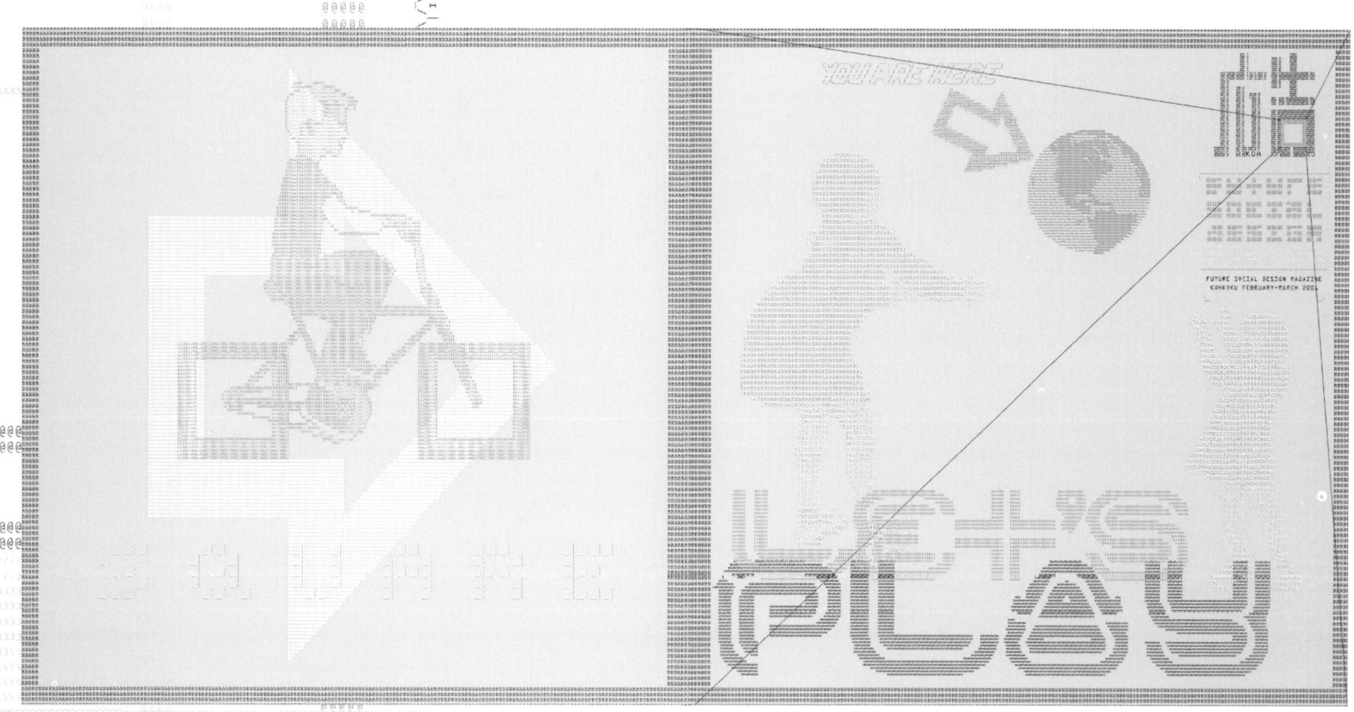

And he adds, **"When you work as a graphic designer you risk producing a bunch of 'propaganda'. I find it incredible that no one ever questions this."**

His attitude towards the profession makes him feel offended by the Modern Movement, considering that its defenders have betrayed its original philosophy: **"It was a visual language that was supposed to give shape to a socialist utopia and instead it became the standard language of capitalism."** Barnbrook does not believe that a designer has to limit himself to being a sort of neutral messenger: **"I don't trust the capitalist system enough to do it."** he says.

MARTIN LUTHER
IS DEAD
X
KARL MARX
WAS RIGHT
マルティン・ルターの失効×カール・マルクスの台頭＝
現代の経営者に突きつけられた超難題
Martin Luther is dead x Karl Marx was right =
mega-challenges for the modern manager
mega-challenges
for the modern manager

extract from "Funky Business" by J.Ridderstråle & K.Nordström

「ファンキービジネス」（須田泰成＆中山ゆーじん訳）より

見ようによっては人間も商品と同じことである。人間は鏡をもってこの世に生まれてくるのでもなければ、私は私である、というフィヒテ流の哲学者として生まれてくるのでもないから、人間は最初はまず他の人間のなかに自分を映してみるのである。人間ペテロは、彼と同等なものとしての人間パウロに関係することによって、はじめて人間としての自分自身に関係するのである。しかし、それとともに、またペテロにとっては、パウロの全体が、そのパウロ的な肉体のままで、人間という種属の現象形態として認められるのである。

カール・マルクス「資本論」（岡崎次郎訳：大月書店国民文庫）より

In a sort of way, it is with man as with commodities. Since he comes into the world neither with a looking glass in his hand, nor as a Fichtian philosopher, to whom “I am I” is sufficient, man first sees and recognises himself in other men. Peter only establishes his own identity as a man by first comparing himself with Paul as being of like kind. And thereby Paul, just as he stands in his Pauline personality, becomes to Peter the type of the genus homo.

Extract from “Das Kapital” by Karl Marx

Thonik

Thonik
Amsterdam, Holland

"The Concept is the Style"

Founded in 2000 by Thomas Widdershoven (1960) and Nikki Gonnissen (1967), **Thonik** is one of the Dutch design studios with the greatest international projection.

Thomas studied design at the Rietveld Academy (Amsterdam) after first reading philosophy, and Nikki studied at the Hogeschool voor de Kunsten (Utrecht). They have been living and working together continuously since 1993, producing original and innovative graphic work with their personal approach to design from a conceptual standpoint.

Their style, if we might call it that, could be defined as a determinate attitude to the commission – they are the ones who decide what the client needs, and not the other way round – and by the development of work processes strongly founded on conceptualisation.

For Thonik the fundamental thing is the idea and, although they resort to common elements in many of their projects, the ideas are what determine the process. For them **"if the idea is good, the rest flows naturally."**

The aesthetic aspect, the formal, the composition hardly play an important role. Everything comes down to taking the original concept to its most logical conclusion, in doing so employing common formal solutions and a single font for most of their jobs – **Avenir** by Adrian Frutiger.

Thonik is at the forefront of a whole generation of young designers who, adopting a less servile stance vis-à-vis the commission, explore the frontiers of the profession in order to play a role more akin to that of strategists, conceptual artists or bandleaders than to graphic designers, in the traditional sense of the term.

HETHE
BESTE
VANOF
WIM T.
SCHIP
HARRY RUHÉ PERS

› Following pages:
The Best of Wim T. Schippers
Front cover, back cover
and inside pages

The Best of Wim T. Schippers
Catalogue

Year: 1997
Client: Centraal Museum, Utrecht

Font used: Helvetica

The Catalogue as an Autonomous Piece

Thonik designs art catalogues and books in a quite unconventional manner, presenting the artist's work as an extension of itself, instead simply reproducing it through images. **"A catalogue is meaningful when it can function as autonomous piece."**

In the design of the catalogue about Wim T. Schippers – artist who belongs to the Fluxus movement – for the Centraal Museum of Utrecht, Thonik employs the text in the image of the cover, playing with the font and colour in order to posit a bilingual solution in the title.

"In book design, especially those dedicated to artists, a photographic image is usually put on the cover. A typographic image, on the other hand, helps the book to look more like a book," Thomas argues.

Thonik had to accommodate two languages – English and Dutch – on the pages of this catalogue. Thus, instead of designing a traditional mockup where the use of typographic styles (bold, italics, etc.) is a frequent compositional resource for distinguishing texts in different languages, Thonik resolves the problem by superposing the texts in green and red, and includes two transparent plastic sheets – green

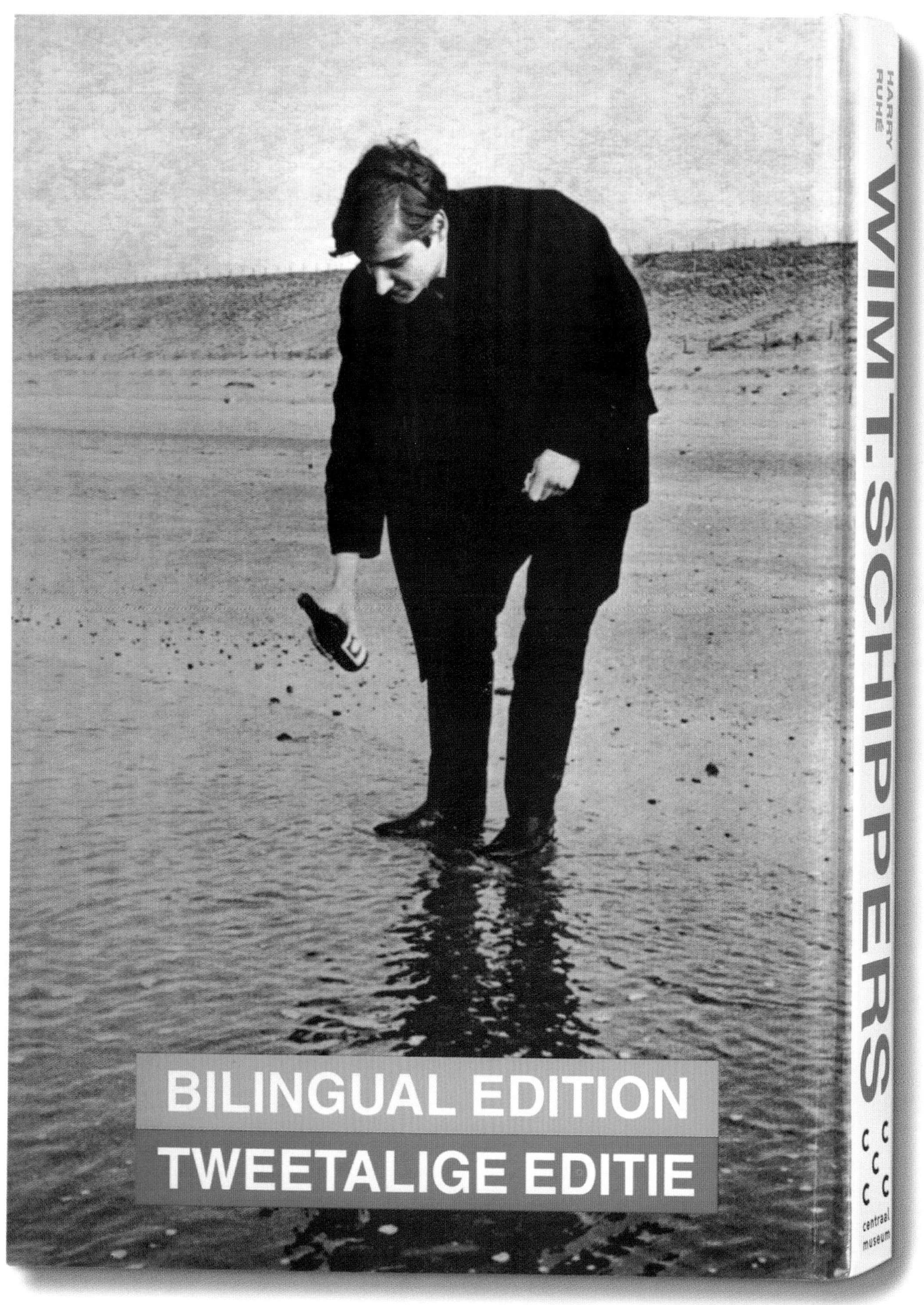
BILINGUAL EDITION
TWEETALIGE EDITIE
HARRY RUHE
WIM T. SCHIPPERS
centraal museum

HETHE BESTE VAN OF WIM T. SCHIP PERS

HARRY RUHÉ

Waldolala

Chapter eleven
Elfde Hoofdstuk

In which the television adventures of a night-club owner are debated, and The Onan sinks ingloriously

Waarin de televisieavonturen van een nachtclubeigenaar worden behandeld, en De Onan roemloos ten onder gaat

De Molière van Nederland. Dát was Wim T. Schippers volgens Gied Jaspars. In een interview met de Haagse Post legde hij uit waarom: 'Ik ken niemand die zulke ad remme dialogen kan schrijven. (...) Molière. In die termen van grootte denk ik. Als Wim iets maakt, kun je nooit zeggen

Al in het vr
Assemblag
ningen krijg
zilveren pe
teksten ged
jaren lang w
een boek 'v
for Advanc
tiek van de
Verenigde S
pelijke werk
Ook in de s
een belang
voor, inclus
gen die daa
het wel lukt
dig gesleut
gevallen (lijk

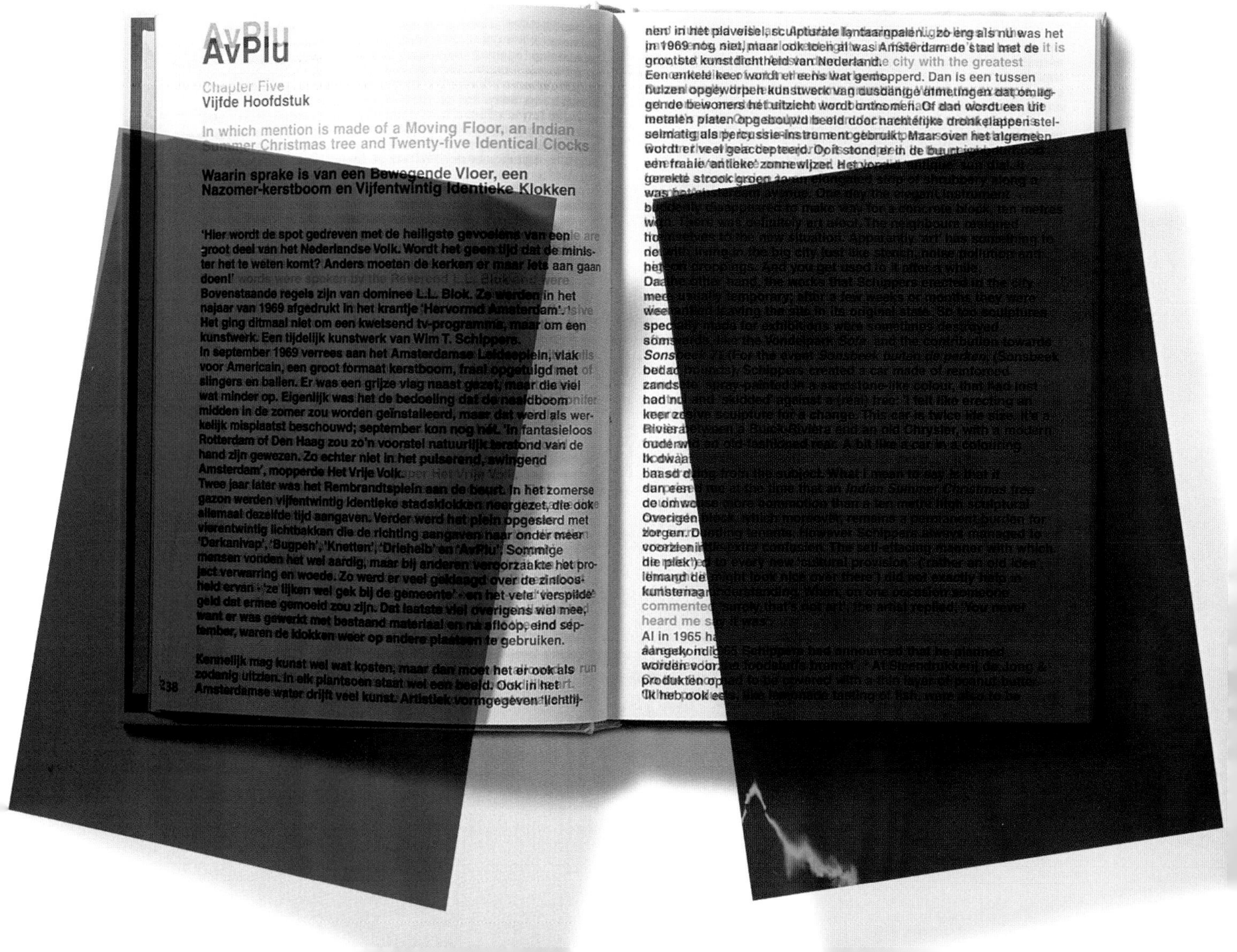

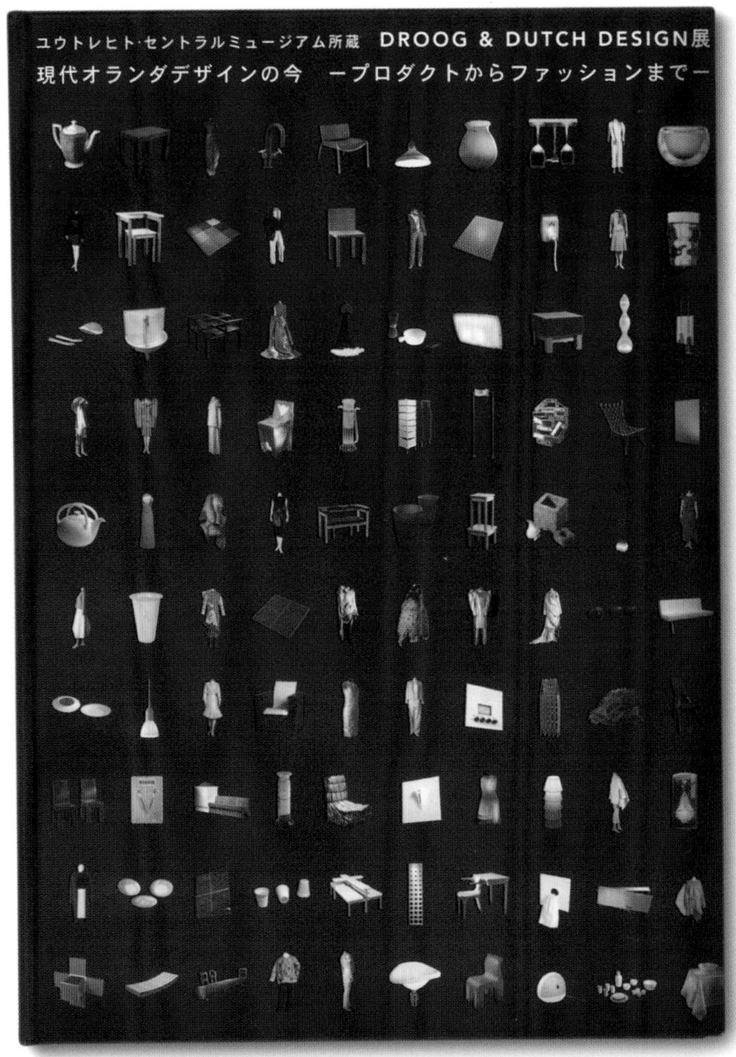

and red – in the book so that the texts can be visualised in one language or the other.

The images, printed as duotones with these same two inks, also acquire a double reading.

At the front of the book, and in the most typical Fluxus style, is attached an envelope with a small selection of full colour lamina reproductions of Schippers's work.

To underscore the conceptual aspect and avoid questions of personal taste intervening in the design process, Thonik manages the different options (formats, colours, types of paper, fonts, etc.) by first establishing a set of parameters which are later repeated with greater or lesser frequency. This is the case with the font, where the habitual choice is Avenir.

"At first we thought about using FF Meta typeface as the 'Helvetica' of the nineties. Until we realised that the 'Helvetica of the nineties' was Helvetica typeface, so we used it for the Wim T. Schippers catalogue. But Helvetica had become the new font for designers and everyone was using it, so we opted for another font. We liked Avenir. It's like a Futura but much friendlier, less geometric. The 'O' is very rounded and the uppercase 'R', for example, is much better than the Helvetica."

Conscious or not, the fact is that with these somewhat restrictive measures in the shaping of their projects Thonik are creating their own identity. What they adopt as a standard to emphasise the importance of the concept ends up generating a particular style: the Thonik 'style'.

Droog & Dutch Design
2000

Cover and inside pages

Catalogue for an exhibition at the Centraal Museum (Utrecht) combining Dutch fashion with objects designed by the Droog Design studio.

Over an absolutely black background, the objects are shown as if they were icons, playing with the proportions and the perspectives of visualisation.

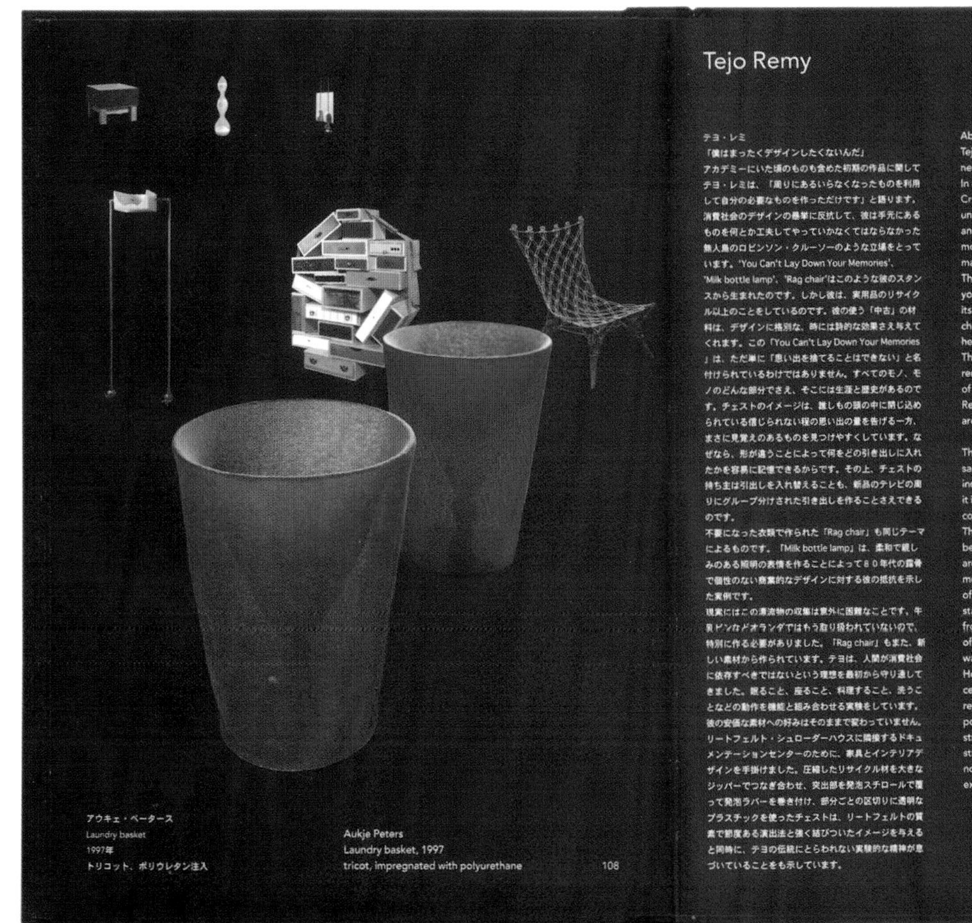

Tejo Remy

テヨ・レミ
「僕はまったくデザインしたくないんだ」
アカデミーにいた頃のものも含めた初期の作品に関してテヨ・レミは、「周りにあるいらなくなったものを利用して自分の必要なものを作っただけです」と語ります。消費社会のデザインの暴挙に反抗して、彼は手元にあるものを何とか工夫してやっていかなくてはならなかった無人島のロビンソン・クルーソーのような立場をとっています。'You Can't Lay Down Your Memories'、'Milk bottle lamp'、'Rag chair'はこのような彼のスタンスから生まれたのです。しかし彼は、実用品のリサイクル以上のことをしているのです。彼の使う「中古」の材料は、デザインに格別な、時には詩的な効果さえ与えてくれます。この「You Can't Lay Down Your Memories」は、ただ単に「思い出を捨てることはできない」と名付けられているわけではありません。すべてのモノ、モノのどんな部分でさえ、そこには生涯と歴史があるのです。チェストのイメージは、誰しもの頭の中に閉じ込められている信じられない程の思い出の量を告げる一方、まさに見覚えのあるものを見つけやすくしています。なぜなら、形が違うことによって何をどの引き出しに入れたかを容易に記憶できるからです。その上、チェストの持ち主は引出しを入れ替えることも、新品のテレビの周りにグループ分けされた引き出しを作ることさえできるのです。
不要になった衣類で作られた「Rag chair」も同じテーマによるものです。「Milk bottle lamp」は、柔和で親しみのある照明の表情を作ることによって８０年代の露骨で個性のない商業的なデザインに対する彼の抵抗を示した実例です。
現実にはこの漂流物の収集は意外に困難なことです。牛乳ビンなどオランダではもう取り扱われていないので、特別に作る必要がありました。「Rag chair」もまた、新しい素材から作られています。テヨは、人間が消費社会に依存すべきではないという理想を最初から守り通してきました。眠ること、座ること、料理すること、洗うことなどの動作を機能と組み合わせる実験をしています。彼の安価な素材への好みはそのままで変わっていません。リートフェルト・シュローダーハウスに隣接するドキュメンテーションセンターのために、家具とインテリアデザインを手掛けました。圧縮したリサイクル材を大きなジッパーでつなぎ合わせ、突出部を発泡スチロールで覆って発泡ラバーを巻き付け、部分ごとの区切りに透明なプラスチックを使ったチェストは、リートフェルトの質素で節度ある演出法と強く結びついたイメージを与えると同時に、テヨの伝統にとらわれない実験的な精神が息づいていることをも示しています。

About his earliest work, part of which was made at the academy, Tejo Remy tends to say that he just made things "that he needed, preferably from discarded objects in his environment". In reaction to consumer terrorism, he acts as a kind of Robinson Crusoe, a man who has to survive with what is available on an uninhabited island. The chest of drawers, the milk bottle lamp and the rag chair were created in this way. However, Remy does more than merely recycle appliances. The "second-hand" materials that he makes create often have a poetic quality. The title of the chest of drawers is obvious: "You can't lay down your memories". Each object, even each part of an object has its own life, its own history. On the one hand the image of the chest refers to the chaotic store of memories in everyone's head, while on the other hand it makes it easier to find things. This is because the different drawers make it easier to remember where objects are stored. Moreover, the owner of the chest can decide himself how drawers are arranged. Remy even made an item where the drawers were grouped around a brand new television.

The rag chair, made from discarded clothes continues on the same theme. The milk bottle lamp does not bear the same individual stamp. However, because of its soft, friendly light it is an example of Remy's protest against the hard, impersonal, commercial design of the 1980s.
The production of these beachcomber's objects proved to be more difficult in practice than expected. The milk bottles are no longer produced in the Netherlands. Consequently they must be specially produced. The rag chair is also made of new material. Tejo Remy has stuck to one of his original starting-points, the idea that people should be independent from consumer society. He experiments with a combination of functions in mobile objects: sleeping, sitting, cooking and washing all in one. His love of cheap materials has not changed. He designed the interior and furniture for the documentation centre next to the Rietveld Schröder house. Chests of pressed recycled material, connected by large zips, a counter clad with polyurethane foam, rolled polyurethane rubber seperated by strips of transparent plastic create an image that contrasts strongly with the sober, controlled drama of Rietveld's work, but nonetheless breathes the same spirit of unconventionality and experiment. (IvZ)

アウキェ・ペータース
Laundry basket
1997年
トリコット、ポリウレタン注入

Aukje Peters
Laundry basket, 1997
tricot, impregnated with polyurethane

108

El Mundo

Rodrigo Sánchez
Madrid, Spain

"The Presence of the Letter"

Rodrigo Sánchez has a degree in journalism from the Universidad Complutense de Madrid. It was during his time at university that he became familiar with newspaper design and took the decision to specialise in the field.

During his latter years at the university he combined his studies with a job as an editor and layout artist at the Madrid dailies **ABC** and **Cinco Días**.

Rodrigo was a founding member of the daily **El Sol** (Madrid, 1990-1992). There he met Roger Black and Eduardo Danilo. This experience was a point of inflection in his professional career: **"I learned to understand a type of design that goes beyond the purely aesthetic and purely informative; a design that takes typography, blank spaces and images much further than I could have ever imagined."**

The knowledge and experience he acquired in those years facilitated his getting a job at another daily, **El Mundo**, as head of graphics for the Sunday supplement and colour sections.

Cover **Metrópoli** no. 365
Quieres ser una estrella del rock?

Proposals and final cover
(right-hand page)

"The aesthetic reference for the cover of this issue is the sort of concert posters with hand-done fonts where the typography and words are mixed, adapting perfectly to format of the poster.
On this occasion we tried to follow as closely as possible that aesthetic, with a heterodox font done by hand specially for this project. Once we had finished the design of the font we got down to combining the colours in order to differentiate the different words and phrases and make it as legible as possible."

LA REVISTA DE MADRID
Nº 365
DEL 23 AL 29 DE MAYO DE 1997
LOCALES DE ENSAYO
ESCUELAS
TIENDAS
SALAS DE CONCIERTOS
RADIO
DISCOGRAFICAS INDEPENDIENTES
CONCIERTOS
ESTUDIOS

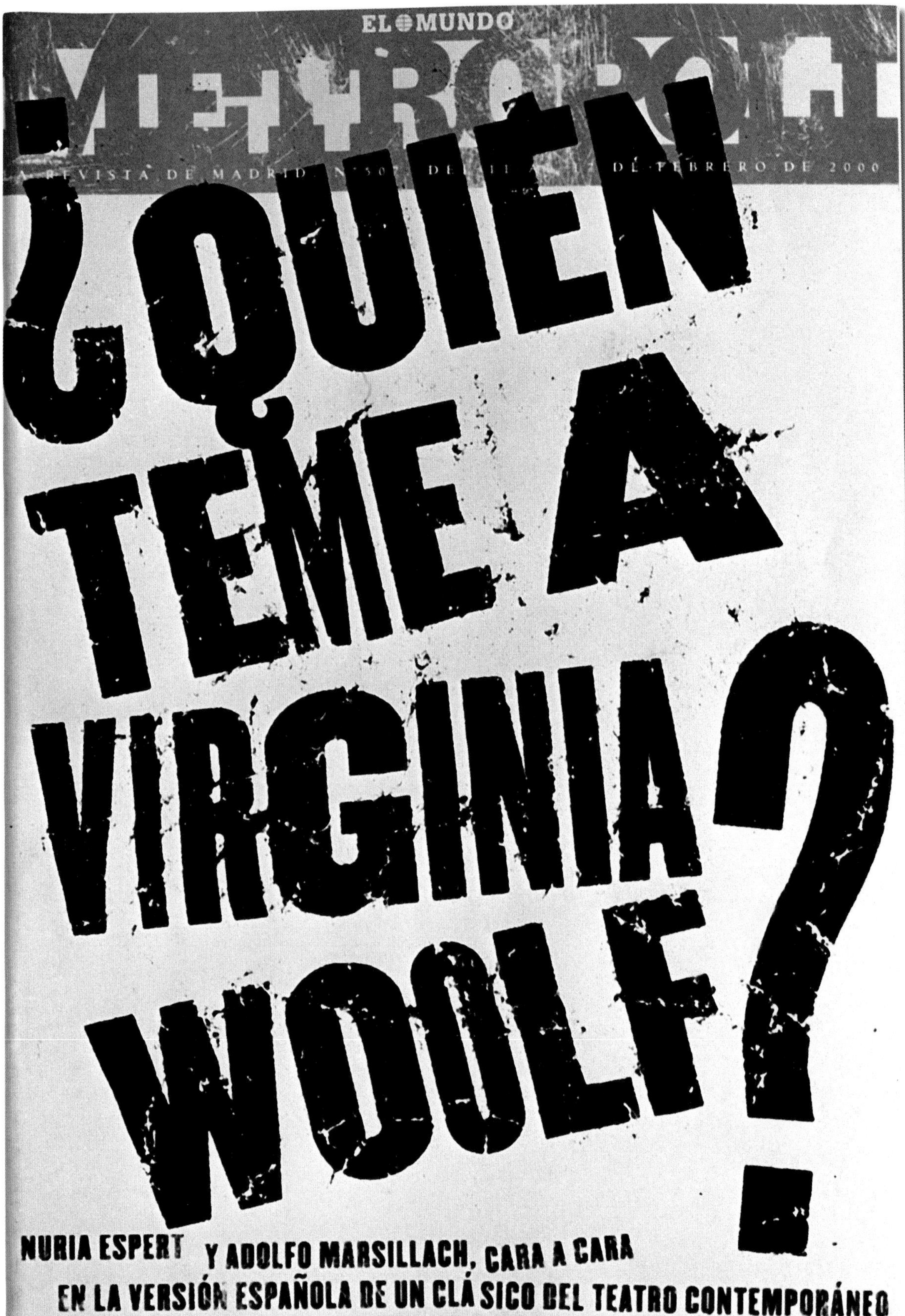

EL MUNDO

METRÓPOLI

LA REVISTA DE MADRID. Nº 507. DEL 11 AL 17 DE FEBRERO DE 2000

¿QUIÉN TEME A VIRGINIA WOOLF?

NURIA ESPERT Y ADOLFO MARSILLACH, CARA A CARA EN LA VERSIÓN ESPAÑOLA DE UN CLÁSICO DEL TEATRO CONTEMPORÁNEO

‹ Cover **Metrópoli**. February, 2000
¿Quién teme a Virginia Woolf?

Cover **Metrópoli**. July, 1998
Armageddon

"A meteorite hurtles towards Earth. The impact will wipe out all life on the planet. We applied a Photoshop effect to give the sensation of speed. Thus, with a simple title – that of the film – and with a blurred background text – the biblical text of the apocalypse – we get a meteoritic cover."

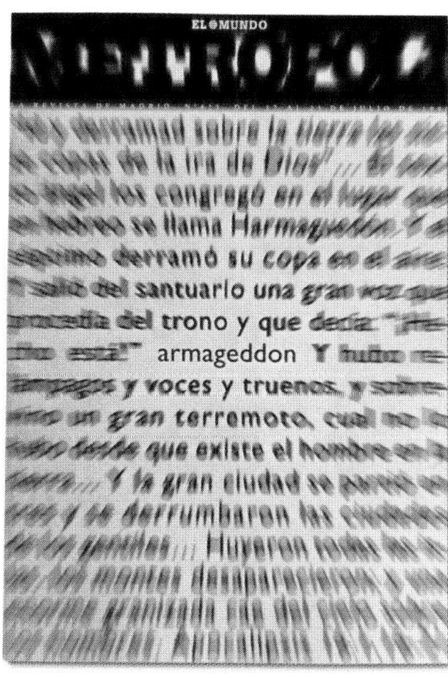

Cover **Metrópoli**. October, 2000
George Clooney / O'Brother

"In my work I often pay homage to Saul Bass, one of my great graphic design idols."

Cover **Metrópoli**. April, 1997
1st Madrid International Film Festival

"For this cover our reference was the modular and constructivist compositions of the Soviet and German avant-garde."

Metrópolis
Weekly supplement

Client: El Mundo, Unidad Editorial, SA.

20 x 28.5 cm. 92 pages. Full colour printing. Weekly

The Typography is the Message

Metrópoli is the entertainment and leisure supplement for the city of Madrid of the daily El Mundo. The content focuses on providing information about premieres, the latest in film, music and theatre, recommended restaurants, bars, shops and so on. In short, all the entertainment choices for Madrid residents in their free time and on weekends.

The circulation is local – the Madrid metropolitan area and surrounding communities – and the target public is the family, addressing the entertainment demands of all age groups.

"There's no politics or finance, sports only rarely... No one expects anything original from a publication that only informs about entertainment events in a city, apart from the faces of famous actors and actresses..." Rodrigo comments.

But Metrópoli has begun to raise eyebrows with the way it presents its themes on the cover. Not content with being a cold showcase for the theme that it refers to, Rodrigo opts for involving himself and, as far as possible, making the cover part of it. The cover itself becomes newsworthy, either as a complement to the spectacle or as a part of it. For Rodrigo, the fundamental thing in the cover is the involve-

EL MUNDO
METRÓPOLI
LA REVISTA DE MADRID. Nº581. DEL 13 AL 19 DE JULIO DE 2001
Shrek,
un ogro poco convencional
de un cuento
de hadas
poco convencional
en una película de animación poco convencional

‹ Cover **Metrópoli**. July, 2001
Shrek

"The graphic work for 'Shrek' emerged out of the impossibility of commissioning an illustration to the newspaper's habitual artists. I needed a quick solution, so I opted to do the drawing myself. And the sort of painting I'm best at is lettering. I just had to use an image of the film character as the background and start covering it with letterings of varying thickness and size and in the appropriate orientation according to the parts of the character."

Cover **Metrópoli**. November, 1999
Italian restaurants

"Bar codes give you a lot to play around with. In this case they are the spaghetti. We wanted to do a simple yet impactive cover. Even the bar code corresponds to that day's issue of our newspaper."

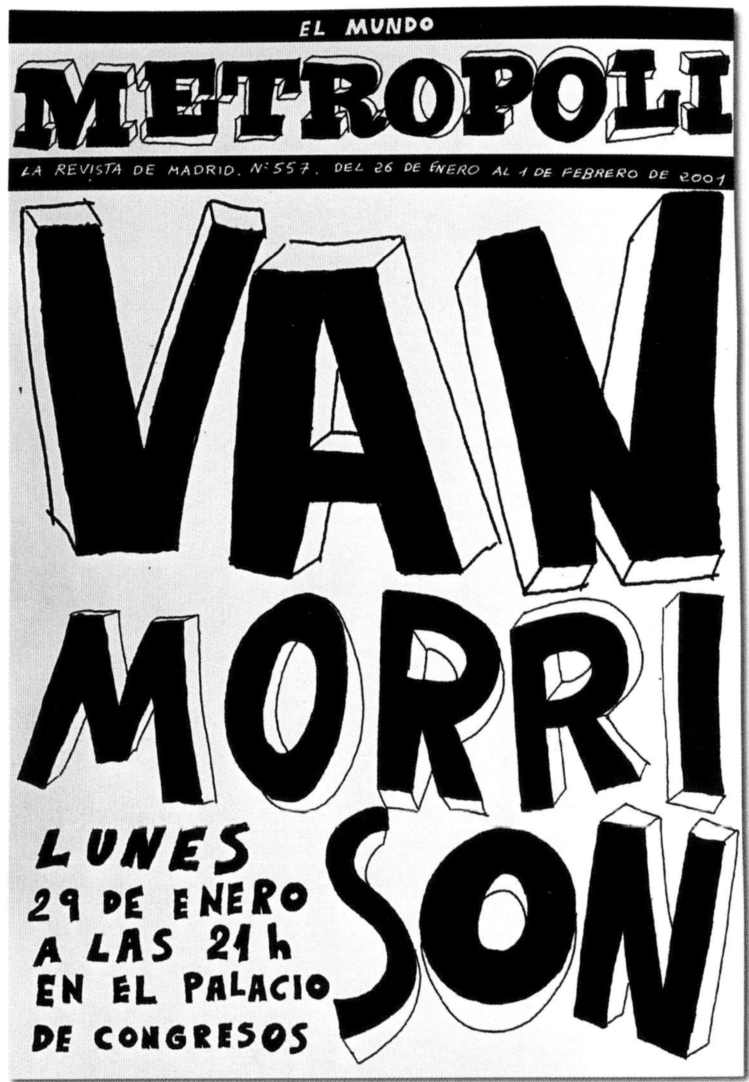

Cover **Metrópoli**. February, 2001
Van Morrison

ment in the chosen theme: **"Any project must start with the need to communicate an idea to a possible reader or viewer,"** he explains.

He uses such resources as enlarging or shrinking of the body of text and the size of the image, absence or exaggeration of the blank space, excess or economy of elements, irony and sense of humour, and so on. For the design team the aim is to surprise the reader with the choice of a good idea and its subsequent graphic realisation.

The starting point for the graphic execution is the font. For Rodrigo, the font **"is the direct message, without excesses, without obstacles, without ornamentation, without problems. The font is the image, the drawing, the design. There is nothing more beautiful and better designed than a letter."**

According to Roger Black, typography is the essential design element for magazines, because magazines essentially consist of words. Rodrigo agrees with this statement and takes the cover as his starting point: **"A typographic cover demands, general speaking, twice the time required for doing a cover with a photo or an illustration as its base."** And he adds, **"Designers often associate, sometimes unconsciously, certain typefaces with certain emotions or sensations. There is also a residual aesthetic culture that comes into play which associates themes or atmospheres with certain typographic styles."** All of this is determinate in the choice of a certain type of lettering for a cover theme.

When he works with the font, and throughout the work process, Rodrigo bears in mind a series of factors, such as surprise, clarity, size and impact, which determine the result of the final work.

In his own words: **"The surprise may appear without your looking for it, or some-**

El Mundo

Cover **Metrópoli**. January, 2001
Children's film

Proposals and final cover

"In this case my daughter Sofía was responsible for the font. I wanted a somewhat more elaborate work than what a child would do spontaneously, and so I asked Sofía to do the work with water and brushes of different thicknesses."

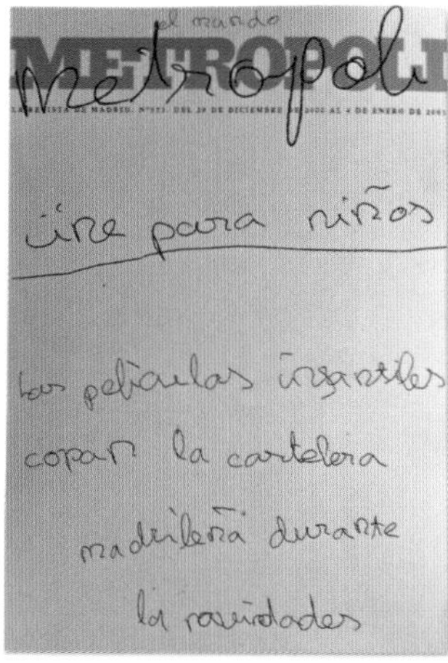

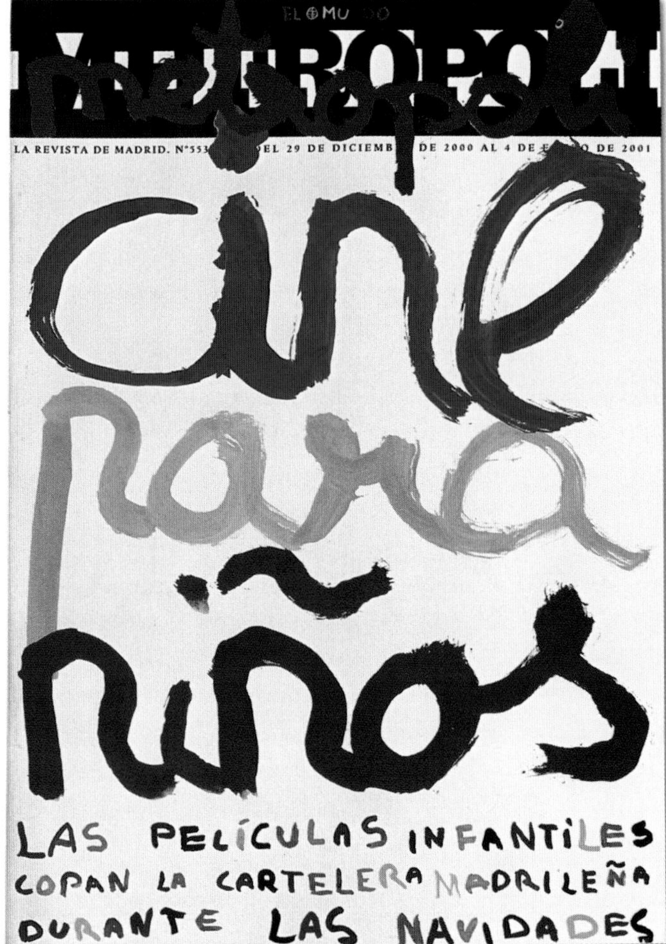

times the surprise is the 'non-surprise'. Clarity does not necessarily mean legibility, but rather clarity in the message that you wish to get across. The design of the typography transmits the emotion of the message. The size of the lettering helps you shout or whisper. The force or impact will depend on the application of all these parameters."

› Following page:
Cover **Metrópoli**. March, 1997
101 Dalmatians

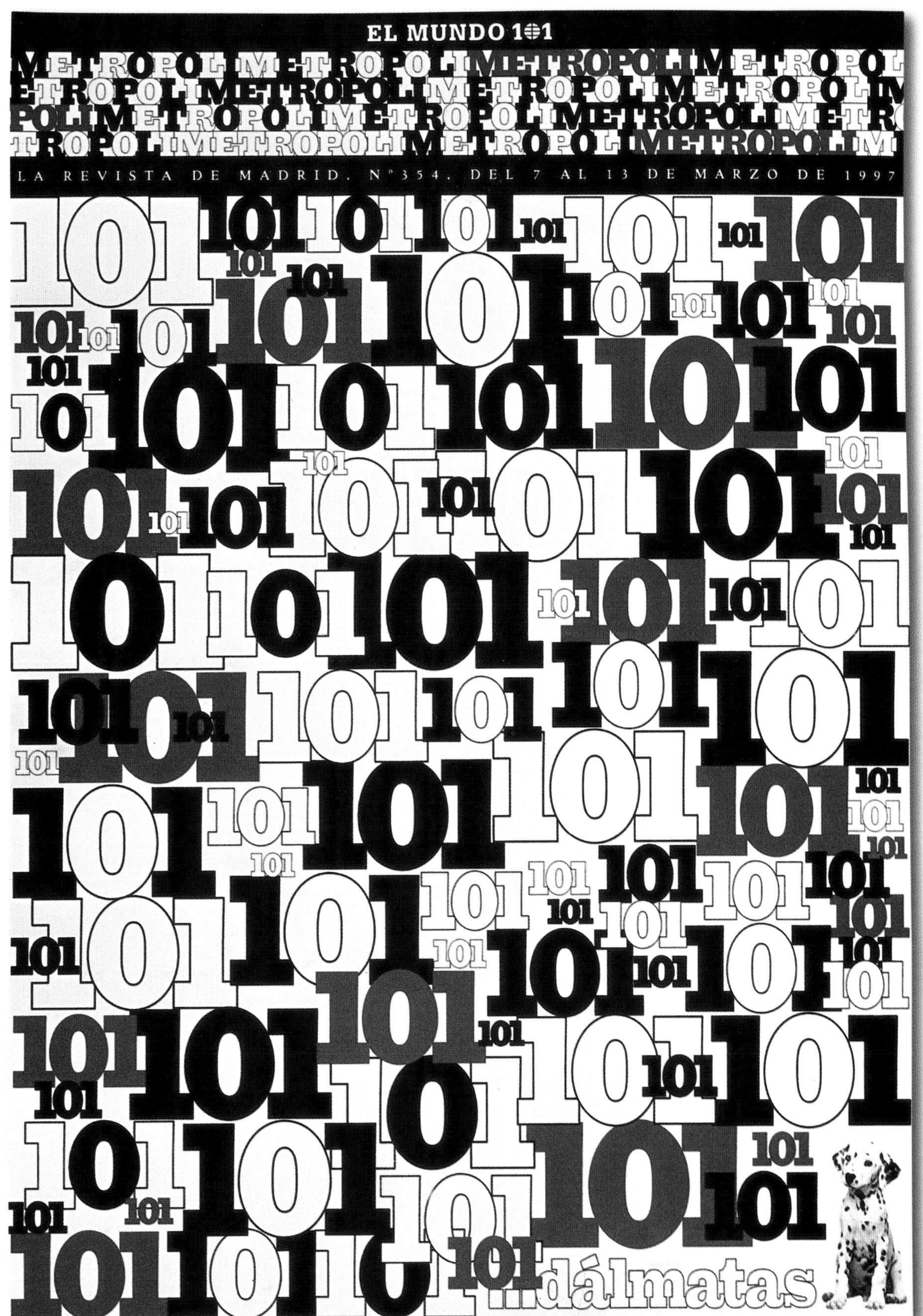
EL MUNDO 101
METROPOLI
LA REVISTA DE MADRID. Nº354. DEL 7 AL 13 DE MARZO DE 1997
101
...dálmatas

Jop van Bennekom

Jop van Bennekom
Amsterdam, Holland

"The Magazine as an Art Form"

Jop van Bennekom (1970) works as a designer and art director for a number of clients in the cultural and fashion fields. He teaches at the Rietveld Academy in Amsterdam and is also the editor of the architecture magazine **Forum**, as well as the creator and editor-in-chief of the magazine **Re-Magazine**.

In his publishing work he draws together all the elements that comprise the design such that the final product becomes an integrated piece.

His work reveals an air of freedom that allows him to take certain risks. As a creator, he approaches his projects from a personal perspective. In his view, **"those things that start from a personal point of view are the ones that can open new horizons."**

Re-Magazine

Covers numbers 4, 5 and 7
2000-2001

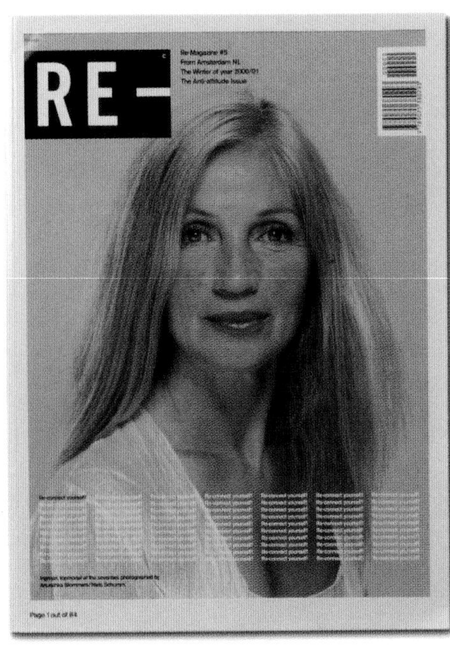

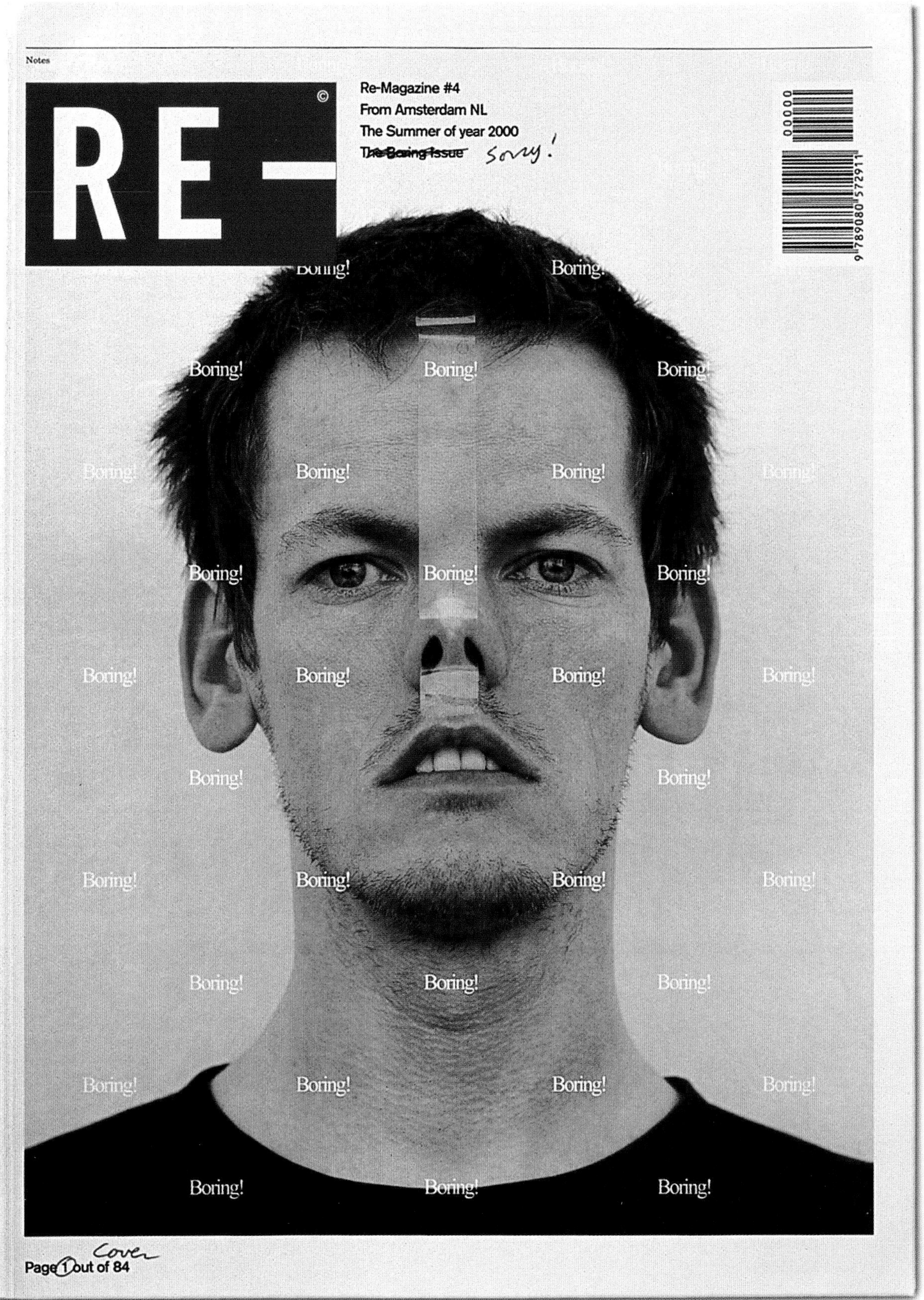
Notes
RE–
©
Re-Magazine #4
From Amsterdam NL
The Summer of year 2000
~~The Boring Issue~~
Sorry!
00000
9 789080 572911
Boring!
Cover
Page 1 out of 84

Re-Magazine, number 4
2000

Inside pages

Page 6 out of 84

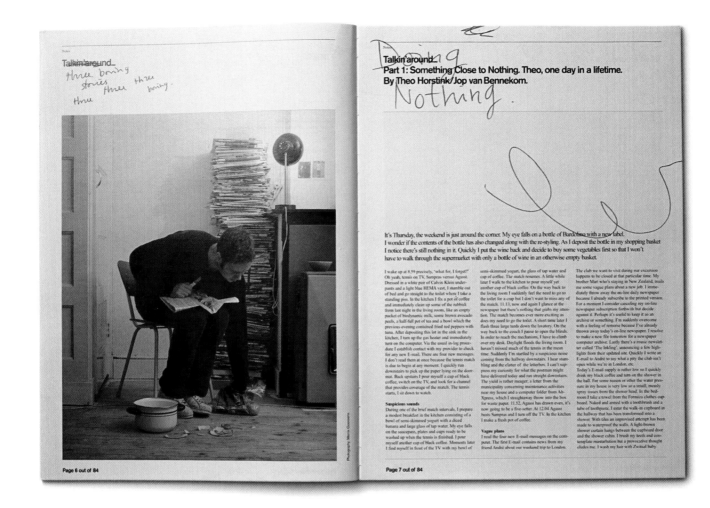

Talkin'around...
Part 1: Something Close to Nothing. Theo, one day in a lifetime.
By Theo Horstink/Jop van Bennekom.

It's Thursday, the weekend is just around the corner. My eye falls on a bottle of Bardolino with a new label. I wonder if the contents of the bottle has also changed along with the re-styling. As I deposit the bottle in my shopping basket I notice there's still nothing in it. Quickly I put the wine back and decide to buy some vegetables first so that I won't have to walk through the supermarket with only a bottle of wine in an otherwise empty basket.

Page 7 out of 84

Re-Magazine
Magazine

Year: 1997
Client: Re-Foundation

Fonts used: Times, Helvetica

22 x 29.5 cm. 84 pages. Full colour printing. Quarterly

Re-Thinking a Magazine

At first glance the design of Re-Magazine might appear formal and of little interest. But as one turns the pages, behind those friendly studio portraits, that orderly and clean layout, one perceives something disturbing.

Jop experiments with graphic stereotypes, with predictable references. He can design a magazine as if it were a novel or an instruction manual, with the aim of generating new meanings through a particular manner of composing the elements on the page. He likes to play with conventionalisms; to decontextualise the page typographically with the intention of suggesting other meanings. According to Jop, the key is in **"the layerness of meaning that needs to be balanced ... like a photographer sets up his lights to create magic in the image."**

What is experimental about Re-Magazine is not so much in the shaping of the contents but in the texts and the concepts worked with.

Re-Magazine is a design conceived in 1997 as a final academic project for the Jan van Eyck Academy. The magazine is not explicitly linked to any particular professional field, but rather deals with ideas associated with contemporary culture that in some way affect

Thank you Post-It.
Freestylin': an analysis by Wilfried Nijhof and Jop van Bennekom.
Photography by Maurice Scheltens / Not!

FreeStylin' Looking at forms of boredom. Creating clouds of text.

Page 16 out of 84 16

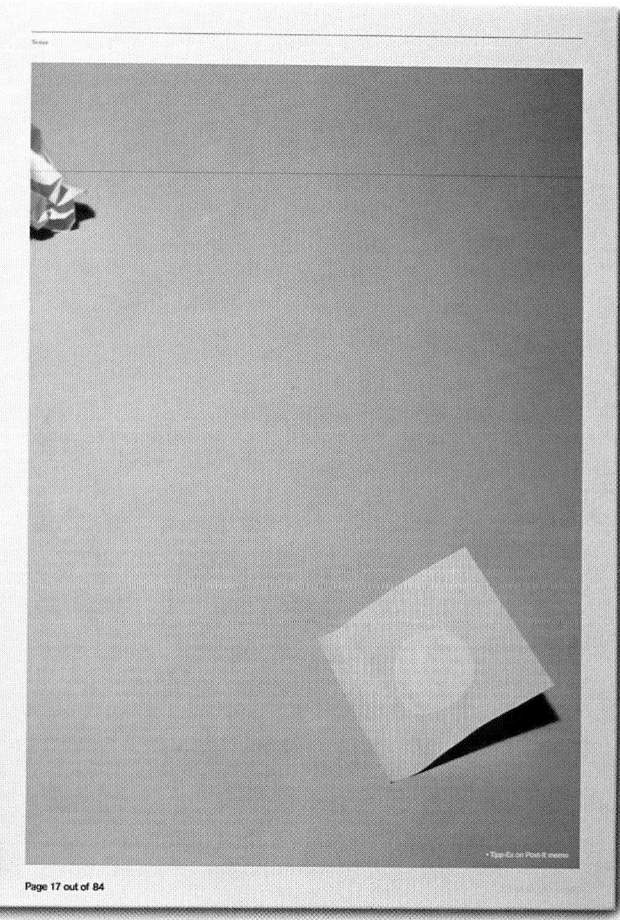

or concern Van Bennekom personally.

Jop takes a new approach to each issue, reacting to the world around him: **"I see a magazine as a work in itself. Like a band that releases a CD or a theatre group doing a play. It's a different approach towards the medium magazine which I have to explain every time."**

The magazine thus becomes a means of relating, a personal form of expression; ultimately, a form of art.

When he embarks on a job, Jop starts with an idea which provides the basis for the rest of the work, both the content and the form of the issue. Hence, one of the aims is to integrate all the elements that make up the magazine, including the publishing.

The font, from this standpoint, is just another element, contributing to eliminate the separation that might exist between the design and content.

Maintaining a graphic line recognisable as a publication, each issue of Re-Magazine presents differences in the design of its pages, with the intention of adapting it to the guidelines set.

Jop starts with the formal aspects, constructing a reticule as a foundation: **"I need a grid in order the break it,"** he says. **"The repetition of a grid turns into a harsh, obsessive and omnipresent system that battles its own organisational principle."**

Jop constructs a clean, balanced – almost aseptic – mockup in which white absorbs a good part of our attention. The texts follow a premeditated order, in certain contradiction with their content. The images are carefully executed and afforded a space commensurate with their importance.

As for the font, Job conceives it as a way of speaking, – **"Talking in a certain tone of voice;**

Re-Magazine, number 5
2001

Inside pages

tender, ironic, demanding, demanding..." He uses common sense in selecting his typefaces but avoids overly obvious choices: **"With the choice of a certain typeface I try to direct the meaning of a text. A very informal text set in a formal classic serif typeface I achieve an interesting contrast."**

Despite high circulation and international distribution, Jop does not compromise on the content or design. He works freely, without any sort of constraints and without taking into account any specific target audience for his magazine:

"There's the one that buys the magazine, the one that steals it and the bum who finds it in a trashbin."

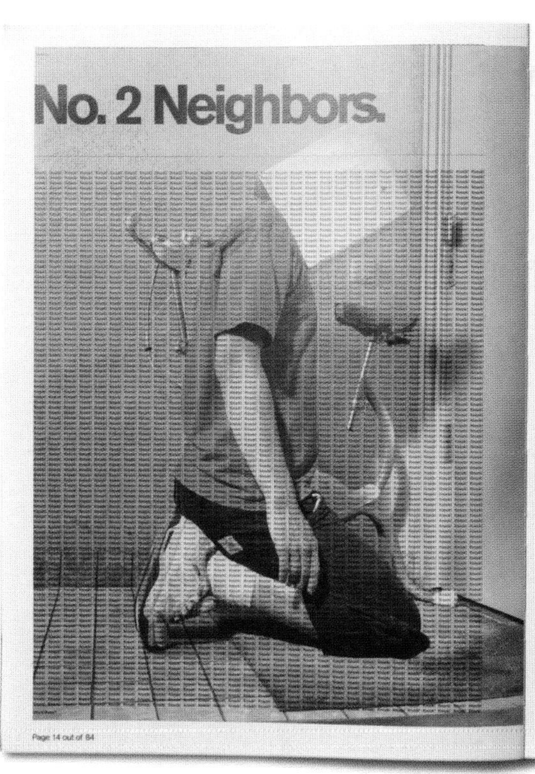

Re-connect attempt No. 2:
Neighbors.
Re-connect with neighbors you don't know.
Meet your neighbors, introduce yourself.
Hi, it's me!
Text: Jop van Bennekom/ Lemert Engelberts.
Photography: Misha de Ridder.

Ms. 47-f

Ms. 47-c

Page 15 out of 84

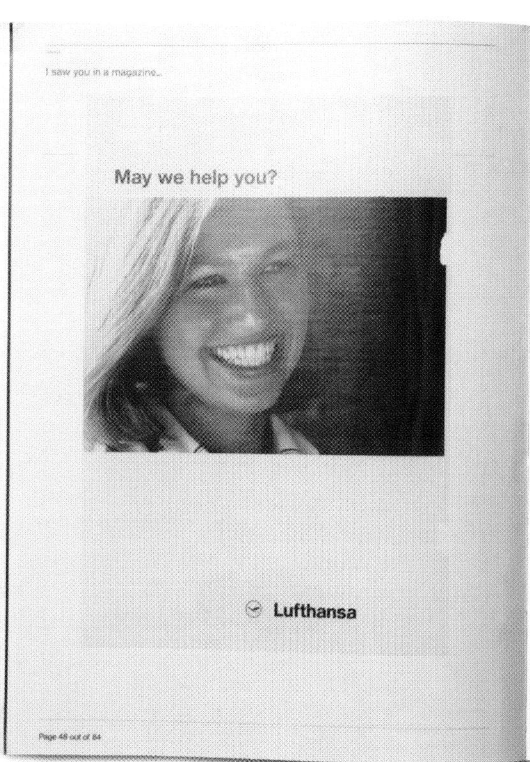

No. 9 Media.

Re-connect attempt No. 9:
Media.
Re-connect with an old issue of National Geographic.
Say hi to a face in the magazine.
Strike up a conversation.
Text: Jop van Bennekom.

May we help you?

Page 49 out of 84

Cahan & Associates

Cahan & Associates
San Francisco, United States

"The Importance of the Process"

Bill Cahan founded the **Cahan & Associates** agency in 1984. Since then he has obtained national and international recognition for his work on corporate and institutional projects, catalogues, packaging and company reports. In their graphic projects Cahan & Associates exemplify decidedly concept-based work:

"We're not interested in things that just look good, behind each project there must be a good idea."

Theirs are projects in which the commercial strategy determines the route to take. For Cahan, although the relationship between the two is often very close, strategy is more important than style. The success of a graphic solution can depend on that:

"A good design won't save a bad product, though a good product will depend on a good design to be successful."

Maxygen Annual Report
2000

Cover and double inside pages

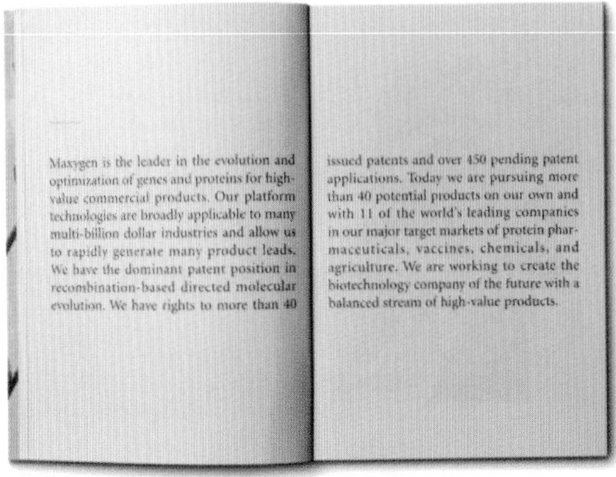
Maxygen is the leader in the evolution and optimization of genes and proteins for high-value commercial products. Our platform technologies are broadly applicable to many multi-billion dollar industries and allow us to rapidly generate many product leads. We have the dominant patent position in recombination-based directed molecular evolution. We have rights to more than 40 issued patents and over 450 pending patent applications. Today we are pursuing more than 40 potential products on our own and with 11 of the world's leading companies in our major target markets of protein pharmaceuticals, vaccines, chemicals, and agriculture. We are working to create the biotechnology company of the future with a balanced stream of high-value products.

Klein Bicycles Catalog
1997

Cover and inside pages

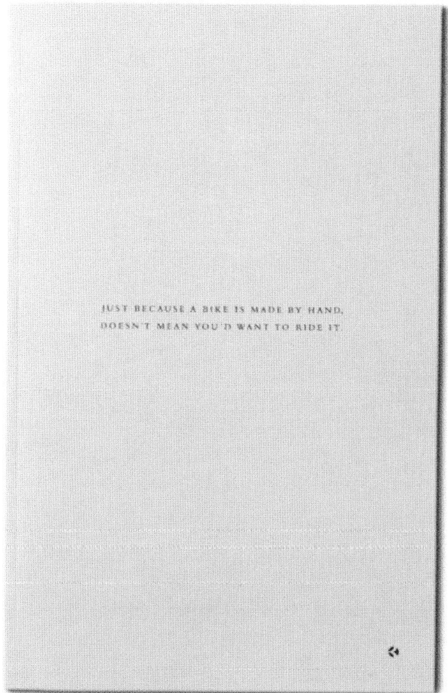

JUST BECAUSE A BIKE IS MADE BY HAND,
DOESN'T MEAN YOU'D WANT TO RIDE IT.

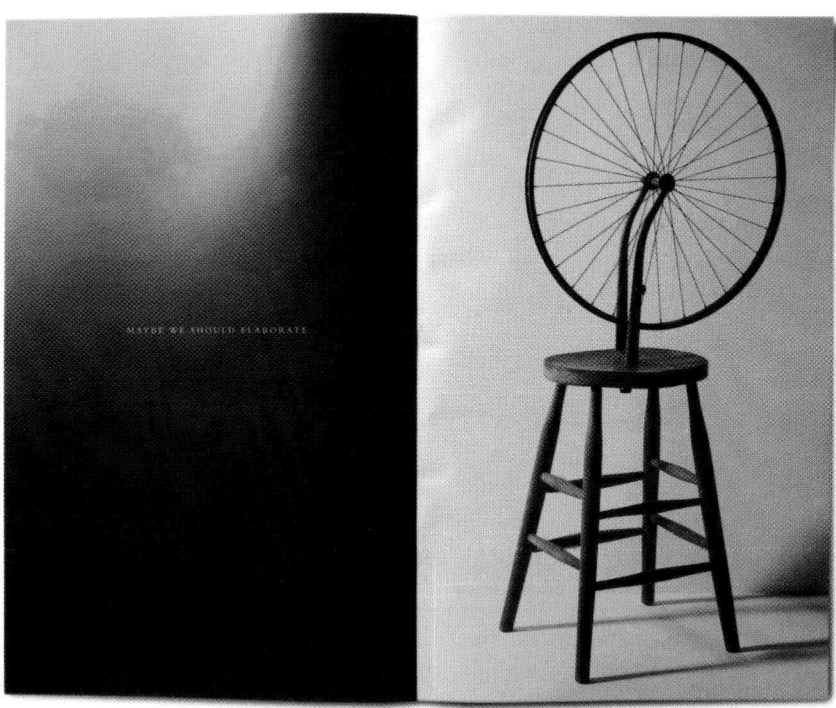

MAYBE WE SHOULD ELABORATE

Klein
Product catalogue

Year: 1998
Client: Klein Bicycles

Fonts used: Bembo

16,5 x 23.5 cm. 96 pages. 2 inks. Six-monthly

Elegance as Strategy

In graphic design, the superficial elements are easier to deal with than what is found in the inner layers and comprises the 'soul' of any project. For any designer, the challenge is to achieve a surface that is transparent enough to allow what is inside to shine through.
At the **Cahan & Associates** agency emotion forms part of this surface, thus drawing the reader in towards the content. Emotion is, for Cahan, **"necessary for presenting any product"**. That includes the editorial design projects done for a long list of corporations for whom the agency designs catalogues and annual reports, concentrating on the different changes in strategy that mark the companies.

"Each job is different given that it reflects different realities and contexts," comments Bill Cahan, head of the agency. **"Our reports not only have to inform and contain very precise information, but they have to entertain at the same time. They have to be different in order to transmit their strategic message clearly and intelligibly."**

The design process developed at Cahan & Associates allows them to avoid graphic solutions too close to the corporate contexts. In his

Klein Bicycles Catalog
1997

Double inside pages

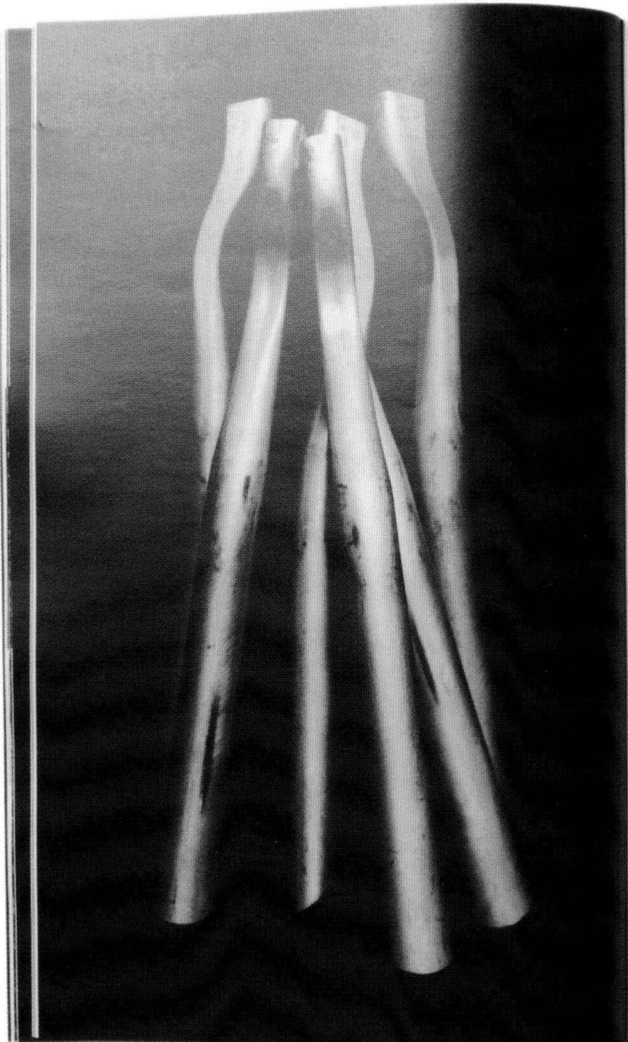

KLEIN

PULSE

Considering that Klein has made its reputation over the last 20 years as being extremely detailed, precise and ultimately exclusive, the use of the word 'value' with a Klein has not been a common adjective. Gary Klein just doesn't like to make anything but the best. Enter the Pulse series: dollar for dollar, ounce for ounce, feature for feature, the best mountain bike value of all time. At a featherweight 3.4 lbs., every Pulse is built with Klein Power Tubing, a relatively new Klein development which shaves tube weight by varying wall thicknesses only internally, as opposed to the time consuming process of also tapering externally. While the Attitude is slightly lighter than the Pulse, the weight is relative. Compared to any other manufacturer's top of the line aluminum frame, you'll likely find the Pulse lighter, stronger and better handling, because even though it provides great value, it's still a Klein.

approach to the content, Cahan goes beyond the information facilitated by the client. His goal is to find a concept, a true story that the readership can relate to so that they will take the company into consideration and remember their products and technology. **"It's not easy at all to find the right story. And often they don't provide us with the necessary the plots."** And he continues: **"We aren't satisfied with what the client gives us. We spend a lot of time with our clients, reading about their businesses, marketing plans, industry trends, anything that can give us different perspectives on the company. The key is in understanding the client and grasping their strategy."**

As in a competition, a single project is developed at the same time by several people within the agency. By delegating work to several designers, Cahan guarantees that the work is undertaken in a climate of greater freedom than if a single designer bore the entire responsibility for the commission. At the same time, this allows the client to see a variety of graphic solutions.

For the product catalogue designed for Klein, Cahan based his strategy on showing in detail those technological – their aerospace engineering – and conceptual elements which best define Klein as a brand name and which differentiate them from their competitors. **"What the client was asking for was a piece that would speak of the high quality of their bicycles, as a basic sales pitch, and that was different from the rest of the bicycle catalogues."**

The spirit that Cahan succeeds in capturing with graphics evokes an air of maturity that contrasts with most bicycle catalogues aimed at a younger public. Klein targets the customer who can spend more money on a presumably better quality bicycle.

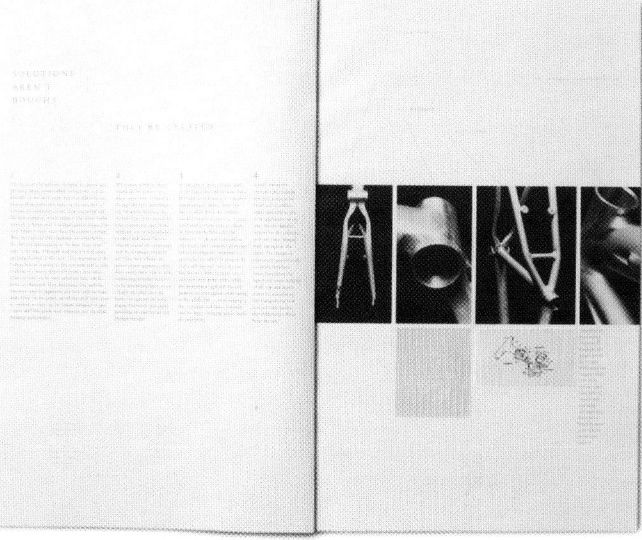

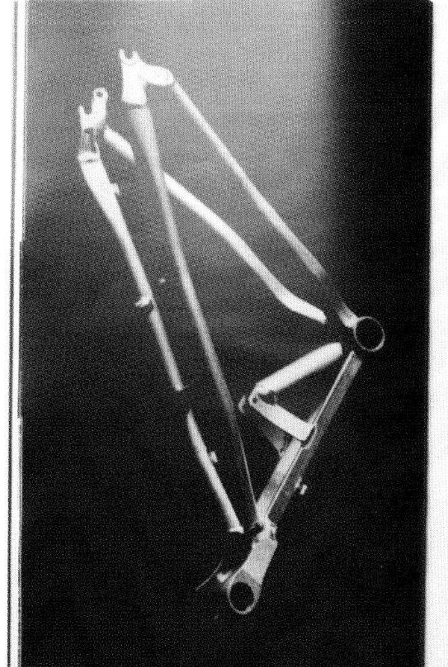

KLEIN
MANTRA
Most full suspension bikes have been designed as if the world was all downhill. But a good portion of land out there is flat and the rest is all uphill. The Mantra differs from most full suspension bikes in that it actually climbs better than a lot of hardtails, flies across the flatlands and still provides big bump performance when going downhill. Like all Kleins, the Mantra is super lightweight (up to five pounds lighter than comparably priced full suspension bikes). And the oversized Klein Torque Control Beam is connected to an ultra-stiff Unified Rear Triangle, which allows the Mantra frame to be more laterally rigid than many hardtails. The point of connection is an over-sized pivot—the Klein Spot-On Pivot location (explained in detail by Gary Klein on page 15), making for the most efficient full suspension bike on the market.

Along with the font, the photographic image helps create an elegant and sophisticated atmosphere by giving value to the details.

The Klein catalogue is a good example of how Cahan & Associates succeeds in expressing emotion through an elegant use of graphic elements.

Mario Eskenazi

Mario Eskenazi
Barcelona, Spain

"The Art of Loving the Letter"

Mario Eskenazi (Buenos Aires, 1945) discovered his passion for graphic design while studying architecture at the University of Córdoba (Argentina).

Magazines such as **Graphis**, **Idea** and **Gebrauschgraphic** and professionals the likes of Paul Rand, Müller Brockmann and Allan Fletcher set the standards for a whole generation of young designers who, like Mario, felt the need to learn and make design not only a profession but a lifestyle as well.

Largely self-taught, Mario learns from his own point of view as a designer, observing, from day to day, everything around him and allowing it to become part of his character.

Mario Eskenazi set up his first studio in 1975 in Barcelona, where he went on to produce a great deal of graphic work. His sensitivity and love of fonts would be mirrored in the majority of his projects – for which he has received numerous awards, including the Spanish National Design Award in 2000.

Traganews Magazine.
1999

Magazine in newspaper format for the Tragaluz restaurant in Barcelona.
The cover is dominated by the number of the issue, which contains images referring to the leading articles.
The texts are composed with Rockwell typeface.
The mockup maintains a variable structure that permits a versatile layout of the contents – text and images.

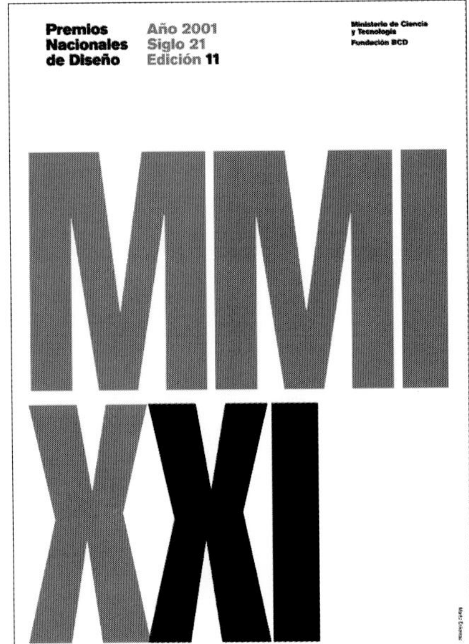

Poster announcing the 2001 **Spanish National Design Awards**

Traganews, no. 1
1999

Cover and inside pages

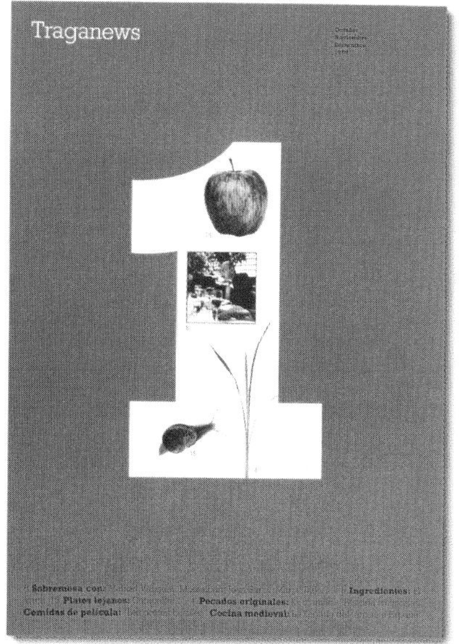

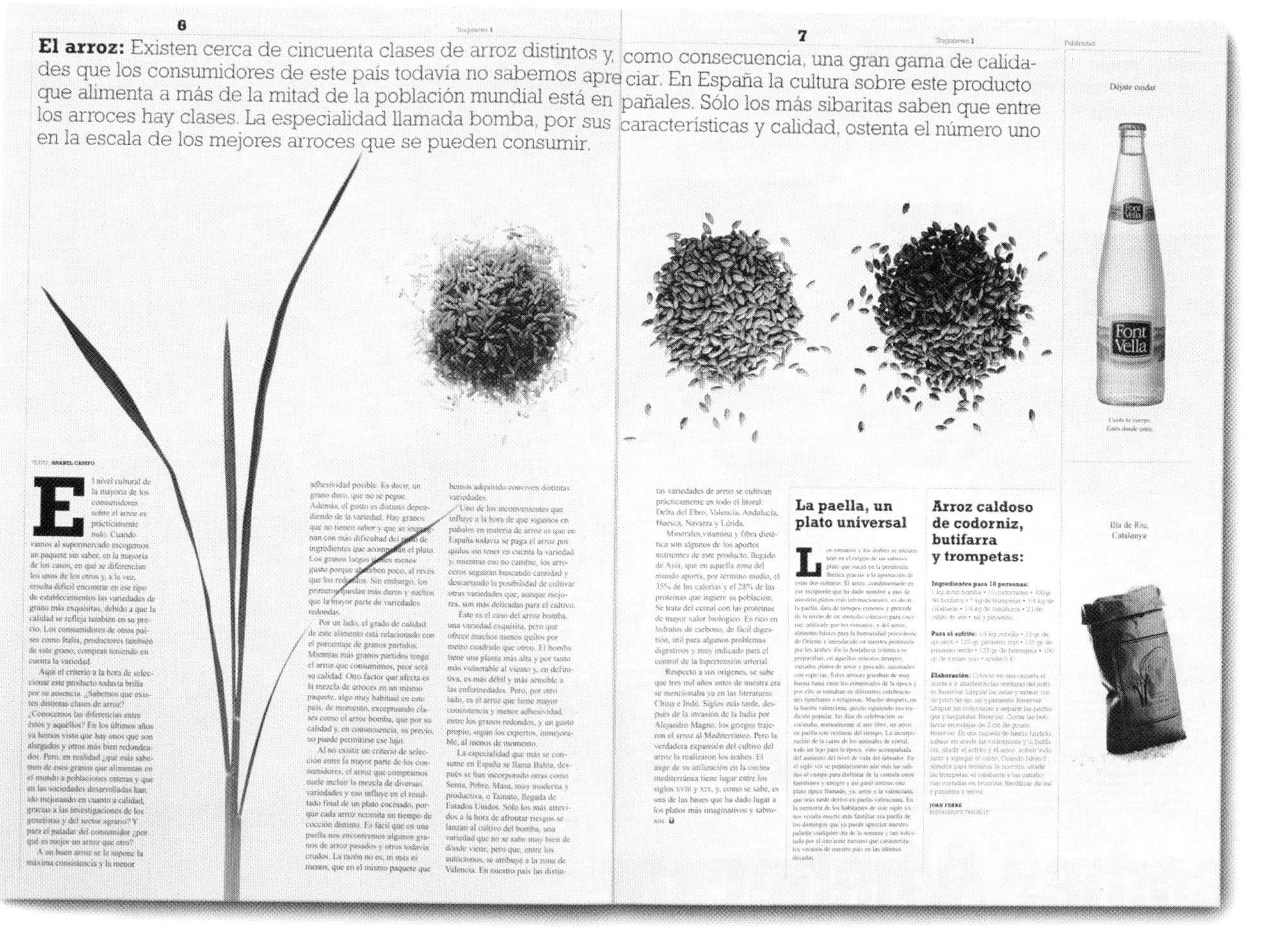

6 Traganews 1

El arroz: Existen cerca de cincuenta clases de arroz distintos y, como consecuencia, una gran gama de calidades que los consumidores de este país todavía no sabemos apreciar. En España la cultura sobre este producto que alimenta a más de la mitad de la población mundial está en pañales. Sólo los más sibaritas saben que entre los arroces hay clases. La especialidad llamada bomba, por sus características y calidad, ostenta el número uno en la escala de los mejores arroces que se pueden consumir.

TEXTO: CAMPO

El nivel cultural de la mayoría de los consumidores sobre el arroz es prácticamente nulo. Cuando vamos al supermercado escogemos un paquete sin saber, en la mayoría de los casos, en qué se diferencian los unos de los otros y, a la vez, resulta difícil encontrar en ese tipo de establecimientos las variedades de grano más exquisitas, debido a que la calidad se refleja también en su precio. Los consumidores de otros países como Italia, productores también de este grano, compran teniendo en cuenta la variedad.

Aquí el criterio a la hora de seleccionar este producto todavía brilla por su ausencia. ¿Sabemos que existen distintas clases de arroz? ¿Conocemos las diferencias entre éstos y aquéllos? En los últimos años ya hemos visto que hay unos que son alargados y otros más bien redondeados. Pero, en realidad ¿qué más sabemos de esos granos que alimentan en el mundo a poblaciones enteras y que en las sociedades desarrolladas han ido mejorando en cuanto a calidad, gracias a las investigaciones de los genetistas y del sector agrario? Y para el paladar del consumidor ¿por qué es mejor un arroz que otro?

A un buen arroz se le supone la máxima consistencia y la menor adhesividad posible. Es decir, un grano duro, que no se pegue. Además, el gusto es distinto dependiendo de la variedad. Hay granos que no tienen sabor y que se impregnan con más dificultad del resto de ingredientes que acompañan el plato. Los granos largos tienen menos gusto porque absorben poco, al revés que los redondos. Sin embargo, los primeros quedan más duros y sueltos que la mayor parte de variedades redondas.

Por un lado, el grado de calidad de este alimento está relacionado con el porcentaje de granos partidos. Mientras más granos partidos tenga el arroz que consumimos, peor será su calidad. Otro factor que afecta es la mezcla de arroces en un mismo paquete, algo muy habitual en este país, de momento, exceptuando clases como el arroz bomba, que por su calidad y, en consecuencia, su precio, no puede permitirse ese lujo.

Al no existir un criterio de selección entre la mayor parte de los consumidores, el arroz que compramos suele incluir la mezcla de diversas variedades y eso influye en el resultado final de un plato cocinado, porque cada arroz necesita un tiempo de cocción distinto. Es fácil que en una paella nos encontremos algunos granos de arroz pasados y otros todavía crudos. La razón no es, ni más ni menos, que en el mismo paquete que hemos adquirido conviven distintas variedades.

Uno de los inconvenientes que influye a la hora de que sigamos en pañales en materia de arroz es que en España todavía se paga el arroz por quilos sin tener en cuenta la variedad y, mientras eso no cambie, los arroceros seguirán buscando cantidad y descartando la posibilidad de cultivar otras variedades que, aunque mejores, son más delicadas para el cultivo.

Éste es el caso del arroz bomba, una variedad exquisita, pero que ofrece muchos menos quilos por metro cuadrado que otros. El bomba tiene una planta más alta y por tanto más vulnerable al viento y, en definitiva, es más débil y más sensible a las enfermedades. Pero, por otro lado, es el arroz que tiene mayor consistencia y menor adhesividad entre los granos redondos, y un gusto propio, según los expertos, inmejorable, al menos de momento.

La especialidad que más se consume en España se llama Bahía, después se han incorporado otras como Senia, Pebre, Masa, muy moderna y productiva, o Tainato, llegada de Estados Unidos. Sólo los más atrevidos a la hora de afrontar riesgos se lanzan al cultivo del bomba, una variedad que no se sabe muy bien de dónde viene, pero que, entre los autóctonos, se atribuye a la zona de Valencia. En nuestro país las distintas variedades de arroz se cultivan prácticamente en todo el litoral: Delta del Ebro, Valencia, Andalucía, Huesca, Navarra y Lérida.

Minerales, vitamina y fibra dietética son algunos de los aportes nutrientes de este producto, llegado de Asia, que en aquella zona del mundo aporta, por término medio, el 35% de las calorías y el 28% de las proteínas que ingiere su población. Se trata del cereal con las proteínas de mayor valor biológico. Es rico en hidratos de carbono, de fácil digestión, útil para algunos problemas digestivos y muy indicado para el control de la hipertensión arterial.

Respecto a sus orígenes, se sabe que tres mil años antes de nuestra era se mencionaba ya en las literaturas China e Indú. Siglos más tarde, después de la invasión de la India por Alejandro Magno, los griegos trajeron el arroz al Mediterráneo. Pero la verdadera expansión del cultivo del arroz la realizaron los árabes. El auge de su utilización en la cocina mediterránea tiene lugar entre los siglos XVIII y XIX, y, como se sabe, es una de las bases que ha dado lugar a los platos más imaginativos y sabrosos.

7 Traganews 1

La paella, un plato universal

Arroz caldoso de codorniz, butifarra y trompetas:

Ingredientes para 10 personas:

Para el sofrito:

Elaboración:

JOAN FERRÉ

Publicidad

Déjate cuidar

Font Vella

Cuida tu cuerpo. Cuida donde estés.

Illa de Riu, Catalunya

La Memoria del Cine
Colección Paidós. 1999

Jacket, title page and cover

For the design of this collection of books by film directors Mario employs such typical film resources as stills and sequences.
On the jacket, over an image of the author/director, the name and title are laid out like a sequence of stills. This same composition is repeated on the end paper and hard cover, maintaining the same conceptual unity throughout the collection.

Paidós Asterisco
Paidós collection. 1999

Covers

The idea for the jacket design is suggested by the name of the collection – asterisk. Each one features a different font and the associated asterisk is employed as an ornamental element.

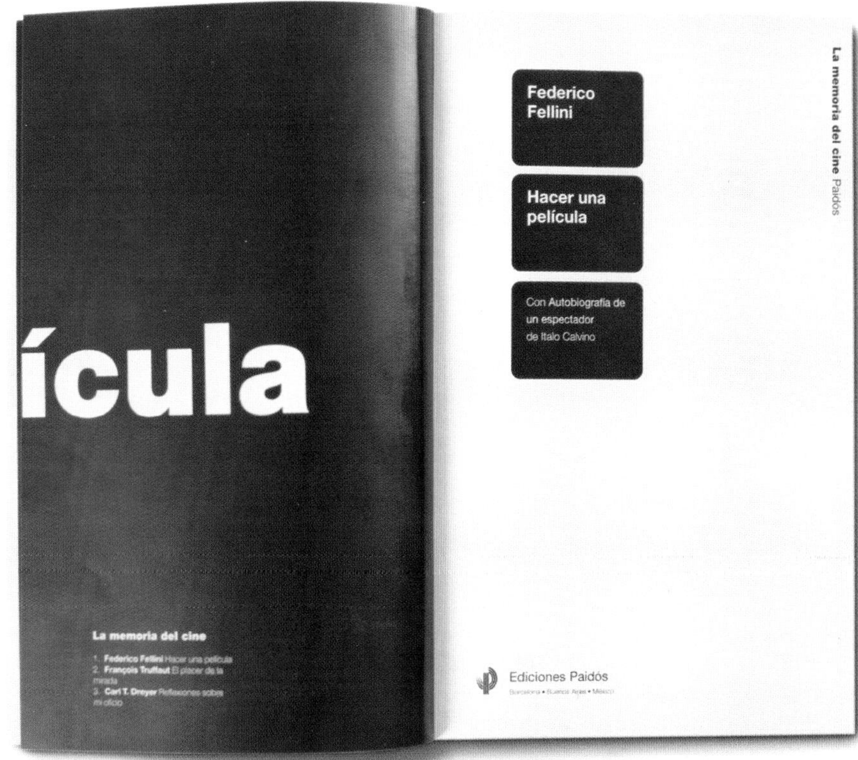

John Gribbin
****
El pequeño libro de la ciencia
PaidósAsterisco
5

Pierre Bourdieu Loïc Wacquant
****
Las argucias de la razón imperialista
PaidósAsterisco
6

El arte
de amar
Erich
Fromm
Paidós Edición del centenario de Erich Fromm

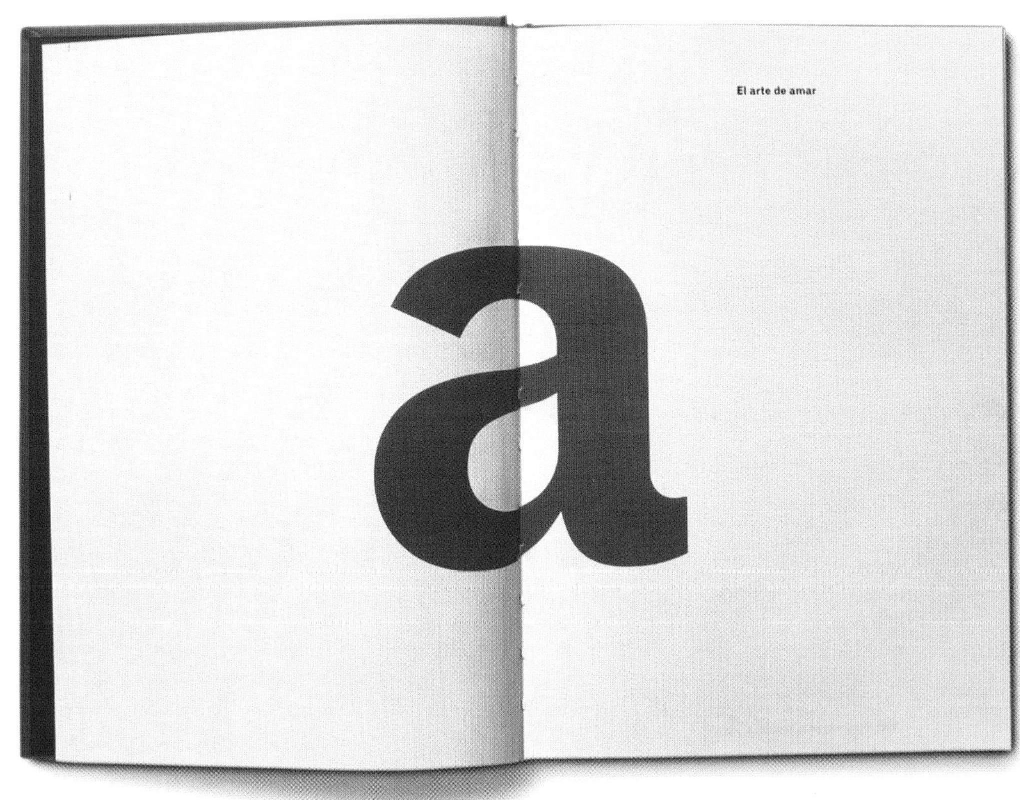

El Arte de Amar
Book-homage to Erich Fromm

Year: 1999

Design: Mario Eskenazi, Diego Feijoo
Client: Editorial Paidós

Fonts used: Grotesque (Monotype)

15.5 x 22 cm. 164 pages. 2 inks

Publishing Identity

Since founding his Barcelona studio, Mario Eskenazi has worked intensively in the publishing world. His works for the Paidós publishing house set a standard in Spanish publishing graphics.

Mario conceives the book as a whole, a single element that includes the jacket, the back jacket, the hard cover, the flyleaves and the title page, as well as the inside pages.

A concept of unity that goes beyond the single edition and also carries over into collections. Each collection designed for Paidós has its own mark of identity: an identity that Mario attains with an intelligent use of font on the jacket.

Mario understands font **"as the fundamental element of the work of a designer. Something like the foundation on which any project is built."**

El Arte de Amar was the book chosen by Paidós to pay homage to Erich Fromm on the centenary of his birth.

"It was the sort of project you dream of," Mario says. **"The book speaks of love, attempting to explain it. But it does so in text – intellectually. So, how do you show that?"**

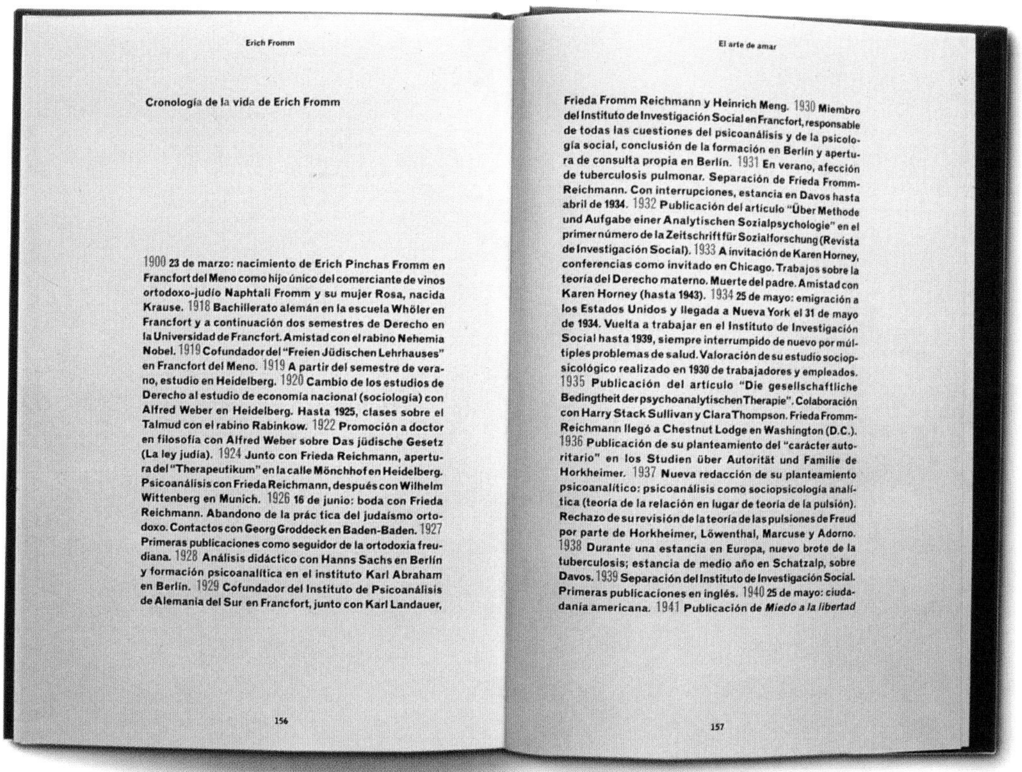

Cronología de la vida de Erich Fromm

1900 23 de marzo: nacimiento de Erich Pinchas Fromm en Francfort del Meno como hijo único del comerciante de vinos ortodoxo-judío Naphtali Fromm y su mujer Rosa, nacida Krause. 1918 Bachillerato alemán en la escuela Whöler en Francfort y a continuación dos semestres de Derecho en la Universidad de Francfort. Amistad con el rabino Nehemia Nobel. 1919 Cofundador del "Freien Jüdischen Lehrhauses" en Francfort del Meno. 1919 A partir del semestre de verano, estudio en Heidelberg. 1920 Cambio de los estudios de Derecho al estudio de economía nacional (sociología) con Alfred Weber en Heidelberg. Hasta 1925, clases sobre el Talmud con el rabino Rabinkow. 1922 Promoción a doctor en filosofía con Alfred Weber sobre Das jüdische Gesetz (La ley judía). 1924 Junto con Frieda Reichmann, apertura del "Therapeutikum" en la calle Mönchhof en Heidelberg. Psicoanálisis con Frieda Reichmann, después con Wilhelm Wittenberg en Munich. 1926 16 de junio: boda con Frieda Reichmann. Abandono de la prác tica del judaísmo ortodoxo. Contactos con Georg Groddeck en Baden-Baden. 1927 Primeras publicaciones como seguidor de la ortodoxia freudiana. 1928 Análisis didáctico con Hanns Sachs en Berlín y formación psicoanalítica en el instituto Karl Abraham en Berlín. 1929 Cofundador del Instituto de Psicoanálisis de Alemania del Sur en Francfort, junto con Karl Landauer,

Frieda Fromm Reichmann y Heinrich Meng. 1930 Miembro del Instituto de Investigación Social en Francfort, responsable de todas las cuestiones del psicoanálisis y de la psicología social, conclusión de la formación en Berlín y apertura de consulta propia en Berlín. 1931 En verano, afección de tuberculosis pulmonar. Separación de Frieda Fromm-Reichmann. Con interrupciones, estancia en Davos hasta abril de 1934. 1932 Publicación del artículo "Über Methode und Aufgabe einer Analytischen Sozialpsychologie" en el primer número de la Zeitschrift für Sozialforschung (Revista de Investigación Social). 1933 A invitación de Karen Horney, conferencias como invitado en Chicago. Trabajos sobre la teoría del Derecho materno. Muerte del padre. Amistad con Karen Horney (hasta 1943). 1934 25 de mayo: emigración a los Estados Unidos y llegada a Nueva York el 31 de mayo de 1934. Vuelta a trabajar en el Instituto de Investigación Social hasta 1939, siempre interrumpido de nuevo por múltiples problemas de salud. Valoración de su estudio sociopsicológico realizado en 1930 de trabajadores y empleados. 1935 Publicación del artículo "Die gesellschaftliche Bedingtheit der psychoanalytischen Therapie". Colaboración con Harry Stack Sullivan y Clara Thompson. Frieda Fromm-Reichmann llegó a Chestnut Lodge en Washington (D.C.). 1936 Publicación de su planteamiento del "carácter autoritario" en los Studien über Autorität und Familie de Horkheimer. 1937 Nueva redacción de su planteamiento psicoanalítico: psicoanálisis como sociopsicología analítica (teoría de la relación en lugar de teoría de la pulsión). Rechazo de su revisión de la teoría de las pulsiones de Freud por parte de Horkheimer, Löwenthal, Marcuse y Adorno. 1938 Durante una estancia en Europa, nuevo brote de la tuberculosis; estancia de medio año en Schatzalp, sobre Davos. 1939 Separación del Instituto de Investigación Social. Primeras publicaciones en inglés. 1940 25 de mayo: ciudadanía americana. 1941 Publicación de *Miedo a la libertad*

paradójica predominó en el pensamiento chino e indio, en la filosofía de Heráclito, y posteriormente, con el nombre de dialéctica, se convirtió en la filosofía de Hegel y de Marx. Lao-tsé formuló claramente el principio general de la lógica paradójica: "Las palabras que son estrictamente verdaderas parecen ser paradójicas".[20] Y Chuang-tzu: "Lo que es uno es uno. Aquello que es no-uno, también es uno". Tales formulaciones de la lógica paradójica son positivas: *es y no es*. Otras son negativas: *no es esto ni aquello*. Encontramos la primera expresión en el pensamiento taoísta, en Heráclito y en la dialéctica de Hegel; la segunda formulación es frecuente en la filosofía india.

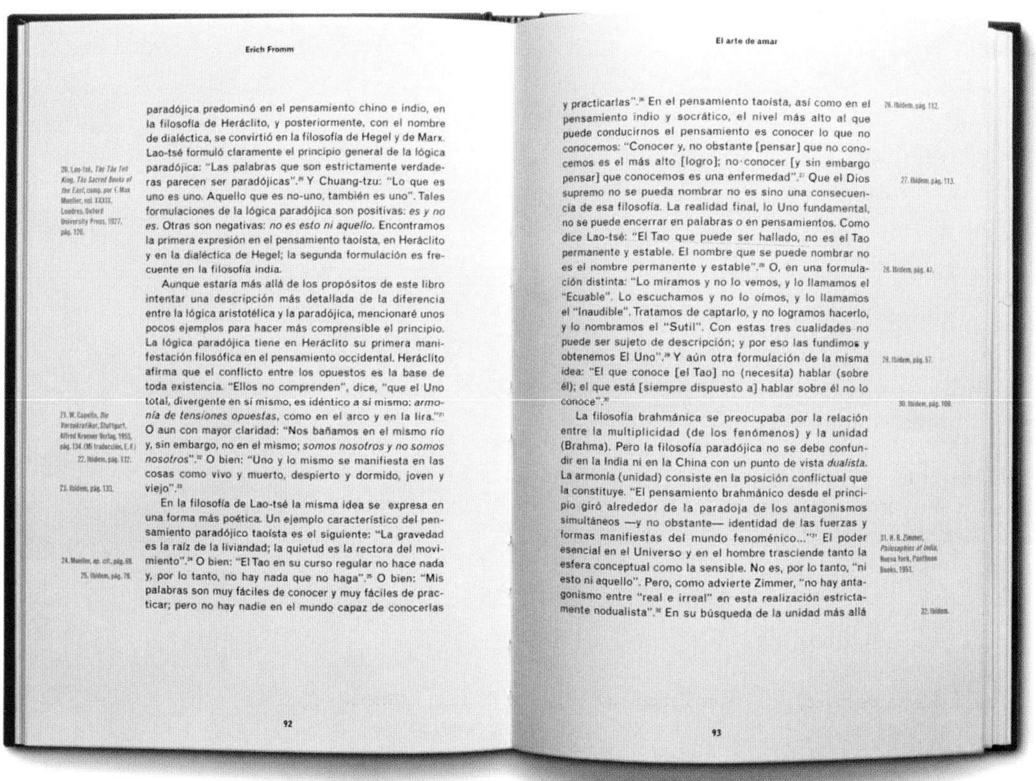

20. Lao-tsé, *The Tâo Teh King, The Sacred Books of the East*, comp. por F. Max Mueller, vol. XXXIX, Londres, Oxford University Press, 1927, pág. 120.

Aunque estaría más allá de los propósitos de este libro intentar una descripción más detallada de la diferencia entre la lógica aristotélica y la paradójica, mencionaré unos pocos ejemplos para hacer más comprensible el principio. La lógica paradójica tiene en Heráclito su primera manifestación filosófica en el pensamiento occidental. Heráclito afirma que el conflicto entre los opuestos es la base de toda existencia. "Ellos no comprenden", dice, "que el Uno total, divergente en sí mismo, es idéntico a sí mismo: *armonía de tensiones opuestas*, como en el arco y en la lira."[21] O aun con mayor claridad: "Nos bañamos en el mismo río y, sin embargo, no en el mismo; *somos nosotros y no somos nosotros*".[22] O bien: "Uno y lo mismo se manifiesta en las cosas como vivo y muerto, despierto y dormido, joven y viejo".[23]

21. W. Capelle, *Die Vorsokratiker*, Stuttgart, Alfred Kroener Verlag, 1953, pág. 134. (Mi traducción, E.F.)

22. Ibídem, pág. 132.

23. Ibídem, pág. 133.

En la filosofía de Lao-tsé la misma idea se expresa en una forma más poética. Un ejemplo característico del pensamiento paradójico taoísta es el siguiente: "La gravedad es la raíz de la liviandad; la quietud es la rectora del movimiento".[24] O bien: "El Tao en su curso regular no hace nada y, por lo tanto, no hay nada que no haga".[25] O bien: "Mis palabras son muy fáciles de conocer y muy fáciles de practicar; pero no hay nadie en el mundo capaz de conocerlas

24. Mueller, op. cit., pág. 68.

25. Ibídem, pág. 78.

y practicarlas".[26] En el pensamiento taoísta, así como en el pensamiento indio y socrático, el nivel más alto al que puede conducirnos el pensamiento es conocer lo que no conocemos: "Conocer y, no obstante [pensar] que no conocemos es el más alto [logro]; no-conocer [y sin embargo pensar] que conocemos es una enfermedad".[27] Que el Dios supremo no se pueda nombrar no es sino una consecuencia de esa filosofía. La realidad final, lo Uno fundamental, no se puede encerrar en palabras o en pensamientos. Como dice Lao-tsé: "El Tao que puede ser hallado, no es el Tao permanente y estable. El nombre que se puede nombrar no es el nombre permanente y estable".[28] O, en una formulación distinta: "Lo miramos y no lo vemos, y lo llamamos el "Ecuable". Lo escuchamos y no lo oímos, y lo llamamos el "Inaudible". Tratamos de captarlo, y no logramos hacerlo, y lo nombramos el "Sutil". Con estas tres cualidades no puede ser sujeto de descripción; y por eso las fundimos y obtenemos El Uno".[29] Y aún otra formulación de la misma idea: "El que conoce [el Tao] no (necesita) hablar (sobre él); el que está [siempre dispuesto a] hablar sobre él no lo conoce".[30]

26. Ibídem, pág. 112.

27. Ibídem, pág. 113.

28. Ibídem, pág. 47.

29. Ibídem, pág. 57.

30. Ibídem, pág. 100.

La filosofía brahmánica se preocupaba por la relación entre la multiplicidad (de los fenómenos) y la unidad (Brahma). Pero la filosofía paradójica no se debe confundir en la India ni en la China con un punto de vista *dualista*. La armonía (unidad) consiste en la posición conflictual que la constituye. "El pensamiento brahmánico desde el principio giró alrededor de la paradoja de los antagonismos simultáneos —y no obstante— identidad de las fuerzas y formas manifiestas del mundo fenoménico..."[31] El poder esencial en el Universo y en el hombre trasciende tanto la esfera conceptual como la sensible. No es, por lo tanto, "ni esto ni aquello". Pero, como advierte Zimmer, "no hay antagonismo entre "real e irreal" en esta realización estrictamente nodualista".[32] En su búsqueda de la unidad más allá

31. H. R. Zimmer, *Philosophies of India*, Nueva York, Pantheon Books, 1951.

32. Ibídem.

Quien no conoce nada, no ama nada. Quien no puede hacer nada, no comprende nada. Quien nada comprende, nada vale. Pero quien comprende también ama, observa, ve... Cuanto mayor es el conocimiento inherente a una cosa, más grande es el amor... Quien cree que todas las frutas maduran al mismo tiempo que las frutillas nada sabe acerca de las uvas.

Paracelso

Mario used red – the colour of passion – to express this universal sentiment. And he places it in different ways on the pages of the book.

As a typographic element he took the letter 'A' – first letter in the words 'arte' and 'amar'- and plays with it in an attempt to symbolise both concepts.

The book title appears in relief on the cover, an incitement to caress it, stimulating the tactile experience, sensuality. The letter 'A' in white over a red background made Mario think of putting all the 'A's' on the inside pages in red, which, over the white background of the paper, evokes little red drops.

Mario laid out the text in single columns, in the traditional manner, with the aim of making the book easy to read. He reserved a wide outer margin for the book's numerous many footnotes. To differentiate them from the rest of the text, in black, these margin notes are also in red.

This edition of El Arte de Amar thus becomes something of an object in itself. The visual and poetic experience that Mario proposes with his design forces us to reflect on the act itself of designing a book. This is meant to be a stimulating experience and its design is meant to be an act of love, as Mario suggest to us with this example.

NL.Design

Mieke Gerritzen
Amsterdam, Holland

"Text as Manifesto"

Mieke Gerritzen (Amsterdam, 1962) studied audiovisual communications at the Rietveld Academy. After a brilliant professional early career she founded her own design studio, **NL.Design**.

Mieke defines NL.Design as a company permanently under construction dedicated to the development of graphic projects for all types of media, print or digital. It also serves her as platform from which, with the participation of other professionals, she publishes books and organises events such as **The International Browserday**.

Mieke cannot be considered as 'just a designer', since the scope and aims of her work embrace a much larger realm: graphic communications, social activism, pedagogy, and so on. Indeed Mieke considers her work to be closely tied to society and politics, and graphic design to be a confluence of a number of disciplines. Thus, on many of her projects, she has worked with other designers, artists and writers.

Catalogue of Strategies. Book. 2001

Cover

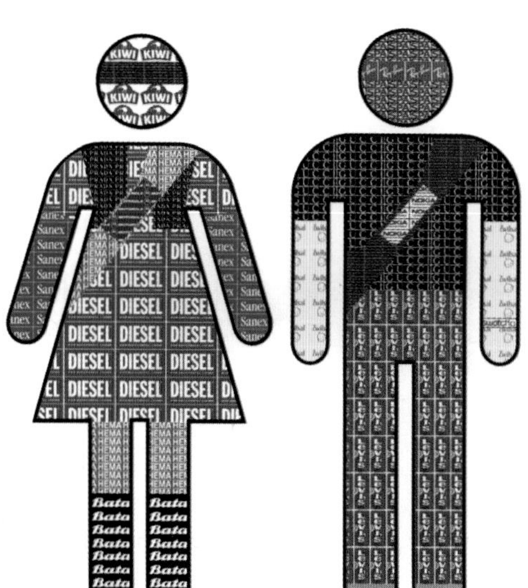

Dressed Icons
Cover design for BNO magazine, 2000.

"I like working with standard images, icons that form part of our visual culture. For me there's nothing more standard than the universal language of pictograms."

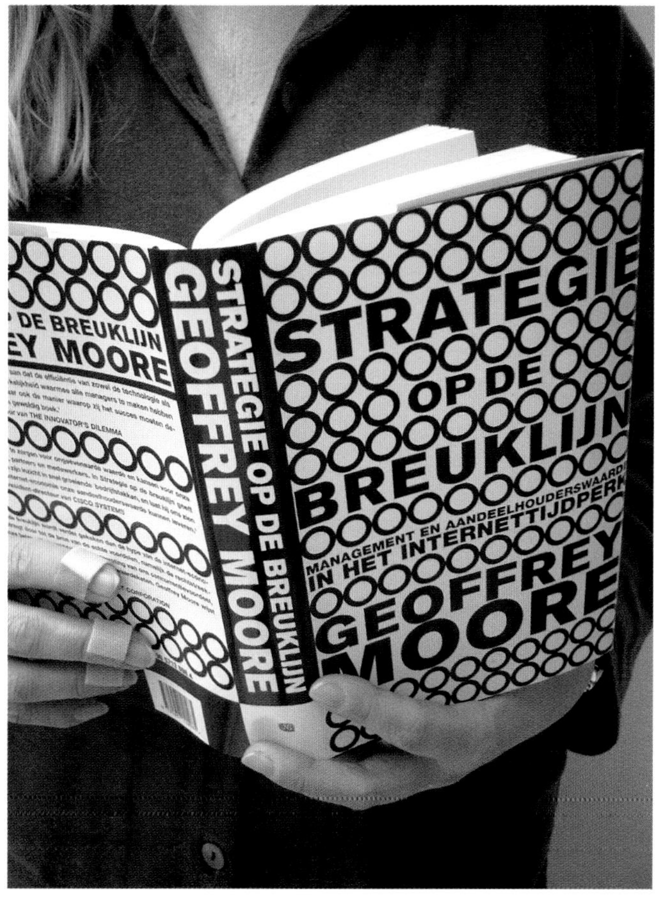

Book jackets for **Nieuwezijds**, Amsterdam

Cover designs for books about the new economy.

Everyone is a Designer!
Manifesto for the Design Economy
Book-manifest

Year: 2000
Client: NL.Design

Font used: Helvetica

10 x 15 cm. 140 pages. Full colour printing

The Project as a Social Commitment

Mieke Gerritzen's commitment to social issues has grown in recent years, at a time when the digital revolution has begun to have an impact on the design world.

Where originally the designer was seen as that professional dedicated to giving form and content to the future of communications, we now face a new, more complex situation in which economic power dominates all possible spaces.

For Mieke Gerritzen this new situation posits an interesting challenge for the entire profession, forcing it to relocate itself in its new space. She considers that **"new media and the so called new economy have been giving us more limitations ... Speculating on what the Internet will become in the future has become a business in itself. Managers have taken over from art-directors and the creative workforce in general. Design is now a product of commerce (sic)."**

Her book Everyone is a Designer! Manifest for the Design Economy, published by Mieke herself and Geert Lovink through **NL.Design**, is a reaction to this situation in which the commercialisation of the profession results in products of poorer and poorer quality.

Everyone is a Designer!
Manifesto for the Design Economy

Cover and inside pages

Originally published in postcard-size format (10 x 15 cm), Everyone is a Designer! is a 'manifesto' in book form that includes declarations, slogans, texts, opinions by a long list of designers, artists, critics and communications specialists. Paraphrasing Joseph Beuys's famous declaration 'everyone is an artist', the content deals with the world of the new technologies and how they are transforming our view and understanding of the world. The book sets its sights on the new economy and expresses critically – and ironically – some of the contradictions and dangers it harbours.

In the design of this book, as in most of her works, Mieke employs a graphic language which perhaps recalls the typographic oeuvre of Piet Zwart and Paul Schuitema, pioneering figures in 20th-century Dutch design.

In the patent austerity, often compensated by the use of colour and contrast, the importance of the font in the creation of geometric spaces recalls those avant-garde compositions.

Mieke uses font and colour as basic resources. The strength of the messages resides in their compositional simplicity and the use of an in-your-face sans serif. In the absence of the images, the font itself becomes image, at times accompanied by iconographic elements – pictograms or symbols – that acquire typographic value.

Her preference for sans serifs, specifically Helvetica, in her graphic works has its logic, according to Mieke, **"in the search for neutrality."** A supposed neutrality that facilitates the transmission of the messages but that, in my view, plays a leading role in expressing the contents authoritatively and provocatively.

In Everyone is a Designer!, the font is the medium and the message at the same time, given that the font supplies the necessary force for the text to acquire the value of a manifesto.

"We live in a fundamentally visual culture. That means that we can be much more expressive when we use text."

GOOD
DESIGN
GOES
TO HEAVEN
BAD
DESIGN
GOES
EVERYWHERE

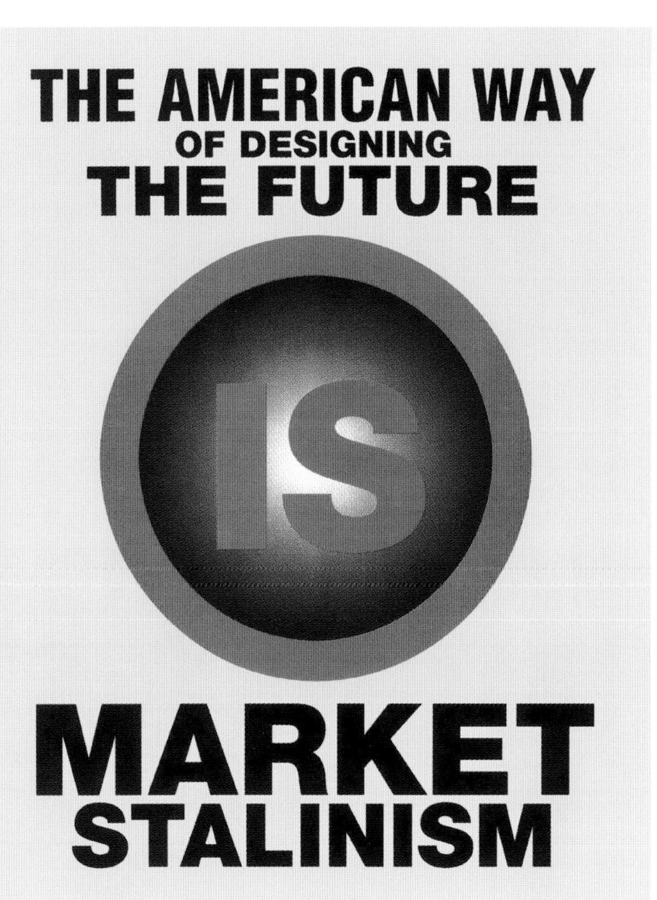

THE AMERICAN WAY
OF DESIGNING
THE FUTURE
IS
MARKET
STALINISM

Everyone is a Designer!
Manifesto for the Design Economy

Inside pages

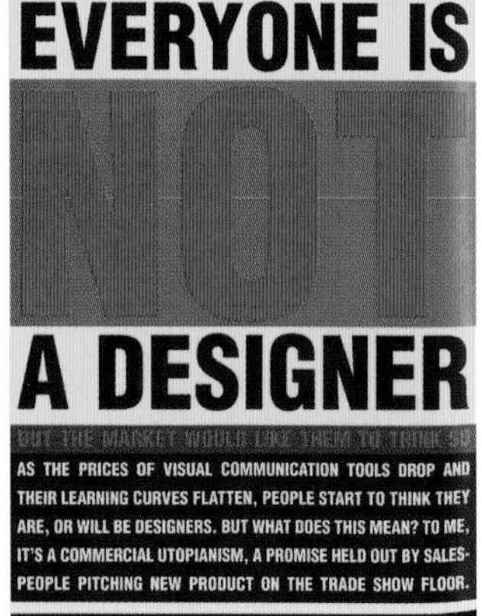

› Following page:
Sloganisms, by Geert Lovink, from the book Catalogue of Strategies

DRINKS
DRUGS
AND
TOBACCO
ARE
CUSTOMIZED
INTERFACES

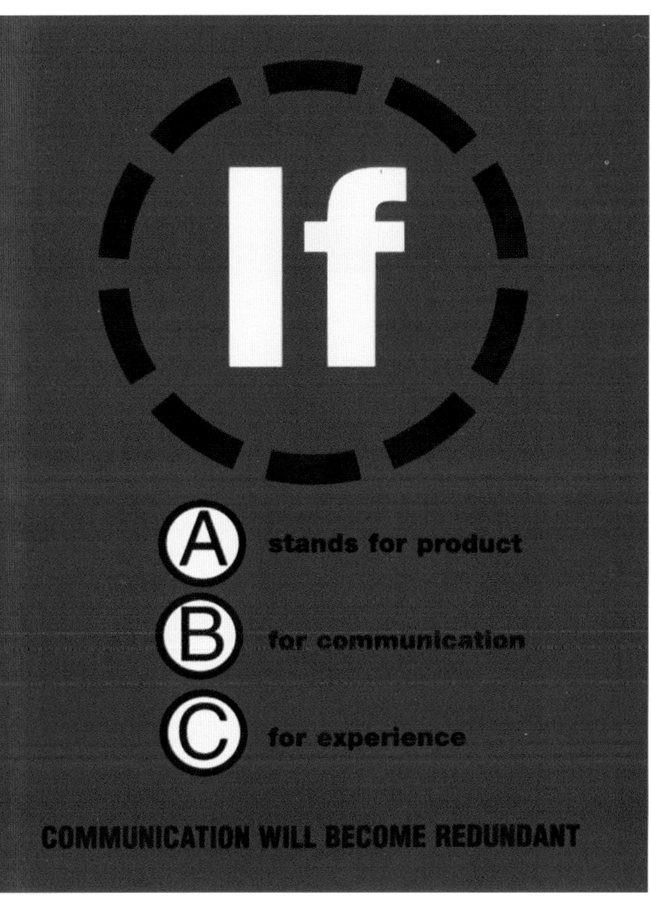
If
A stands for product
B for communication
C for experience
COMMUNICATION WILL BECOME REDUNDANT

DESIGN MUST ANSWER THREE QUESTIONS: IN A WORLD THAT IS CONTINUALLY TRANSFORMED BY COMPUTERS AND COMMUNICATION TECHNOLOGIES, HOW CAN DESIGN HELP US FIND OUR WAY THROUGH THAT SPRAWLING LANDSCAPE, MAKE US AT HOME IN IT, AND MAKE SENSE OF IT?

DIGITAL SYSTEMS DEMAND AN AESTHETIC OF UNFINISH. DESIGN MOVES FROM THE REALM OF VISUAL PROBLEM SOLVING TO THE FLUID FIELDS OF EXPERIENCE CREATION, OFTEN UNBOUNDED IN BOTH TIME AND FORM.

BOOKMARKS 2000:
www.cashing.com
www.funds.com
www.newconomy.com
www.greed.com
www.shallow.com
www.buymore.com
www.iwanttobefirst.com
www.funds.com
www.capital.com
www.emission.com
www.stock.com
www.hype.com
www.sales.com
www.financialclimate.com

SLOGAN

THOSE WHO DO NOT KNOW MEDIA HISTORY HAVE

ONLINE SHOPPING WARRIOR AS KULT

WWW.J'ACCUSE.COM THEORY IS JUST SOMETHING

BUNIX: THE WORLD'S FIRST OPEN S

THE CREATIVE DESTRUCTION O

CAPITALISM SEES THE INTERNET A

WHERE TO CLICK IF YOU WANT TO FIT IN (FROM

ALL HOPE THAT DESIGN CAN BRING SALVA

DON'T STOP THINKING ABOUT T

JOB OPPORTUNITY: MOBILE PHONE ASSIS

OPEN MONOPOLIES FOR AN OPEN SOCIETY AFTE

VIRTUAL COMPANIES ARE PAPER TIGERS AUFBRUCH

THE GLOBAL PROVINCE AND RHETORIC AFTER H

VIRTUAL FAILURES (CONFERENCE

ITS GOLDEN AGE, CONCEPTUAL RENAISSANCE, NIH

THEY CAN'T ALL BE TRUE (JOHAN SJERPSTRA) WE WI

THE WILL TO DESIGN: OVERCOMING

DECIDE OR CONSUME TOOLKI

EXTEND YOUR COZY FEELING (BALENO) HA

REVOLUTIONS 'R' US NO RECONCIL

LEAD ME TO THE WRONG SI

IOMICS:

E FREEDOM TO BYPASS IT MILLENNIAL DISEASE:

RIDEAL DIGITAL RARITY BECOMES INDISPENSABLE

DON'T UNDERSTAND, SO WE DON'T INVEST IN IT (WARREN BUFFETT)

RCE RELIGION™ DIGITAL VISIONS:

POSTMODERNISM (BOOK TITLE)

DAMAGE AND ROUTES AROUND IT

SITE) MEET THE UNCANNY PROSUMERS

ON SHOULD BE ELIMINATED (GENC GREVA)

E INTERNET YOU ARE ONLY HUMAN ONCE

NT IN CYBERSPACE NO ONE KNOWS YOU'RE AN ARTIST

THE CULTURE CLASH (BOOK TITLE)

R NETZE: KYBERNETIK DER TAT

EGGER: WHY DO WE REMAIN IN THE INTERNET?

LE) KNOW YOUR WIRED ENEMY VIRTUAL EMPIRE:

STIC MOMENT I HAVE WRITTEN SIX THEORIES ON CYBERCITIES

E WHERE THE CONSUMERS ARE (NEW CHINESE SAYING)

TERTAINMENT T-SHIRT: RESISTANCE IS FERTILE

UILD YOUR OWN INTERNET OBSERVATORY

E YOU HEARD ABOUT MINISPACE?

ION WITH ARTIFICIAL NATURE (GRAFFITI)

OF VIRTUALITY (SONG TEXT)

Plazm

Joshua Berger, Pete McCracken, Niko Courtelis, Enrique Mosqueda
Portland, United States

"The Magazine as a Cultural Contribution"

Founded in 1991 by a team of artists, **Plazm** is a creative platform dedicated to identity project development, advertising design and communications in general.

Plazm gives free rein to its experimental ambitions with its own self-published magazine – **Plazm** – and an independent font development studio.

The designers and artists of the Plazm studio believe firmly in teamwork. Thus their work is based on mutual collaboration and the creative input of each member in order to develop their projects as far as possible.

Plazm

Cover **Plazm** no. 17 designed by Ed Fella

Plazm

Cover no. 26. 2001
Cover no. 25. 2000
Cover no. 16. 1997

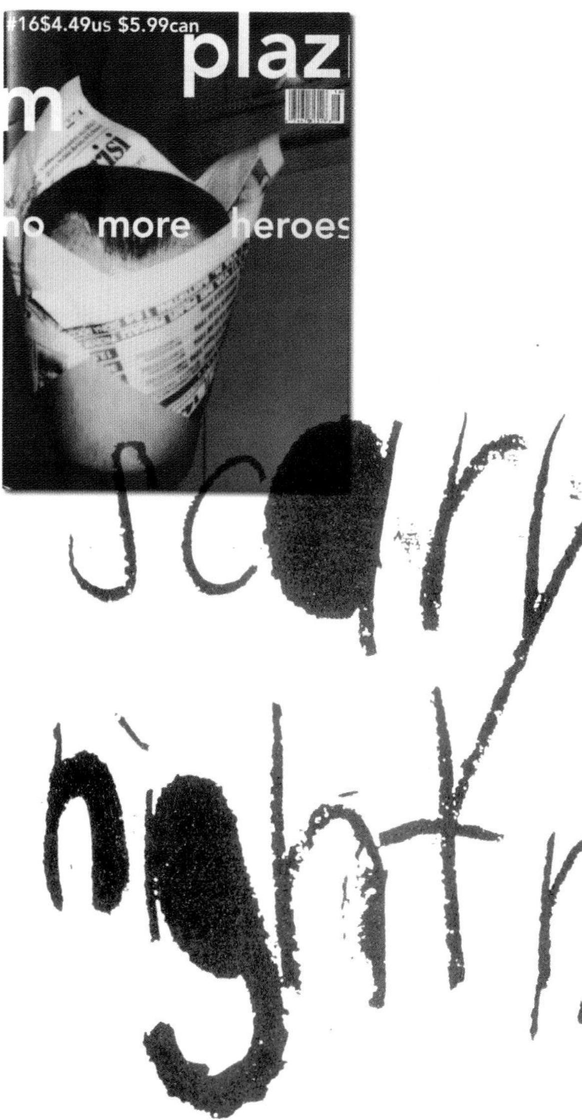

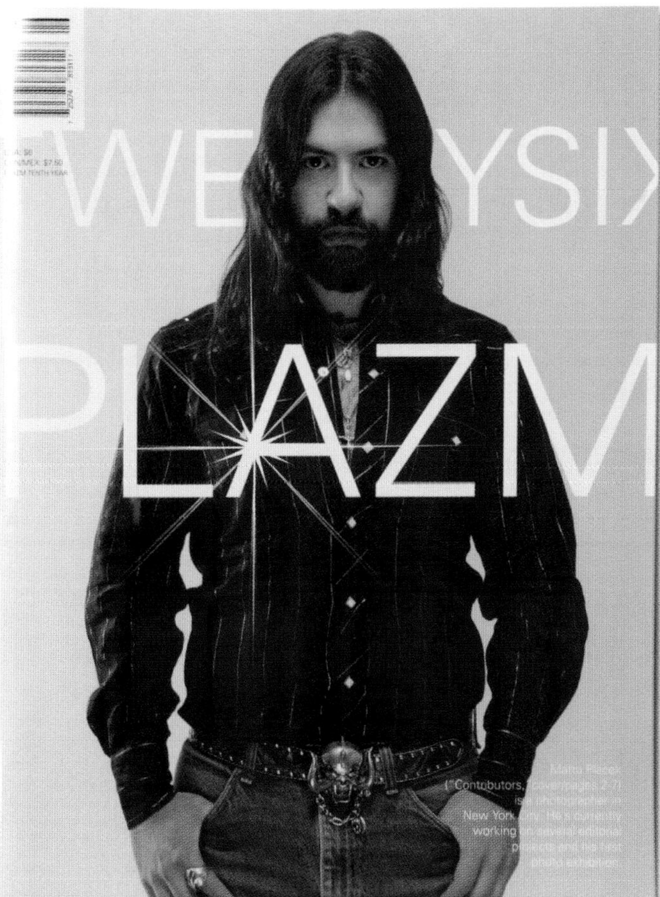

Plazm Magazine
Magazine

Year: Since 1991
Client: Plazm

23 x 30.5 cm. 68 pages. 1 ink / Full colour printing. Quarterly

Editorial Independence

Plazm magazine was created by a group of professionals concerned with showing the diversity of emergent forms of cultural and artistic expression not otherwise covered in the printed media.

Artists who have never published their works appear beside their internationally recognised counterparts. Anything that might be considered marginal due to its social or political implications has a place in the magazine.

Its readers are as diverse as the type of material that captures their attention: **"we target any type of reader, regardless of race, age or gender."**

Plazm is an independent magazine that enjoys absolute freedom in choosing its contents and establishing its editorial standards.

"We can publish photographs that don't form part of any advertising campaign, present artists that never show their work, reviews of books that nobody has ever heard of or poems by unknown authors," says Plazm editor-in-chief, Jon Raymond. **"Plazm uses its independent character to give a voice to the people and events that would be passed over by history. In some way, we like**

Plazm Magazine

Contents page from **Plazm** no. 15
(Below) Double page from **Plazm** no. 21

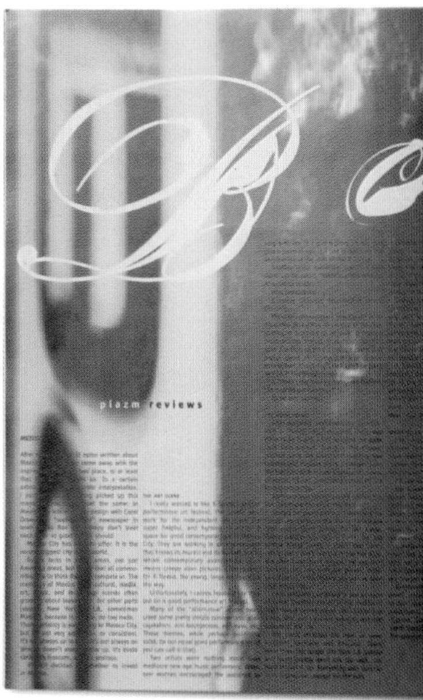

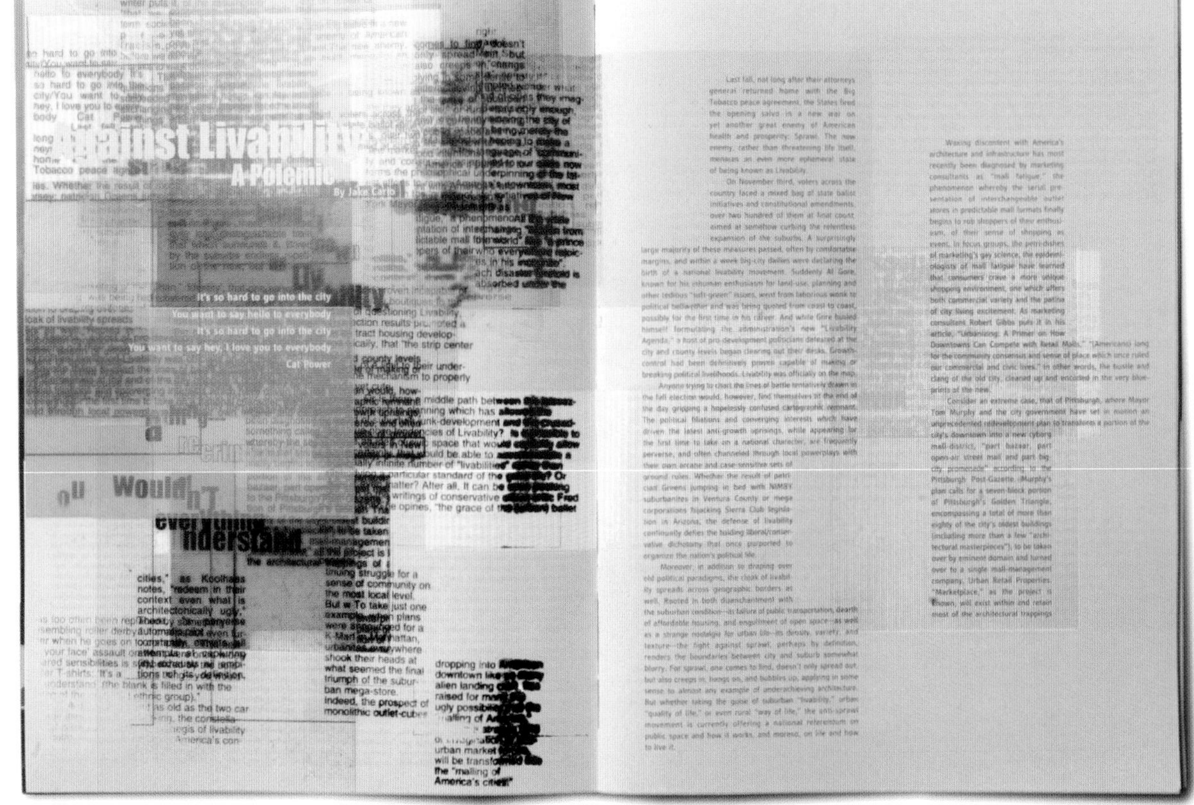

Plazm Magazine

Double page from **Plazm** no. 15
Double page from **Plazm** no. 21
(Below) Double page from **Plazm** no. 25

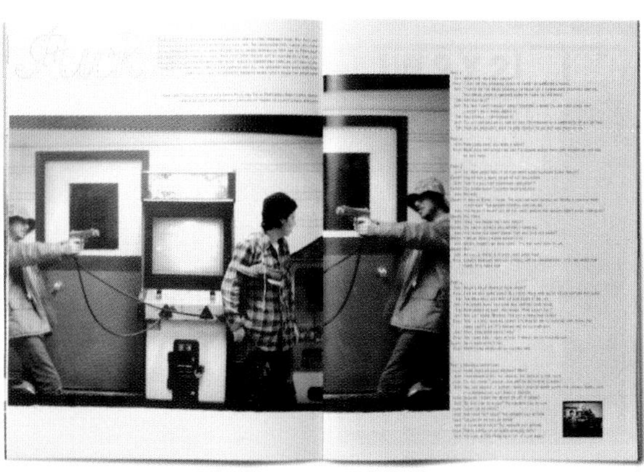

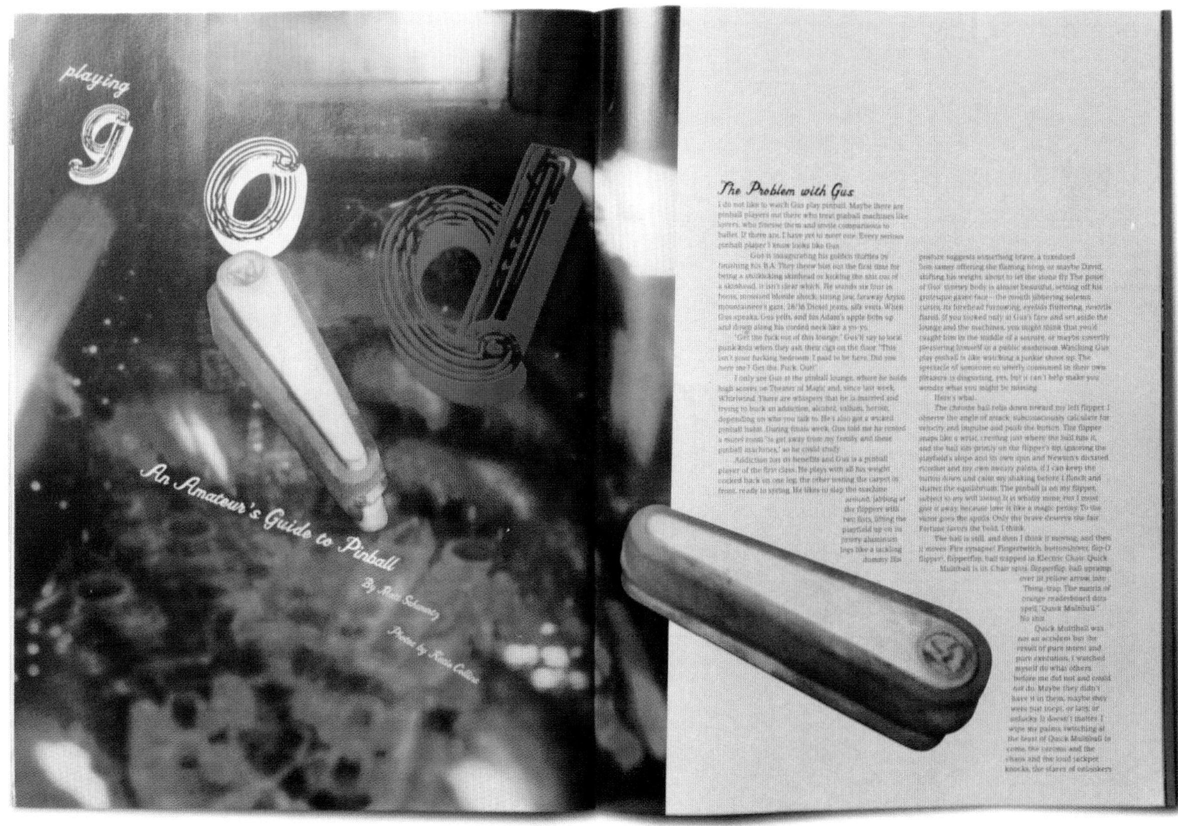

Plazm no. 17

Double-page article

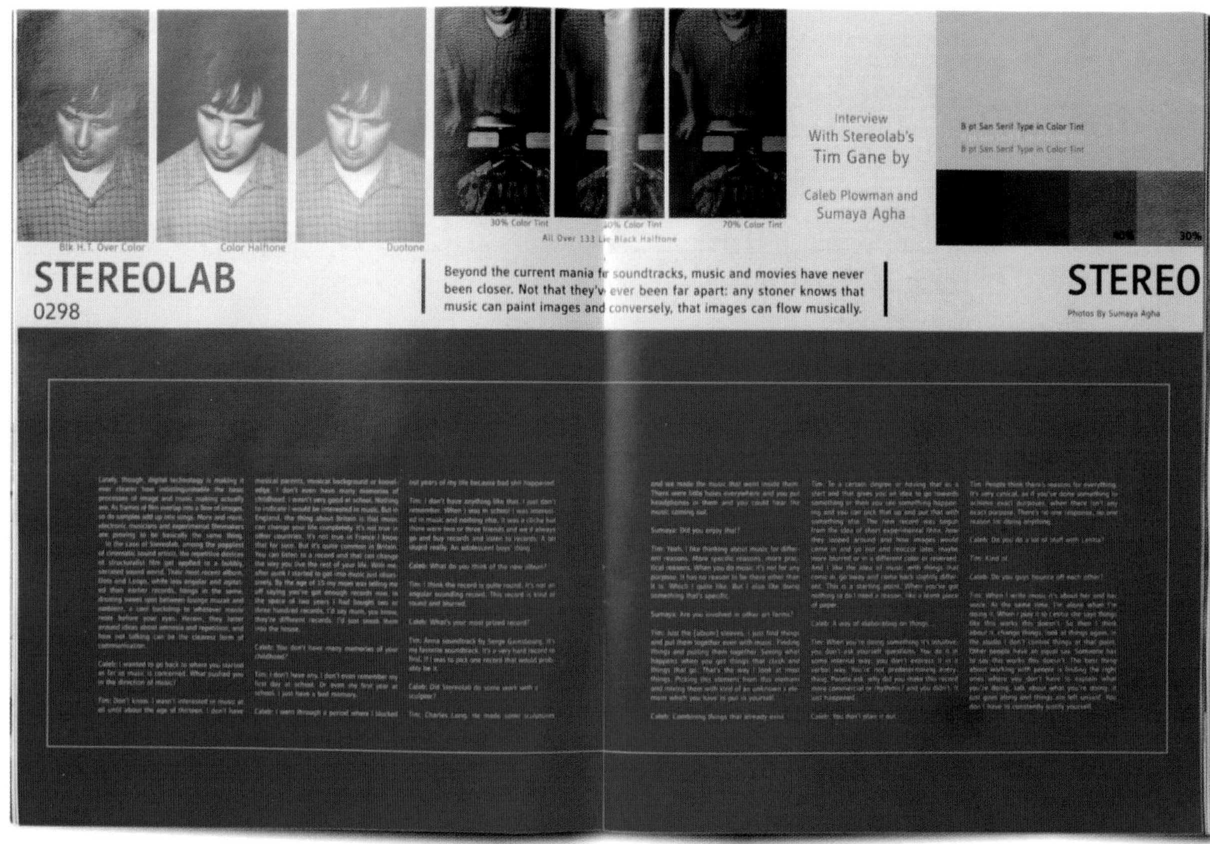

Blk H.T. Over Color

Color Halftone

Duotone

30% Color Tint

70% Color Tint

All Over 133 Line Black Halftone

Interview With Stereolab's Tim Gane by

Caleb Plowman and Sumaya Agha

8 pt San Serif Type in Color Tint

8 pt San Serif Type in Color Tint

30%

STEREOLAB

0298

Beyond the current mania fo soundtracks, music and movies have never been closer. Not that they've ever been far apart: any stoner knows that music can paint images and conversely, that images can flow musically.

STEREO

Photos By Sumaya Agha

to think that the magazine Plazm contributes to constructing a written history different from the official one."

As for the design of the magazine, Plazm feeds off collaboration from designers, artists and writers who find in its pages space for expression. The design is closely linked to the editorial contents, a fundamental factor in the success of a publication based on striking a balance between words and images, between the communication of ideas and the exploration of forms.

The work process is based on conceptualisation and collaboration between the different professionals involved in the making of the magazine.

They are not bound to any style in particular. They create their own fonts depending on the contents. Thus the magazine serves as a platform for the use of their typographic designs, for their diffusion and marketing.

The choice of font is deliberate and is grounded in the above-mentioned conceptual base. Joshua defines quite clearly what font means to him: **"The font bears meaning beyond the information that it transmits. It expresses contents through its legibility, through the cultural and ideological references, through its historical context and through its capacity for reproduction."**

Plazm magazine forms part of the permanent collection of the San Francisco Museum of Modern Art.

Plazm no. 15
1997

Cover designed by Art Chantry

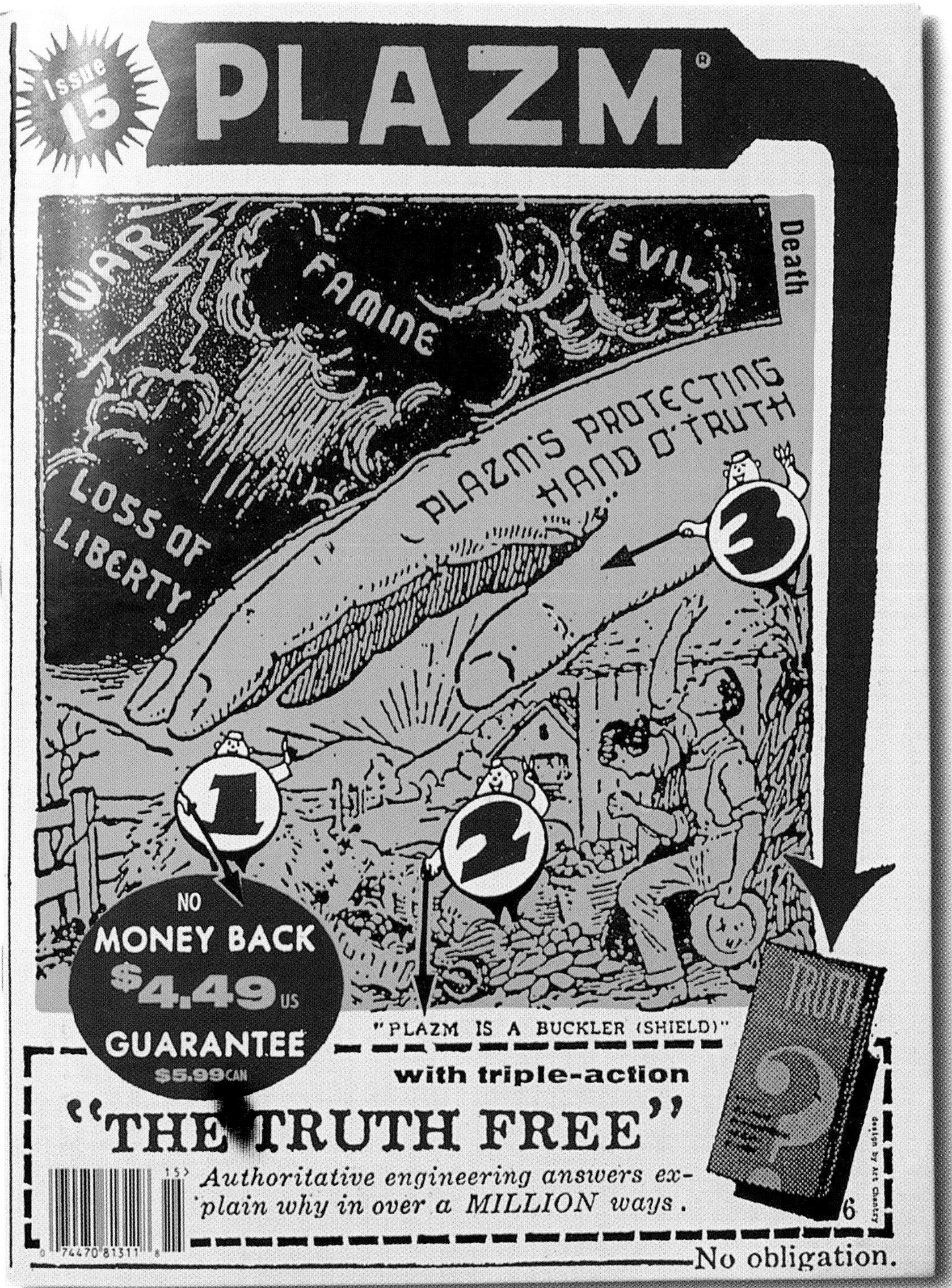

Directory

Alfonso Meléndez
Gran Vía 69
28013 Madrid
Spain
T. [+34] 91 547 97 20
alfatipo@interlink.es

Appetite engineers
Martin Venezky

218 Noe Street, San Francisco
California, USA 94114
T. 415 252 8122
martin@appetiteengineers.com
www.appetiteengineers.com

Barnbrook Design
Jon Barnbrook

10-11 Archer street
Studio 12
London W1V 7HG
United Kingdom
T. [+44] 0 207 287 3848
studio@barnbrookdesign.co.uk
www.barnbrookdesign.co.uk

Bis]
Sant Pere 17, 2º
17600 Figueres (Girona)
Spain
T. [+34] 972 67 43 33
alex@bisdixit.com
www.bisdixit.com

Cahan & Associates
171, 2nd Street. 5th floor
San Francisco, CA 94105, USA
T. 415 621 0915
www.cahanassociates.com

Eumogràfic
Perot Rocaguinarda 6
08500 Vic (Barcelona)
Spain
T. (+34) 93 889 48 77
vic@eumografic.com

Santa Eulàlia 21, 2n
08012 Barcelona
Spain
T. (+34) 93 459 10 19
bcn@eumografic.com
www.eumografic.com

El Mundo, Unidad Editorial SA
Rodrigo Sánchez

Pradillo 42
28002 Madrid
Spain
rodrigo.sanchez@el-mundo.es
www.elmundo.es

Frost Design
Vince Frost

The Gymnasium
Kings way place, Sans Walk
London EC1R OLU
United Kingdom
vince@frostdesign.co.uk
www.frostdesign.co.uk

Grafica
Pablo Martín

Pl. Ramon Berenguer el Gran 1, 2º 2ª
08002 Barcelona
Spain
T. [+34] 93 315 18 19
pablo@grafica-design.com
www.grafica-design.com

Grrr
Apartado de Correos 22.081
08080 Barcelona
info@grrr.ws
www.grrr.ws

HumanGraphics
Pasaje poniente 14
08840 Viladecans (Barcelona)
Spain
ensermagazine@hotmail.com
www.enserhumano.com

Jop van Bennekom
Prinsengracht 397 sous
1016 HL Amsterdam
The Netherlands
mail@re-magazine.com
www.re-magazine.com

Labomatic (U)
88 bis, Rue du Faubourg du Temple
75011 Paris
France
labomatic@labomatic.org
www.labomatic.org

Mario Eskenazi
Pl. Berenguer el Gran 1, 4º 1ª
08002 Barcelona
Spain
T. [+34] 93 319 23 69
m-eskenazi@m-eskenazi.com

Max Kisman
95, Bols Avenue. Mill Valley. California
CA 94941, USA
T. [+1] 415 380 8303
maxk@maxkisman.com
www.maxkisman.com

Media Vaca
Vicente Ferrer

Salamanca 49
46005 Valencia
Spain
T. [+34] 96 395 69 27
mediavaca@retemail.es
www.mediavaca.com

Moniteurs
Ackerstrasse 21-22
10115 Berlin
Germany
T. [+49] (0) 30 24 34 560
info@moniteurs.de
www.moniteurs.de

NL.Design
Mieke Gerritzen

Rozenstraat 147
1016 NR Amsterdam
The Netherlands
T. [+31] (0) 20 620 49 38
mieke@nl-design.net
www.nl-design.net

Orange Juice Design
Garth Walker

461, Berea Road
Durban 4001
South Africa
garth@oj.co.za
www.oj.co.za

Pentagram
Angus Hyland

11 Needham Road
London W11 2RP
United Kingdom
T. [+44] (0)20 7229 3477
email@pentagram.co.uk
www.pentagram.com

Peter Bil'ak
Zwaardstraat 16 (lokaal 0.11)
2584 TX, Den Haag
The Netherlands
peterb@rainside.sk
www.peterb.sk

Planet Base
Sebastián Saavedra

Pasaje Maluquer 16, bajos
08022 Barcelona
Spain
T. [+34] 93 417 18 61
sebastian@planetbase.net
www.planetbase.net

Plazm Media
PO Box 2863
Portland, OR 97208. USA
T. 503 528 8000
design@plazm.com
www.plazm.com

ReDesign
Bulharská 16, 110 00
Prague 10
Czech Republic
redesign@ti.cz
www.redesign.cz

Social
Paul Driver

Regents Park House. Regent Street
Leeds LS 27QJ
United Kingdom
paul@socialuk.com
www.socialuk.com

Tau Diseño
Felipe IV 8, 2º izda.
28014 Madrid
Spain
T. [+34] 91 369 32 34
spain@taudesign.com
www.taudesign.com

Thonik
Weesperzijde 79 D
1091 EJ Amsterdam
The Netherlands
T. [+31] (0) 20 468 35 25
studio@thonik.nl
www.thonik.nl

Why Not Associates
22c Shepherdess walk
London N1 7LB
United Kingdom
T. [+44] (0)20 7253 2244
info@whynotassociates.com
www.whynotassociates.com

Andreu Balius
Milà i Fontanals 14-26, 2º 2ª
08012 Barcelona
Spain
T. [+34] 93 459 16 52
andreu@typerepublic.com

Andreu Balius Planelles is a graphic designer and type designer, creator of the font project Garcia fonts & co. and the Typerware studio in Barcelona. He studied Sociology at the Autonomous University of Barcelona and graphic Design at the IDEP School.

He combines work at his studio with type project development and teaching. He is an Associate Professor at the School of Social Sciences and Communications of the Pompeu Fabra University in Barcelona.

He has received Excellence in Type Design awards from both the Type Directors Club (New York, 2002) and the association Typographique Internationale, 2001.

Thanks to:

Raquel Pelta,
Jaume + Miquel Anton,
Jutta Nachtwey
Vanessa, Silvia and Toni (IndexBook)
Sylvia van de Poel (BIS Publishers)
Nathalie Le Stunff (Pyramyd)
Pedro Lopez (NovaEra)
Albert Gea

And to all the designers that have so generously contributed to making this book possible.

Designed by: Andreu Balius
Fonts used: Stainless + Dispatch,
designed by Cyrus Highsmith

Dedicated to Raquel